NARRATIVES FROM THE SEPHARDIC ATLANTIC

INDIANA SERIES IN SEPHARDI AND MIZRAHI STUDIES

Harvey E. Goldberg and Matthias Lehmann, editors

NARRATIVES FROM THE SEPHARDIC ATLANTIC

Blood and Faith

Ronnie Perelis

Indiana University Press

Bloomington and Indianapolis

This book is a publication of

Indiana University Press
Office of Scholarly Publishing
Herman B Wells Library 350
1320 East 10th Street
Bloomington, Indiana 47405 USA

iupress.indiana.edu

Manufactured in the United States of America

Library of Congress Cataloging-in-Publication Data

Names: Perelis, Ronnie, author.
Title: Narratives from the Sephardic Atlantic : blood and faith /
    Ronnie Perelis.
Description: First edition. | Bloomington and Indianapolis : Indiana
    University Press, 2017. | Series: Indiana series in Sephardi and
    Mizrahi studies | Includes bibliographical references and index.
Identifiers: LCCN 2016045755 (print) | LCCN 2016046921 (ebook) |
    ISBN 9780253024015 (cloth : alk. paper) | ISBN 9780253024091
    (e-book)
Subjects: LCSH: Crypto-Jews—Spain—Biography. | Carvajal, Luis
    de, 1567?-1596. | Mello, João Manuel Cardoso de. | Montezinos,
    Antonio de, active 17th century.
Classification: LCC DS135.S8 A165 2017 (print) | LCC DS135.S8
    (ebook) | DDC 970.004/924009246—dc23
LC record available at https://lccn.loc.gov/2016045755

1   2   3   4   5   22   21   20   19   18   17

To Tammy, for your love and faith

וְאֵרַשְׂתִּיךְ לִי, לְעוֹלָם; וְאֵרַשְׂתִּיךְ לִי בְּצֶדֶק וּבְמִשְׁפָּט, וּבְחֶסֶד וּבְרַחֲמִים.
וְאֵרַשְׂתִּיךְ לִי, בֶּאֱמוּנָה; וְיָדַעַתְּ, אֶת-יְהוָה.

Contents

Acknowledgments

While a visiting professor at Brandeis University, the social historian, Silvia Arrom, invited me to lunch. She also offered to look over my manuscript beforehand. I welcomed a set of new eyes to help reorient the project. When we met, she handed me a copy with copious notes and one big idea. She saw Benedict Anderson's *Imagined Communities* written all over my analyses of spiritual discovery and textual encounters. It took a social historian to see the centrality of the networks of family and community to the life stories of the religious adventurers and dreamers I studied. By the end of our lunch I saw how Carvajal's, Macedo's, and Montezinos's stories were linked together by the double bond of sociobiological and spiritual family. It was also clear to me at that moment that looking at their self-narratives through the lens of family would both contextualize them within their historical moment and tell us something new about religion, family, and the construction of identity in the early modern world. That was a very productive lunch!

And so it goes that this project has benefited from spiritual fathers, mothers, brothers, and sisters whose erudition and generosity have enriched almost every page of *Narratives from the Sephardic Atlantic*. Kathleen Ross guided me through the earliest stages of this project with an eye for detail, patience, and respect for my intuitions. She was a keen reader and sensitive listener who did not let me hide behind vague and shiny ideas. At the earliest stages of my research, Yosef Kaplan was a steady guide as I explored the contours of the Western Sephardic Diaspora. I was a graduate student he had never met, writing to him from afar, and yet he always returned my emails with detailed comments and useful leads. His encouragement and guidance have enriched this project in countless ways, and I continue to learn from his scholarship and *gentileza*.

Colleagues near and far have offered careful notes, challenging critiques, and suggestions that helped transform my drafts into this book: Jonathan Schorsch, Claude Dov Stuckzynski, Will Stenhouse, Debra Kaplan, James Amelang, Richard Kagan, Holly Snider, Emily Colbert Cairns, Hilit Surowitz-Israel, Steve Fine, Laura Leibman, and Adam Zachary Newton. The anonymous readers at the University of Indiana Press provided me with penetrating questions and useful suggestions. The editorial staff at Indiana University Press and, in particular, Matthias Lehmann and Harvey Goldberg, have guided this book with grace to its publication.

An earlier version of chapter 3 appeared as "Blood and Spirit: Paternity, fraternity and religious self-fashioning in Luis de Carvajal's spiritual autobiography" in *Estudios Interdisciplinarios de América Latina y el Caribe* (Vol. 23, No. 1, July 2012). I wish to thank Prof. Raanan Rein and the editors of EIAL for their comments. The chapters on Carvajal also benefited from comments made by the participants in the Foro de Estudios Inquisitoriales at the Colegio de México where I presented my research on May 12, 2015. In particular I would like to thank Gabriel Torres Puga and Jesús del Prado Plumed for their warm hospitality and subtle insights into the case of the Carvajal family. My reading of Montezinos's narrative began as a paper delivered at the First Lavy Symposium, "Atlantic Jewry in an Age of Mercantilism," held at Johns Hopkins University in the spring of 2005. The comments and questions of the participants were invaluable as that paper turned into " 'These Indians are Jews!': Lost Tribes, Crypto-Jews and Jewish Self-Fashioning in Antonio de Montezinos' Relación of 1644" in *Atlantic Diasporas: Jews, Conversos, and Crypto-Jews in the Age of Mercantilism, 1500–1800* (JHU 2008). The essay benefited greatly from Richard Kagan's and Philip Morgan's careful eye and judicious editing.

Numerous friends answered my email queries both practical and theoretical and asked sharp and provocative questions during conferences: Stan Mirvis, Jesús del Prado Plumed, Carsten Wilke, Francesca Bregoli, Miriam Bodian, Julia R. Lieberman, Matt Goldish, David Graizbord, Asher Salah, Joel Hecker, Erin Graff Zivin, Alan Brill, José Alberto Tavim, and Sarah J. Pearce. This book is richer because of their collegiality and generosity of spirit and honesty.

From my first semester at Yeshiva University I encountered a vibrant intellectual community. My students at the Revel Graduate School, Yeshiva College, and Stern College enriched my thinking and challenged my assumptions. I was blessed to be able to share my love of the texts at the center of this book with my students and to see the experiences of Carvajal, Cardoso, and Montezinos from new perspectives. My colleagues welcomed me and proved to be strong allies and friends. David Berger and Mordechai Cohen, at the helm of the Bernard Revel Graduate School, offered unwavering support for this project. The deans of both YC and Stern have worked hard to create an environment where scholarship and passionate teaching are valued and supported. Dr. Herbert Dobrinsky continues to lead the Sephardic Studies program at YU with passion and conviction. This book benefited from his hard work supporting Sephardic history and culture at YU for over fifty years. Steve Fine has been an indispensable friend and mentor during my years at YU; thank you for the tea and conversation.

The following grants gave me the opportunity to explore archives and libraries, consult experts, and pursue my research with greater ease: the Coca-Cola Travel grant (1997 and 2001); the Mark Uveeler Special Doctoral Scholarship from the Memorial Foundation (2003–4); the Maurice Amado Research Grant

(2003); Tinker Foundation Field Research Grant (2001); and the Siman Sephardic Summer Research Grant (1997). I appreciated the warm invitation of the Center for the Study of Conversion and Inter-Religious Encounter at Ben Gurion University for the summers of 2014 and 2015. The Dr. Kenneth Chelst Book Grant gave me the ability to work with two of my talented students, Daniel Atwood and Elisha Fine, on the revision of the manuscript. The librarians at several institutions provided invaluable assistance in tracking down materials: the librarians at Yeshiva University, especially the intrepid librarians of the Inter-library loan department; the National Library in Madrid; the National Library of Israel; the University of Pennsylvania; the Center for Advanced Jewish Studies in Philadelphia; and the Jewish Theological Seminary's rare book room, where an under-supervised summer job reviewing their collection of Spanish and Portuguese books led the way to this book.

The cover of this book is graced with a dreamlike vision of fathers and sons by the Mexican artist Eduardo Cohen. His widow Esther Shabot generously offered the image and was happy that her late husband's painting was connected to work exploring themes close to his heart.

My siblings and siblings-in-law have supported me in this ongoing project. I have learned so much about brotherhood from each of you.

To my soul brothers: Danny Birnbaum, Daniel Frommer, Michah Gottlieb, Sagi Kfir, Morris Levin, David Marmor, Jamie Shear, and Val Vinokur. Thank you for helping me laugh, for giving me perspective, and for being loving witnesses to the twists and turns of this project.

My parents, Joseph and Dorita Perelis, believed in my dream so many years ago—when it all seemed like a fantastic long shot! They gave me the confidence to pursue an uncharted path and to make my own way. I am forever thankful for their sacrifices, their courage, and their *joie de vivre*. They gave me roots, they gave me motherlands and mother tongues, and they taught me to love stories and story-telling. I can never thank them enough.

My in-laws, Marcia and David Jacobowitz, have been a part of this book from its earliest stages. I thank them for the big and small: for all the ice cream dates with the kids so I could work an extra hour; for the public talks they attended where they began to see just what their son-in-law was spending so much time on; for their unfailing support and love throughout this journey; and for celebrating each milestone.

To my children, *luz de mis ojos*: Reyna Sarah, Abie Shahar, Batsheva Rachel, and Emanuela Nitza. They have grown up during the writing of this book. They ground me and make me laugh, wonder, and learn new things about myself every day. This book changed as I developed as a father. I understood the same stories in new ways because of my ongoing life with them. I am amazed by their creativity, big-heartedness, and curiosity.

To my Tammy, my partner, who has been in the trenches with me and helped me see light at those dark moments, who has sustained me and inspired me throughout. She balanced empathy with a love of truth. She understood my passion for this project from the very beginning. She got what was underneath it all and I do not have enough words to thank her.

NARRATIVES FROM THE SEPHARDIC ATLANTIC

Introduction

THE SUBTERRANEAN NETWORKS of New World crypto-Judaism rarely thrived in isolation. Rather, these secret Jewish communities were connected through a complex web of familial, economic, and cultural ties to a global network of fellow conversos and openly professing Jews living throughout Europe and the Americas.[1] With commercial links solidified through marriage, business and family were inseparable. Real-world affiliations made of "blood and treasure" were intertwined with a longing for family in metaphorical and spiritual terms. Individual crypto-Jews found paternity and brotherhood with like-minded religious searchers for a family of spirit inseparably connected with their family of flesh and blood. *Narratives from the Sephardic Atlantic* explores the dialectical relationship between the socioeconomic iteration of family and its more spiritual, metaphorical expression within the context of the early modern Sephardic Atlantic.

Autobiographical texts offer a unique lens through which to consider the relationship between blood and faith. As the authors reflect on their lives, both their biological families and their larger social circles form an essential part of their own development. However, there are other figures—teachers and friends, enemies and strangers—who also help shape the autobiographer's life. In more spiritually tinged narratives, these individuals often become essential to the dynamic of awakening and enlightenment driving the retelling of the author's experience.

This book looks at three autobiographical texts written by individuals caught within the matrix of inquisitorial persecution, expanding global trade, and crypto-Jewish activity in the early modern period. Luis de Carvajal the Younger (1567–96), also known as Joseph Lumbroso, moved from Spain to Mexico in 1580, when he was a teenager, and began writing his spiritual autobiography after his first inquisitorial trial in 1589. The Portuguese merchant Antonio de Montezinos (1604–47), recounts his life-changing encounter with the lost tribe of Reuben living in the northern Andes. His account dates to 1644 but was published only in 1650 as part of Menasseh ben Israel's treatise on the fate of the Lost Tribes, *Mikveh Israel/Esperanza de Israel*. Manuel Cardoso de Macedo (1585–1652) was an Azorean Old Christian who first embraced Calvinism before leaving Christianity behind and converting to Judaism. He wrote his spiritual autobiography, *La Vida del buenaventurado Abraham Pelengrino Guer*, while living as a Jew in Amsterdam at some point after the 1620s.

Each text reflects the unique vicissitudes of the author's experience, while at the same time they all share certain basic elements including deep roots in Iberian culture, Atlantic peregrinations, and a hunger for spiritual enlightenment. Providing insight into the workings of family life, as well as the conceptualization of family per se, within the wider converso and Sephardic context, these texts engage a variety of interconnected themes, from the centrality of marriage, to notions of brotherhood, and the push and pull of mercantile and religious commitments. By focusing on family, we are able to make new connections between the texts and their wider context and better appreciate the narrative and psychological dynamics at play within each of these unique autobiographical works.

What makes or breaks family relationships? How does family determine identity? Is there a higher calling that supersedes or even rejects blood relationships? What impact do family and surrogate family relationships have on the ability to write about oneself—to record and map the contours of one's life out of the memories of individual events and interactions? What happens when socioeconomic family ties conflict with religious ideals? These questions become particularly charged under the pressure of Iberian inquisitorial culture with its regime of surveillance and concern with tainted converso blood. While surveillance forces individuals to hide their true allegiances, discriminatory policies inspired by the late medieval Iberian anxiety relating to blood purity (*limpieza de sangre*)[2] raised awareness of ethnic differences between Old and New Christians—an awareness that both joined converts and their descendants in tribal unions and at the same time drove these individuals to hide their Jewish origins in the hope of evading inquisitorial persecution and social stigmatization. How did the Atlantic and the inquisitorial contexts shape the conceptual models available to our three authors to imagine the contours and meanings of their families? These are some of the larger questions animating this book.

Iberian Crypto-Judaism and the Early Modern Atlantic World: A Brief History

The life stories at the heart of this book transpired across the wide expanse of the early modern Atlantic. However, the social and spiritual contours of these individual lives were shaped by historical processes that developed in late medieval Iberia. To understand the transatlantic socioeconomic networks that converso and Sephardic merchants developed during the age of exploration and colonial expansion as well as the complex phenomenon of crypto-Jewish activity in the wider Iberian world, we must return to the summer of 1391.

That summer was witness to a spree of violent, anti-Jewish riots, which began in Seville but soon spread throughout Christian Spain. Angry mobs charged the *aljamas*, offering the choice of conversion or death. The majority of those faced with this option chose the expedient and pragmatic path of conversion. It is impossible to judge the sincerity of these conversions. What is clear is that they were undertaken under violent duress, and while church doctrine forbade forced conversions, once baptized, these Jews were under the wings of the Catholic faith. Some Jews interpreted the tragic and humiliating events of 1391 as a providential sign of the victory of Christianity over Judaism. Faced with the enormity of the rampage, many Jews might have come to finally doubt their own choseness and agree with the Christian argument that they heard for generations—how could God treat his beloved son this way? Eventually, many converts came to sincerely embrace their newly acquired Catholic faith. This group was likely a minority among the first generation of converts, the majority of whom had no intention of becoming Christian when they chose to save their lives at the baptismal font.[3] As Cecil Roth notes, instead of dealing with infidels outside the Church, the events of 1391 produced only a new class of heretics within the Church.[4]

Crypto-Judaism as a large-scale social reality, then, had its birth in 1391, when masses of Jews who suddenly found themselves within the shadow of the Church continued to associate—economically, religiously, and socially—with their former coreligionists, many of whom were family.[5] It is difficult to determine what percentage of these conversos actively attempted to maintain secret Jewish practices. However, regardless of their particular religious convictions and commitments, these conversos did maintain high levels of social cohesion with other conversos and open Jews, and in some instances such social and economic ties encouraged conversos to maintain secret Jewish practices.

For many, their recently acquired Christian identity opened up new economic and social opportunities to participate in previously forbidden areas such as the military and church, as well as allowing them to marry into the nobility. New Christians seemed to excel in all those places where they were once excluded, which in turn drew envy and anger. These reactions, along with the widespread perception that many of these converts were either secretly practicing Judaism or living in a skeptical no-man's-land of Averroistic materialism led to the development of the statutes of Pureza de Sangre (first promulgated in 1449 with the Sentencia-Estatuto of Toledo) and the establishment of the Spanish Inquisition in 1481. These conditions made life for Spanish New Christians difficult, regardless of their actual religious orientation.[6]

The Catholic Monarchs Ferdinand and Isabel completed the centuries-long Christian struggle to regain Iberian territory from Muslim domination with the conquest of Granada on January 2, 1492. With the *reconquista* complete, the Catholic Monarchs turned toward the internal issue of the conversos and their Jewish brethren. From the newly reconquered Alhambra palace the Catholic Monarchs made the fateful decision to expel the Jews of Spain. The Edict of Expulsion lays out the legal and ethical necessity of the expulsion of the Jews of Spain by arguing that the presence of an open and vibrant Jewish community within Spain made it impossible for the conversos to fully integrate themselves into the Church. The authors of the edict point out that despite multiple attempts to limit contact between Jews and conversos on the part of the monarchy and the Church, the Jews, "always attempt by whatever ways and means to subvert and detract faithful Christians from our holy Catholic faith and separate them from it and attract and pervert them to their cursed belief and opinion, instructing them in the ceremonies and observances of their law, convening assemblies where they read to them and teach them what they must believe and observe according to their law."[7] The edict continued to enumerate the methods and practices used by Jews to corrupt their former coreligionists. By inciting and enabling the conversos to Judaize, the Jews of Spain were in effect responsible for "great injury and damage to our Holy Catholic faith" and as such were guilty of a capital offense. After mercifully trying multiple other solutions, the crown was forced to act for the good of the Christian republic and expel the Jews from their ancestral homeland.[8]

In April of 1492, from the newly conquered Alhambra palace in Granada, the Catholic Monarchs, Ferdinand and Isabella, signed the edict of expulsion, offering the choice of conversion or expulsion to the country's Jews. While many left, the majority stayed.[9] In effect, the phenomenon of less than sincere conversions that occurred in 1391 repeated itself within the newly unified Catholic kingdom.[10] In Spain itself, however, the phenomenon of crypto-Judaism steadily dwindled after the expulsion; without the presence of practicing Jews, it was harder for those who remained—many of whose religiosity in either direction was often dubious—to continue their crypto-Jewish life.[11] Ironically, it was the discrimination against conversos inspired by the mentality and the restrictive rules associated with *limpieza de sangre* that proved to be one of the few factors that helped many of these converts maintain their Jewishness.

The majority of those who chose exile over conversion to Catholicism in 1492 found haven and welcome in Portugal. This was short lived: in 1497 there was a mass forced conversion of the Portuguese Jewish community.[12] In contrast to the gradual and unsystematic assaults on Spanish Jewry (itself a heterogeneous group), this totalizing act of the conversion of an entire community—whose religious commitment was manifest by their choice of exile over conversion—created a distinct and resilient form of crypto-Judaism.[13] The fact that the Portuguese crown promised the converted Jews protection from inquisitorial investigation for twenty years meant that those who desired to maintain their attachment to Judaism could do so in secret with little danger. This initial twenty years was extended, and it was only with the establishment of the Portuguese Inquisition in 1536 that a steady stream of Portuguese conversos started relocating to more favorable areas.[14] Y. H. Yerushalmi argues that this long period of grace allowed the

Portuguese converso community to develop an elaborate system of secret rituals and education, which maintained the "Jewishness" of these forced converts for several generations.[15]

External sociological forces also shaped the Jewishness of the Portuguese conversos. Early on we find examples of forced converts who took full advantage of their new status and seemed to care little for their ancestral Judaism. A small but significant group easily assimilated into Portuguese society, even marrying into elite families in the same way that Castilian and Aragonese conversos did in the generation after 1391. However, the majority of the Portuguese converts found it challenging to fully enter into Portuguese society. Portuguese Jews and conversos formed the backbone of the emerging merchant class, becoming in essence their own socioeconomic cast. In his study of the seventeenth-century political theorist Martín González de Cellorigo, Claude B. Stuczynski illustrates some of the structural and conceptual issues behind the conversos' ethnic exclusion. Cellorigo identified the New Christians in Portugal as a "Fifth Estate," unable to assimilate into the wider body politic. Their mercantilist activities kept them outside the socioeconomic patterns of the traditional classes of the nobility, clergy, and peasants.[16] Even after their conversion they were referred to and referred to themselves as the Gente da Naçao, or the "Men of the Nation," indicating a sense of social solidarity and a shared culture.[17] Their Old Christian neighbors throughout the Iberian world viewed them as a distinct class whose commitment to the Church could not be fully trusted. This social ostracism meant that even those Portuguese converts who desired to live as good Catholics were seen as different from other believers and for the most part functioned within their own social orbit— marrying and engaging in business with other conversos and thus keeping themselves separate from the wider Portuguese society.

The Portuguese Inquisition's investigations of and prejudice against New Christians further solidified the Jewishness of many otherwise Christianized conversos. Regardless of their actual Judaizing before their arrest, many conversos embraced Judaism *after* their brutal encounter with the Inquisition. As we will see in all three cases at the center of this book, the experience of prison and inquisitorial investigation could inspire a discovery of Judaism or catalyze a latent Jewishness into a potent force in the life of the individual prisoner.

Y. H. Yerushalmi has shown how the phenomenon of crypto-Jewish belief and practice, in its most powerful and prevalent form, was created in and "exported" from Portugal. In 1580, Portugal came under the Habsburg crown, allowing for the free transit of Portuguese subjects throughout Spanish territories in Europe and across the Atlantic. As a result, and because the Portuguese Inquisition treated New Christians so harshly that the Spanish Holy Office appeared relatively benign in comparison, New Christians were compelled to seek new commercial opportunities in Spain, the Habsburg-controlled Low Countries, and Italy, as well as the Americas, despite official limitations on converso travel to the American colonies. While most Portuguese New Christians were not interested in maintaining ties to Jewish belief and practice, some conversos were committed to the "Law of Moses"[18] and brought these religious proclivities with them as they traveled throughout the Iberian world. For many Spanish conversos who had become completely estranged from Jewish practice, the influx of these Portuguese New Christians who were actively Jews provided a new opportunity to encounter the religion of their ancestors.[19]

While not all (or even most) of these Portuguese New Christians were actually crypto-Jews, their Jewish origins and atavistic attachment to their former religion were presumed by their Old Christian counterparts. Throughout the Peninsula, the Low Countries, and the Indies, "Portuguese" was synonymous with Jew. The Gente da Nação, or Gente de Negocio as they were often called, were perceived as ubiquitous throughout the global reach of the Spanish Empire. Bishops from Santo Domingo to Río de la Plata complained of the pernicious laxity (or open apostasy) of the Portuguese colonists and traders.[20] This marginalized class of Iberian society was attracted to the fluidity of the New World. For many New Christians, the Americas held a particular promise as a place far from the Inquisition's grasp. Despite restrictions against their voyage to the Indies, by the end of the sixteenth century sizable numbers of New Christians managed to find their way throughout the eastern and western stretches of the Iberian empires.[21]

Recaptured Voices: The Rereading of Transatlantic Converso Autobiography

Travel, exile, and trade became essential features of converso and Sephardic Jewish life in the early modern period. The search for religious freedom often coincided with opportunities for economic success. Trade networks spanning the globe operated through contacts of blood and language, regardless of nationality or religion. One family—possibly made up of devout Catholics, crypto-Jews, and Jews—could have relatives living in every important point along the path of international commerce: the East Indies, Alexandria, Turkey, Venice, Spain, the Americas, and Amsterdam. Conversos traveled along this global circuit to escape persecution or simply to look for adventure and profit.[22]

Their peculiar religious predicament within the Iberian world—namely, their need to hide their Jewish identity—created a matrix of displacement and secrecy, of half-lives and double-identities, along the routes of international commerce and channels of culture they traversed. Many conversos who left Spain and Portugal for the Americas in hopes of escaping inquisitorial persecution or the hounding that came with the *limpieza de sangre* regime returned to Europe after their travels, often to Jewish havens in places like Amsterdam, Hamburg, or Venice, while some wound their way back to Spain or its European possessions.

The present investigation focuses on the experiences of three individuals caught within this dynamic: Luís de Carvajal the Younger, Antonio de Montezinos (aka Aharon Levi), and Manoel Cardoso de Macedo (aka Abraham Peregrino). All three wrote about the convergence of their spiritual and spatial journeys; their writing is testimony to the parallels between transatlantic passage and internal discovery. This book contextualizes these individuals and their writings within their historical moment while uncovering the existential questions driving their narratives.

New World Crypto-Judaism and the Rethinking of Early Modern Spanish Literature

The story of the Jewish presence in the Americas has begun to be told. In the nineteenth century Henry Charles Lea and José Toribio Medina laid the foundations for the historical treatment of inquisitorial activity in the New World. In the 1930s, the Mexican historian Alfonso Toro dedicated a monumental study to the Carvajal family. Wissenshaft scholars such as Mayer Kayserling in his *Biblioteca Española-Portugueza-Judaica* (Strasbourg, 1890) as well as his numerous individual studies related to the Western Sephardim highlighted the Atlantic dimension of this prolific and colorful community. Scholars associated with the American Jewish Historical Society, such as Cyrus Adler and George Alexander Kohut, all dedicated important research to the topic of conversos and open Jews in the Americas.[23] In the 1960s and 1970s, the American scholars Martin A. Cohen, Richard Greenleaf, and Seymour Leibman continued Toro's important work in Mexican Jewish history and were joined by other studies of Jewish life throughout the Americas: colonial Peru (Gunther Böhm), Brazil (A. Wishnitzer and Anita Novitsky), and the Caribbean (I. S. Emmanuel and Mordechay Arbel), to name just a few. Throughout his writings on the Western Sephardim, Yosef Kaplan carefully traces the intricate transoceanic web connecting the Jews of Amsterdam, Hamburg, and London with the wider Atlantic world. Jonathan I. Israel's *Diasporas within a Diaspora* (2002) placed the experiences of these conversos and Western Sephardim within their global economic context.[24]

The phenomenon of crypto-Jewish activity in the New World has been treated from a historical and sociological perspective. References to Portuguese Gente de Nação—their settlement, trade, religious activity—abound throughout colonial documentary sources. Textual reflections of their inner life—poetry, autobiography, correspondence—however, are very rare.[25] This imbalance, it seems, is partially the result of the nature of the material. Few people who live a double life risk leaving behind evidence of their heterodoxy. As a result, the texts I am examining, with the notable exception of Luis de Carvajal's *Vida*, were written once the individuals reached the safety of an open Jewish community, such as Amsterdam, Ferrara, or British Jamaica.

Another issue that has affected the appreciation of these texts lies in the generic nature of much of the material. Prima facie, these texts do not seem to conform to ready-made literary categories, and so they are seen as curious documentary sources. At best, they fill in a historical landscape, and, indeed, the diaries, letters, testimonials, and historical/cosmographic works of Sephardic travelers do contain a wealth of historical data revealing details of their authors' lives and the complex world they lived in. Until this point, however, scholars have ignored the dynamics of representation, performance, and subjectivity that play themselves out in these works. In reorienting the reading of the texts, I will pay attention to these narrative practices and what they can tell us about the interplay between the author's self-image as crafted in these texts and the audience each one hoped to reach.

A reconsideration of colonial travel narratives along the lines of Margarita Zamora's *Reading Columbus* (1993) or Stephen Greenblatt's *Marvelous Possessions* (1991) challenges our notions of both history and literature, opening up a more nuanced and multivalent understanding of the texts, their authors, and the period in which they were written. In a similar fashion, I want to draw the texts by Carvajal, Cardoso, and Montezinos into a dialogue with the broader cultural issues of their historical moment. These individuals lived at the nexus of Iberian, Atlantic, and Jewish cultural, geopolitical, and socioeconomic forces, which can help to shed light on their writings at the same time that these writings illuminate the complexity of their historical moment.

The Authors and Their Works: Brief Sketches

Each author and text will be discussed in greater detail in the chapters that follow. However, for the sake of clarity, I have included these brief biographical and bibliographical sketches of the three authors and their works.

Luis Rodríguez de Carvajal was born in Benavente, Spain, a small town near the Portuguese border, in 1567. He, along with his extended family, followed his uncle, Luis de Carvajal y de la Cueva, to New Spain in 1580 where the elder Carvajal was awarded the governorship of the frontier territory of the New Kingdom of León in northwest Mexico. He began writing his spiritual autobiography after his first inquisitorial trial for Judaizing in 1589. He, along with his mother, sisters, and a large group of conversos, was arrested for a second time in 1595, again for Judaizing. Luis was burned at the stake for his heretical crimes in the auto-da-fé of

1596 in Mexico City. His *Vida* was collected as evidence against him during his second trial and was preserved as part of his trial record.[26]

The Portuguese merchant Antonio de Montezinos (1604–47) spent time in Nueva Granada (modern day Colombia), where, according to his report, he encountered the lost tribe of Reuben living in the northern Andes. After traveling to Amsterdam in 1644, he described this encounter and relayed the Reubenites' message to an eminent group of lay and religious leaders of the Portuguese Jewish community. This oral account found its way into Menasseh ben Israel's *Mikveh Israel/Esperanza de Israel* (1650) where it was presented as the *Relación* or report of Aharon Levi and served as a proof text for the subsequent discussion of the origin of the Americans and the Lost Tribes of Israel. We know very little of his biography except that he was from the Portuguese town of Vila Flor, which had a sizable converso population. From inquisitorial documents we also know that during his time in South America he was arrested on suspicion of Judaizing and released by the Holy Office in Cartagena de Indias. After six months in Amsterdam, Montezinos returned to the New World, joining the Jewish community in Pernambuco where he died a few years later. There is no copy of the original transcript of the *Relación*.[27]

Manuel Cardoso de Macedo (1585–1652) was an Azorean Old Christian who first embraced Calvinism before leaving Christianity behind and converting to Judaism. He discovered Calvinism while studying in England, where his father had extensive business dealings. On a return visit to his family in the Azores, Cardoso was arrested on the basis of rumors of his apostasy from Catholicism. He was sent to Lisbon to stand trial for his heresy. It was in the inquisitorial prison in Lisbon that Cardoso met an accused Judaizer whose supposed crimes inspired Cardoso to rethink his attachment to Calvinism and pointed him towards the Law of Moses. Upon his release in 1609, he made connections with a circle of New Christians with whom he eventually escaped from Portugal for the Jewish communities of northern Europe. It was in Hamburg, his first destination, where he converted to Judaism. He then worked for a short time in Danzig before moving to Amsterdam where he wrote his spiritual autobiography, *La Vida del buenaventurado Abraham Pelengrino Guer*, at some point after the 1620s. A surviving manuscript copy of this text, dated 1769, is preserved in the Etz Hayyim Library and was republished in a critical edition by Bernard Teensma (1976).[28]

1   Audience and Archive

Text, Context, and the Literary Construction of Experience

THE TEXTS AT the center of this study present themselves as straightforward narratives with a clearly defined goal in mind. Montezinos's *Relación de Antonio de Montezinos* reports to the Sephardic congregation of Amsterdam regarding his experiences with the Reubenites in South America and their message of hope to Jews of the diaspora. Luis de Carvajal and Manuel Cardoso de Macedo both tell their readers explicitly that they wrote their spiritual autobiographies in order to recount the glory of God's providence in the world as exemplified in their life stories. However, these texts go beyond their stated purpose. In the process of telling their story, they spill over specific generic parameters and become multivalent narratives which engage in a variety of generic practices.

It is my contention that, as is the case with so many other early modern autobiographic texts, these narratives exhibit a great degree of hybridity. By appreciating the complex textures of each one, we can better understand its composition and relationship to its intended audience(s). This chapter explores the generic practices employed in the three texts and considers the impact of their possible audience(s) on their composition. I want to show how the texts participate within a wider network of writing—in terms of content but more importantly in terms of structure—which I term their "archive."[1]

Montezinos, Carvajal, and Cardoso produced hybrid texts that partake of multiple generic practices to achieve their particular ends. In the early modern Iberian context the shape of a personal narrative would be inspired by or in dialogue with many of the official forms of self-narratives that were composed for juridical or religious purposes, such as the *relación*, the confession, and *vidas de monjas* (nun's lives), as well as the *discurso de la vida*, which begins most inquisitorial interrogations. In the following pages I will explore some aspects of the generic archive out of which these texts developed. My hope is to make the texts more intelligible by inscribing them within certain recognizable generic practices while at the same time highlighting how they employ those practices in creative and subversive ways.

The *Relación* and the Variety of Early Modern Autobiographic Writing[2]

> ¿Hay algo más novelesco que la autobiografía?
>
> Miguel de Unamuno[3]

The diverse, unexpected, and bizarre circumstances surrounding the discovery, conquest, and colonization of the Americas created a situation wherein many of the individuals involved in this imperial project had to report back to their king. Many of these accidental authors were soldiers, sailors, merchants, or clergy who were not trained as humanists—many were barely literate—yet their need to report to their superiors, defend their innocence, or demand their just reward drove them to write their *relaciónes*. These texts were inscribed within the norms and expectations of the notarial arts, but because of the variety of circumstances, the varying literary skills of the authors, and the sheer number of *relaciónes* we begin to see texts that partake of those rhetorical structures—formal address, attention to the facts of a case, and the author's thinly veiled self-interested advocacy for himself—but transcend their standard parameters and become hybrid texts treating varied aspects of the authors' experiences and reflections on the new worlds they encountered. The "literary" nature of these texts—the ways they reflect a subjective grappling with existential issues—found its way into what should otherwise have been dry notarial records because of the heterogeneity of the individuals who wrote them and the often extraordinary experiences they recount.

Thus, Montezinos's *Relación* and the *vidas* of Carvajal and Cardoso, despite presenting themselves as a prima facie "record" or "report" about their author's experience, are in fact multivalent texts that engage in a range of generic practices and employ different narrative modes to tell their stories. These diverse modes of telling complex stories not only pave the way for the creative fancy of fiction, but also point to the constructed nature of language and expand the range of what can be written and communicated. From this perspective, the *relación*—that ubiquitous and supremely utilitarian form of bureaucratic communication—becomes a generic omnibus, a wide-open space for individuals to tell their messy and layered stories. Later in this chapter we will look at other modes of autobiographic discourse and the ways they bleed into each other and inform Carvajal's, Cardoso's, and Montezinos's narratives. Before turning to this broader analysis, however, I focus on Montezinos' *Relación* and its generic construction.

Antonio de Montezinos' *Relación* and the
Documentation of the Fantastic

> All of which I wrote down with such certainty that although within it
> [the account] one reads certain very new things, and for some they
> might be difficult to believe, however, they can be believed without
> a doubt.
>
> Alvar Núñez Cabeza de Vaca[4]

Montezinos's *Relación* presents itself as a straightforward report of Antonio de Montezinos's experiences in the Andes. It begins by noting the date and location where the report was given and the audience before whom it was "declared." The reader is also informed of the names by which the author of the report is known. "On the 18th of Elul of the year 5404, which according to the secular reckoning is [1]644, there arrived to this town of Amsterdam Aharon Levi who in another time in Spain was known as Antonio de Montezinos, and he declared before a diverse group of the Portuguese nation the following report."[5] Despite its reference to the Hebrew date, this scribal introduction to the *Relación* functions within the basic patterns of Spanish notarial writing and shares its trust in the written and authorized word. The exact dates, the clarification of the subject's identity, and the presence of witnesses who heard Montezinos's report follow the guidelines of Spanish legal discourse, which "gave formal, bureaucratic bonding and approval to what the documents contained."[6]

The recorded text of Montezinos' narrative employs the legal formulae common to the *relación* and to contemporary Iberian juridical discourse. It begins with the date and location where the story begins and goes on to provide more dates, locations, and names of individuals whom Montezinos encountered. These details are important for his crafting of a believable story. While his reference to the Indian "Francisco" will become significant as the story unfolds, the mestizo mule driver, "Francisco del Castillo," who is never mentioned again, seems to have no importance for his tale, except that the inclusion of his name strengthen its sense of verisimilitude. I do not consider such a detail a fabrication. The *Relación*, along with so many other "factual reports" of the period, made ample use of the details of its author's experience in order to anchor the narrative in a reality recognizable to its readers.

As a comparison, a more "canonical" example of this rhetorical move can be found in the first chapter of the *relación* that eventually became known as the *Naufragios* (Castaways) of Álvar Núñez Cabeza de Vaca. Cabeza de Vaca begins his account with the date that the expedition began, the name of the captain and the other officers of the fleet, where they first set anchor, and so on.[7] In order to give a "true account" Cabeza de Vaca is compelled to include the names of people and places and the series of dates when events of little note occurred regardless of whether or not they will become important to his overall narrative project(s). These details ground his *relación* within the real and the "verifiable" so that those parts that are essential to his self-presentation as a valiant and responsible leader deserving of reward are part of a larger constellation of "real" events. This is not to assert that Cabeza de Vaca invented these details. Instead, I argue that while they appear superfluous to the narrative, in actuality they are essential to supporting its larger project of presenting a "true" report.

The *Naufragios* and Montezinos's *Relación* share certain thematic and rhetorical commonalities. Both tell the story of a journey into unknown American territory. The protagonists assume an attitude of humility, openness, and respect as well as condescension to indigenous peoples and their cultures. Both relate stories that partake of the fantastic—the discovery of the lost tribes, Cabeza de Vaca's becoming a miracle healer—yet consistently present their experiences with the dry objectivity typical of the *relación*. The generic packaging of these semi-fantastic themes into the rhetorical format of the *relación* orients readers' expectations and predisposes them to consider the text before them as a "factual" narrative.

A text such as the *Naufragios*, or any of the *relaciónes* prepared by soldiers, colonial officials, or clergy working within the colossal infrastructure of the Spanish Empire, was designed for a distinct reader or group of readers, who had a major impact on the composition of any particular report. This intimate dependence between author and his desired audience is readily apparent in the composition of Montezinos's *Relación*. Montezinos lived most of his life as a subject of the Spanish crown, but when he came to Amsterdam and decided to give a report of his experiences with the Reubenites, Montezinos was already Aharon Levi, a "New Jew" whose allegiance lay with his embattled people.[8] The *Relación* was presented before the eminences of the Spanish Portuguese community of Amsterdam, but Montezinos likely hoped that it would reach a wider audience. He hoped to spread the "good news" ("buenas nuevas") of the continued existence of the tribe of Reuben and to impart their particular message of messianic hope to the Jews of the diaspora.[9] By anchoring his narrative within notarial discourse he was better positioned to convince his readers of the validity of his claims.

Notorial discourse, however, was only one vehicle that the *Relación* utilized to substantiate its narrative. Montezinos's text also employs a confessional mode of discourse to establish credibility. As will be discussed at length in chapter 5, the *Relación* is a story of religious awakening and transformation. We meet Montezinos as an assimilated converso seeking his fortune in South America. Through a series of powerful experiences, he embraces his secret Judaism, abandons the allure of the Iberian colonial project, and becomes a fervent messianist, a bearer of the "good news" of an imminent redemption. His own transformation is essential to his narrative and to the practical ends it intended to achieve. Montezinos's own conversion was brought about by his encounter with the Reubenites; consequently, the converted Montezinos becomes living proof of their existence. On a more immediate level, by sharing his experience of conversion, Montezinos certifies his religious credentials for his Sephardic readers: the Montezinos of the *Relación* is committed to the God of Israel and has renounced his former life as a converso. Within the ex-converso community of Amsterdam there was a great deal of anxiety about the religious integrity of its newly "returned" members, and Montezinos's account of his conversion would have strengthened the trustworthiness of his story as a whole.

The insertion of a confessional discourse into a *relación* was not uncommon. Moments of introspection, remorse, and repentance can be found throughout the corpus of New World *relaciónes*, beginning with Columbus's diaries and letters. These confessional moments strengthen the image of the author in the eyes of his readers: He is not only responsible and brave, but also a man of faith and conviction whose word should be trusted. On a personal level, the confessional mode meets the author's need to express the psychological dimension of his experience. Rhetorically it partakes of the proliferation of confessional discourses, both oral and written, within the Counter-Reformation Iberian world.

The authorship of Montezinos's text complicates its generic connection to the *relación* and its status as an autobiographical text. The text is entitled *Relación de Aharon Levi, alias, Antonio de Montezinos*. The reader is informed within the first sentence that the text was "declared" orally by Montezinos before an eminent group of witnesses. While Montezinos supposedly gives an account of his own experience, the *Relación* is recorded in the third person, like a deposition or a transcript of a juridical interrogation: the witness said X or did Y. The strong first-person voice that is classically associated with autobiographical narratives is absent. Its absence is compounded by the fact that the text of the *Relación* is a written transcript of Montezinos's oral report, not his own recording of his experiences in the third person, as in the case of Luis de Carvajal's *Vida*.

The distancing of Montezinos from his text complicates but does not preclude its participation in the autobiographic mode. Montezinos can be considered the text's "corporate" author. Margarita Zamora applies this term to Columbine texts; although they originated with the admiral, they were clearly mediated by those who copied, edited, and circulated his texts.[10] In the case of Montezinos, we can assume that his account suffered a similar amount of mediation. The use of the third person reflects the fact that his story was recorded by a third party. In this sense the *Relación* follows a rhetorical model common to other generic practices, such as the mediated confession of nuns, and the confessions produced through inquisitorial interrogation. In both situations, the subject is required to recount an experience, or his or her entire life, and this autobiographic narrative is then rendered into a written text by a third (often hostile) party. In the next section we will consider how this coercive method of narrative "extraction" informed the production of more "literary" autobiographic and pseudo-autobiographic writing.

Unwitting Autobiographers: Inquisitorial Interrogation and Autobiographic Composition[11]

Confession is an essential aspect of a Catholic's religious life. In confessing their sins, the children of the Church are guided through a process of spiritual cleansing and renewal. The Inquisition hoped that its interrogations and prosecutions of accused sinners would also result in their repentance, atonement, and spiritual illumination. The Holy Office did not consider the punishments it meted out to be retributive; rather, they were to be understood as atonement, "a penance that had to be done in order to make amends for the defendant's injury to God, the Church, and the sacraments."[12] The sinner's confession was an essential step in that process of atonement.[13]

The Inquisitors used a variety of strategies to guide (or coerce) sinners to their eventual confession. Inquisitorial procedures were draped in secrecy. The accused were not told why they were under investigation. Instead, the Inquisitors asked the accused why they thought they were arrested. This placed the accused in a vulnerable position where they would be frightened "into providing them [the tribunal] with a 'truthful' confession that would reveal aspects of their lives that they might otherwise conceal."[14] At the conclusion of three *audiencias*, and before being informed of the charges against them, the accused were warned to search their conscience and provide a "full and complete confession." They were reminded that "the Holy Office is not accustomed to arresting people without having sufficient information that they have said, done, and committed . . . an offense against God and against the Holy Roman Catholic Faith."[15] These warnings framed the acts of autobiographic narration known officially as the *discurso de la vida*.

To expedite the process of confession and to extract details of particular interest to the court's investigation, the Inquisitors would ask the accused a series of basic questions about religious beliefs and practices, as well as particular questions about the individual's family history, especially in the case of New Christians. The Spanish Inquisition saw a direct link between an individual's New Christian background and his or her propensity toward heresy, whether through inherited beliefs and behaviors or more insidiously through a preternatural/atavistic attraction to sin and theological error. This connection between *limpieza de sangre* and heresy informed the structure of the Inquisitors' questions. Originally only conversos were asked these questions but "by the sixteenth century, genealogical queries . . . formed part of most important inquisitorial trials."

Richard Kagan and Abigail Dyer cite a section of the Inquisitor's "Instructions" from 1561, which lays out the basic guidelines for this route of questioning:

> [Inquisitors are to have accused heretics] state their genealogy as expansively as possible, beginning with their fathers and grandfathers, together with all the collateral lines they can remember. [They are also to] state the professions and residences of their ancestors, and the persons to whom they were married, whether they are living or dead, and the children descended from these ancestors and collateral lines. The accused are also to state whether they are married and with [*sic*] whom, the number of times they have been married, and the names and ages of their children. And the Notary will write this genealogy into the transcript, putting [the name] of each person at the start of a line, and listing if any of his ancestors or members of his lineage has been arrested or punished by the Inquisition.[16]

The purpose of this extensive genealogy was to discover networks of possible heretical contagion passed through an extended family. By the 1580s these instructions became more detailed and the resulting autobiographic narrative was aptly termed *el discurso de la vida*. These *discursos* were also expected to include the places where the accused lived and the people with whom he or she had contact. The accused was encouraged and expected to be as accurate and detailed as possible in recounting the *discurso*, "extensively and in great detail."[17]

Within the confines of this coercive atmosphere lie the parameters for a rich area of autobiographic activity. Kagan and Dyer refer to the life stories narrated and recorded in these *discursos* as "inquisitorial autobiographies." The *discursos de la vida* were not freely composed accounts of the individual's life experience. The individuals who gave these *discursos* did so out of necessity and under duress; refusal to confess would often result in the use of torture; the information included in a confession, if incriminating, could result in an auto-indictment of the accused or lead to the arrest of relatives and associates. On a rhetorical level, the *discursos* were guided by certain standardized questions that delimited the narrative's composition. The originality and expressiveness of the *discurso* were further compromised by its transcription. Despite the meticulousness of inquisitorial documentation, errors were inevitable. On a more fundamental level, the narrative was necessarily altered given the specific guidelines the scribes used to standardize their records and in the common practice of recording the narrative in the third person.

These conditions are at odds with a modern conception of autobiography as "the culminating form of individual self-expression."[18] The self who is expressed—the life that is narrated—is mediated by the Inquisitor's questions, the coercive environment of the tribunal, and the rhetorical goals of the accused—their desire to avoid or mitigate prosecution and shield love ones from arrest. The *discurso* is not a self-directed exposition of the accused's life—an account of his or her psychological development. Rather, it is, in David Gitlitz's words, a "lobbying text." The accused are generally lobbying to deflect responsibility for their alleged crimes away from themselves and individuals close to them.[19] The *discursos* share similar mediating structures with other early modern autobiographic practices, most notably the *escritura de monjas*, or nun's literature.

Nuns throughout the Peninsula and the Americas were often asked by their confessors to write down their spiritual autobiographies. These autobiographic acts occurred within a clearly delimited context: The nun could neither initiate the writing nor choose the topic. The confessor decided the scope and focus of the text. Common points of interest were the nuns' experiences in prayer, ecstatic visions, or their account of being "called" to Christ. These autobiographies were undertaken for a variety of reasons: as a way of publicizing the nun's good example, as a spiritual exercise for the individual nun, or as a means of better understanding and supervising her idiosyncratic—and thus hard to control—mysticism.

In her discussion of the *autoría mediatizada*, or mediated authorship, operative within New World *escritura de monjas*, Kathleen Ross describes the central role of the confessor in the composition of these texts:

> The figure of the confessor or of the superior was always present, whether as a protector or as a harsh taskmaster because the nun was forbidden from engaging in a project as personal as writing down her own life story without being authorized or obligated by a male religious authority. . . . For this reason the act of writing is described throughout the *vidas* as an arduous task undertaken out of the love of God and as an act of obligation toward His earthly representative, the confessor.[20]

Narrating one's life was a potentially volatile affair, and thus the confessor had to be the means through which the story was told. However, it was the presence of the confessor that enabled and forced the nun to compose her story.[21] Thus life stories are of a piece with inquisitorial autobiographies in that both are instances of individuals narrating their lives through an intricate structure of mediation.

In his provocative article on "Inquisition Confessions and *Lazarillo de Tormes*," David Gitlitz uses certain aspects of inquisitorial discourse to reexamine the development of early modern Spanish autobiographic writing and its picaresque cousins.[22] Gitlitz argues that there is a clear link between inquisitorial practices of confession-directed interrogation and the rise of autobiographic writing in early modern Spain.[23] The need to account for one's activities and omissions, conversations and associations trained Spaniards—and in particular conversos and intellectuals who were most likely to have to account for their apparent doctrinal lapses—to create a public *vida* that they could present to their interrogators and elude punishment. Following Stephen Gilman (and Américo Castro before him), Gitlitz believes that the conversos possessed an intense and widespread fear of the Inquisition and that this fear was well founded in reality. In the sixteenth and seventeenth centuries the inevitability of inquisitorial persecution meant that "paranoia made perfectly good sense."[24]

In Gitlitz's schema, this looming threat of inquisitorial interrogation conditioned individuals to keep track of the events of their lives and create two "books": "the book of their life as they perceived it, and the book of their life as they hoped the temporal judges might read it, the temporal judges being the neighbors and servants, the business acquaintances and clergy . . . who might at any moment narrate their life to the Inquisition."[25] From this widespread and ongoing internal composition of life-narratives, Gitlitz sees a direct path toward the proliferation of autobiographic writing in sixteenth-century Spain:

> My point is that the likelihood of being called to account—at least for intellectuals and conversos—tended to fragment one's concept of self by requiring one to be constantly aware of how one appeared to others, and to be prepared at any moment to recount the edited version of one's life to an adversarial higher power. In this atmosphere, the ingrained rhetorical techniques of disclosure and evasion, strategies of self-promotion and vindication, and habits of incessant self-monitoring with their associated hyper-consciousness of one's identity as a reportorial voice, so harrowed the psychic soil of Spain that the autobiographical genres easily took root.[26]

Gitlitz argues that inquisitorial confessions share many thematic and generic practices with the other forms of autobiography that "peopled the Spanish literary landscape" in the sixteenth century: "Spaniards had to train themselves to think autobiographically. For intellectuals, and for conversos of any rank or station or religious predilection, survival required habits of thought which prepared one to give an autobiographical account on demand."[27] Drawing on Roberto González-Echevarría's analysis of the *relación*, Gitlitz sees the confessions composed for the consumption of the inquisitorial tribunals as a type of report. As opposed to the egocentric self-reflection of modern autobiography whereby, as Sylvia Molloy puts it, "I am the matter of my book," early modern autobiographic writing is a means to an end.[28] There is always an implicit or explicit reader/addressee, who, moreover, has often demanded the writing in the first place. The self-writer in this context is a reporter who accounts for his or her actions with a definite end in mind: evading punishment, receiving rewards, gaining favor or honor.

We can see this dynamic clearly played out in the first-person picaresque narratives that were written in ironic imitation of the "official" *relaciónes*, inquisitorial *discursos de la vida*, and confessions written by nuns for their confessors. The narrator of the *Lazarillo de Tormes* directs his narrative to an unnamed notable: "Your Mercy wrote asking that I would write to you and relate my case with great detail . . . so that you would have a complete report of my person."[29] It is an accounting to someone who assumes a position of power over the reporting subject. The reporter himself, then, has an end in mind when he is reporting—to make himself look good, pious, valiant, and the like, in order to evade censure or punishment or to gain favor and reward from the reader—and this end is a determining factor in the shaping of the report. Modern readers assume the autobiography to be an "expression of ego, or a presumably true record for posterity"; as Gitlitz, points out however, the early modern autobiographic narrative was a "lobbying document, a means toward an end": "The end governs those facts which are reported and those which are omitted. The end governs the context in which they are framed, the rhetorical palate with which they are colored, and the nuances to which, or away from which, the reader's attention is drawn."[30] In his analysis of inquisitorial trials, Gitlitz sees a progressive development in the narrative strategies employed by suspected Judaizers over successive generations. Interrogations from the first few decades of inquisitorial surveillance reflect "an artless naiveté with which the witnesses describe what they had done or seen."[31] Over time, however, the suspects produced strategically constructed confessional narratives to shift the blame away from themselves: "Later when all the roles had become somewhat ritualized, and the consequences of too-candid speech were widely understood, the confessions exhibit a more guarded hypocrisy."[32]

Those who appeared before the Inquisition were forced to compose a life story. That these stories were given "on demand" and were meant to reflect the verifiable facts of the witness's life did not preclude their narrative inventiveness; in fact, according to Gitlitz, the inquisitorial context was what inspired the careful composition of the *discurso* and cultivated an acute awareness of the audience's/interrogators' taste. The picaresque ironically reflects (or refracts) this discourse back and presents an alternative and subversive *discurso de la vida*. For both González-Echevarría and Gitlitz, the picaresque becomes the funhouse mirror of the official discourses, both secular and ecclesiastical, of empire; it affects a meta-literary "unveiling of the illusion of the power of language."[33] Along the way, however, the official generic practices bleed into each other and open new possibilities for self-expression from within. In the New World *relaciónes*, in the *vidas de monjas*, and in the inquisitorial *discursos de la vida*, we encounter vibrant narratives that make use of a wide register of generic practices and narrative strategies to tell their stories.

Carvajal, Montezinos, and Cardoso all spent time in the jails of the Inquisition and all three had to give their own versions of their lives for the consumption of their interrogators. After these experiences, these three individuals did not go on to write their own ironic inversions of inquisitorial discourse, their own *Lazarillo* or *Don Pablos*. It is possible that the basic structures and narrative modes operative in these texts, and perhaps even the very idea of recording their lives to begin with, had their genesis during the time that these three individuals spent under inquisitorial interrogation in Mexico City, Cartagena de Indias, and Lisbon. This scenario is suggestive and tempting. These texts reveal important markings of inquisitorial discourse; however, it would be erroneous to focus only on this one generic practice as the key to understanding them.

The varieties of autobiographical writing in the early modern Iberian context can rarely be differentiated from each other; rather, they should be seen as a network of interrelated generic practices. While there have been strong arguments made for the development of one genre out of another, I posit a circulation of texts and generic models, each influencing the other. The *relación*, the *vida espiritual*, the auricular confession, and the inquisitorial *discurso de la vida*—not to mention the pseudo-autobiographic picaresque—are interrelated: as they develop, these distinct genres are informed by each other and undergo a subtle ventriloquism of generic practices operating within one text. The *relación* often includes moments of spiritual introspection within its dry official frame. In narrating the soul's search for the divine, spiritual autobiographies veer off their confessional mode and recount vignettes of adventure and exotic travel or reflections on the mundane and quotidian.[34]

Early Modern Self-Fashioning within Its Social Matrix

At the heart of these circulating generic practices is a fundamental "embeddedness" of the author's self-fashioning within his or her intimate and extended social networks. The individual sense of self is formed through the encounter with others who make up his or her social reality. Far from holding back the individual's narrative of self, the encounter with parents, siblings, teachers, friends, foes, and lovers inspires and provides textual scaffolding for the autobiographical text to unfold. Natalie Zemon Davis suggests that autobiographical narratives during the early modern period rarely take on the formal literary structure of the modern autobiography. Instead, early modern autobiographical practices are "embedded" within a range of textual practices: juridical discourse, ledgers, correspondence between business associates, and family documents such as the tradition of writing *tsava'ot* (ethical wills) and personal inscriptions in the family Bible.

Writing about Leon de Modena's *Life of Judah* Zemon Davis places the Venetian rabbi's classic example of Jewish "Renaissance self-fashioning" into a broader generic continuum with earlier and more widespread Jewish autobiographical practices.[35] She sees the scattered examples of early modern Jewish autobiography, mostly from Italy and Germany, as representative of an active and established genre of Jewish writing. The widespread practice among both men and women of writing "ethical wills" and the custom of final deathbed confession, often witnessed by a quorum of ten men (*minyan*), are narrative practices that can be seen as "partway toward self-portrait." "Here one must speak as 'I'; one must reflect on oneself to another."[36] Contrary to those who limit autobiographical writing to texts in which the narrative is focused on the self, Zemon Davis and others discern a wide range of autobiographical practices developed by Jews and their neighbors in these less direct, or more "interested" formats. These "embedded" autobiographical texts provide a wider frame through which to understand the more explicitly autobiographical texts written by Modena and Glukl of Hamlin alongside the converso autobiographies at the center of this study.

Carvajal, Cardoso, and Montezinos write texts that are interested. Each author tells the reader his reason for writing down his experience: to recount the kindnesses that God has performed, to deliver a message of hope to the Jews of the diaspora, and so on. In this sense they are lobbying texts seeking a desired rhetorical end. This is quite far from the modern notion of a work all about the "I." Instead, in the early modern period, people wrote about their lives—engaged in the confrontation with their "self"—by utilizing an intense degree of mediation. These self-narratives were interested texts that were concerned with much more than their author's textual self-confrontation, at the same time that it was by addressing those outside demands that these individuals constructed a space wherein they could address their unfolding notions of self. Zemon Davis counters the idea that the "interestedness" of early modern autobiographical texts precluded any development of consciousness when she writes that "certain forms of embeddedness and most especially in the family could assist in consciousness of self. Not only were kinsfolk imagined as the audience for which the life was recorded, but also playing oneself off against different relatives was a major part of self-revelation."[37] Reading Carvajal, Cardoso, and Montezinos through the lens of family uncovers how their interestedness, and especially their deep embeddedness within their family and communal relationships, do not limit the autobiographical impulse; rather they form the frame, medium, and contours of that literary and psychological activity. The narrative's deep roots in the author's family and social structures does not diminish, but rather energizes the narrative self-fashioning and acts of self-reflection and disclosure.[38]

Writing His Way into the Book of Life: Manuel Cardoso de Macedo's Textual Transformation into Abraham Peregrino

At the beginning of his *Vida*, Manuel Cardoso de Macedo states that he wrote his autobiography as an expression of thanks for God's continuous kindness and mysterious providence: "Seeing the extraordinary means through which the Blessed God used to bring me to His recognition, . . . I wanted to make a memorial to the calamities and turbulent paths through which He brought me to His service, so that I could continually give Him praise for the mercies he enacted on my behalf."[39] It is not clear whom Cardoso had in mind as the intended reader of this "memoria." Was it a solitary exercise, an act of private devotion between himself and God? God is never directly addressed as the reader before whom Cardoso recounts his life. However, at certain moments within the narration Cardoso acknowledges the presence of a hypothetical "good reader" ("bom lector"). While he writes his *Vida* as an act of devotion, it seems likely that the *Vida's* goal was to serve as religious inspiration for others in search of a spiritual home.

The Sephardic community of Amsterdam in the seventeenth century was comprised of ex-conversos and their children. Most of these individuals were sincerely dedicated to normative Judaism; for others, however, the transition from Catholicism to Judaism was more complicated. Whether because of their ignorance of Jewish practice and belief, their difficulty adjusting to a new religious and social reality, or a basic skepticism toward religion in general (à la Spinoza), many of these "New Jews," to differing degrees, experienced doubt, confusion, and ambivalence toward their newly adopted religious life.[40] The Sephardic publishing houses in Amsterdam and in Venice printed a vast array of educational literature geared to this audience of newly "returned" Jews. Most of these volumes were translations of the Bible, the prayer book, and books covering basic points of ritual observance. The rabbis of these communities channeled considerable energy toward writing books of religious inspiration, polemics, and discussions of theological issues of particular interest to those Jews who only recently had lived as Catholics.

This impressive literary output is indicative of a readership looking for guidance and inspiration. Cardoso's *Vida* could have easily been written with this audience in mind. His rejection of Catholicism and Calvinism, his inquisitorial experience, and his heroic embrace of Judaism would make him an exemplary model for those ex-conversos who were filled with doubt and uncertainty about their decision to openly practice Judaism. It should be remembered that many chose to abandon their homes and businesses in Spain and Portugal not because they desired to embrace Judaism but rather in order to avoid inquisitorial persecution. Once in Amsterdam, some joined the Jewish community out of necessity, not conviction. Cardoso, however, chose Judaism despite the mortal danger it placed him in. His example, as textually preserved in his *Vida*, would be a powerful response to those still ambivalent about their religious commitments.

Although this might have been his targeted audience, the text was written in a genre that was almost nonexistent within the Sephardic community: the spiritual autobiography. An examination of Western Sephardic writing in the early modern period reveals a few moments of autobiographical self-reflection lodged within a sermon or a poem. However, it is very rare to find a text dedicated to an autobiographical exposition.[41] The texts of Carvajal, Cardoso, and Montezinos are among the few known examples. The dearth of autobiographical writing among the Western Sephardim, however, was not due to their isolation from Iberian literary influences. These communities were extremely proud of their Iberian heritage, maintaining literary salons, poetic *academias*, and reading the latest masterpieces of the Spanish masters.[42] It is possible that the spiritual autobiography did not find its way into the Sephardic context with the same ease as other Iberian generic forms because its roots lay in auricular confession, a religious practice alien to the normative Judaism these individuals were in the process of embracing.

In Judaism the penitent confesses to God or to the individual he or she wronged in order to gain forgiveness. In contrast to Catholicism, there is no intermediary who is sanctioned, let alone required, to hear one's confession. The model of writing down one's life in order to gain forgiveness and inspire others to seek God's path as exemplified in Augustine and Santa Teresa did not translate easily or obviously into a Jewish context. I believe that this partially explains why there are so few examples of autobiographical writing within the Sephardic community, despite their exposure to and emulation of Iberian cultural and literary models. Cardoso and Carvajal are two exceptions who prove the rule: they were both raised in a Christian environment and experienced their Jewish awakening within a thoroughly Christian context. Thus, they were more likely to see the autobiography as a viable response to their extraordinary religious experiences.

Carvajal's turn toward the spiritual autobiography makes perfect sense considering his thoroughly Catholic upbringing. Despite his family's crypto-Jewish activities, he was educated within the Church and spent time working in the Colegio de Indios in Santiago de Tlaltelolco, where he developed a close relationship with the learned rector Fray Pedro de Oroz. Carvajal was his personal scribe and had access to Oroz's extensive library, where he would have been exposed to confessional autobiographies modeled after Augustine.

Cardoso's early rejection of Catholicism and its sacraments—including the sacrament of confession—did not preclude his exposure to confessional practices. While auricular confession was not allowed in its Catholic form, Calvin encouraged a form of group confession, whereby the community helped the individual through his or her spiritual suffering. It is likely that Cardoso's autobiographical gesture followed a Protestant model of spiritual autobiography to which he would have been exposed during his time in England.

That autobiographical gesture—the textualization of the Christian's inner struggles with the devil and process of gaining "convincement" of being among the "elect"—was common in Calvinist spiritual autobiography. After successfully coming to this place of inner peace and knowledge of being among the elect, the Calvinist could then share his or her experience with "spiritual brethren." In his study of seventeenth-century British autobiography, Paul Delaney explains the importance of this practice to autobiographical writing: "Accounts of successful 'convincements' would be especially useful to those believers who were still enmeshed in the agonies of doubt over their own wickedness and uncertainty of election. From this kind of mutual help and encouragement it was a relatively small step to the writing and publication of formal spiritual autobiographies."[43] In his *Vida* and his trial records Cardoso refers to his extensive participation in Calvinist circles during his time in England, and thus it is not unreasonable to see some of these practices as a model for his choice of recording his trials and tribulations.[44]

It is difficult to fully ascertain why a spiritual autobiography like Cardoso's was so rare within the Western Sephardic diaspora. This cultured and prolific community was in touch with the wider literary trends of their time. Between the voyages of discovery and colonization and the wars of religion, early modern Europe was awash in a dynamic outpouring of personal narrative writing: travel accounts, spiritual autobiographies, and personal histories of persecution at the hands of "infidel" oppressors circulated widely throughout early modern Europe. However, the Western Sephardim, who were so adept at using the cultural practices of their Christian neighbors, overwhelmingly chose to avoid direct reflection on their tumultuous past. Instead they concentrated their literary energies on volumes of ornate baroque poetry as well as drama and didactic religious works. We rarely find instances of autobiography that reflect the move toward Judaism or of their former lives as crypto-Jews. The exceptions prove the rule: our three authors were all educated within a thoroughly Christian environment, with Carvajal actually completing his *Vida* while still in New Spain. Uriel da Costa wrote his *Exemplar vitae humanae* after being expelled from the *kehilah* of Amsterdam. This fascinating document was brought to light only posthumously by his friend, the Christian theologian Philipp van Limborch, as *De veritate religionis christianae: Amica collation cum erudito judaeo* (Gouda, 1687). The repackaging of da Costa's passionate *Exemplar* within an anti-Jewish/pro-Christian polemic casts doubt on the fidelity of Limborch's edition. The absence of da Costa's original manuscript complicates the issue even further. Da Costa's case points to the uneasy place of autobiographies within the Sephardic community. On the whole, only those thoroughly immersed in Christian culture followed this literary practice. Family histories such as the de Pinto manuscript and the texts relating to the life of Fernão Álvares Melo (1569–1632), both of which were collected and studied by H. P. Salomon, rarely discuss the tribulations of Jewish life in the Iberian world or the internal processes involved in openly embracing Judaism. These texts were also meant to be private family documents, not part of a larger communal conversation. While the Sephardic merchants were active travelers, engaging markets throughout the routes of global trade, we have almost no written accounts dedicated to their experience of travel.[45] This short list is certainly not exhaustive, and over time scholars may discover new texts, but the overwhelming impression is that the spiritual autobiography was not a robust genre among the Western Sephardim Whereas the Reformation and the Counter-Reformation used spiritual autobiographies as weapons in their external and internal wars of ideas, Western Sephardi Jews left these works to gather dust in their archives, at most.

In their fascinating monograph *A Man of Three Worlds*, Mercedes García-Arenal and Gerard Wiegers offer an intriguing explanation for the autobiographical silence among the ex-conversos of Amsterdam. They describe the atmosphere of a self-imposed "collective amnesia" within the Sephardic community:

> The New Jews of sixteenth- and seventeenth-century Amsterdam had suffered pain and traumatic experiences in the Iberian Peninsula, which later led them to deny or suppress their collective memory of a "marrano" past. This denial of memory, or "collective amnesia," resulted in a general refusal to acknowledge the fact that generations of Jews had ever been forcibly converted to Christianity; and this refusal clearly made it difficult to admit to the notion of a later "return" to Judaism. The topic of past conversions was strictly taboo among the Jewish community and could not even be mentioned as a way of exalting the Inquisition victims in one's own family. The family chronicle of Isaac Pinto and the works of Miguel de Barrios himself are good examples of genealogical memoirs illustrating the extent to which Amsterdam Jews had suppressed disquieting aspects of their Iberian pasts: the theme of Jewish descent and of a return to a religion that their forebears had been forced to abandon is quite simply never broached. The reason for this silence is clear—these authors had great difficulty in accepting the Christian conversions of ancestors who had been born, and might have been brought up as, Jews. The emotional effect of this denial was kept alive by many factors, and can still be detected even in the works of some contemporary historians.[46]

While Wiegers and García-Arenal see an almost total blocking out of the past, other scholars have pointed out numerous instances when the New Jews of Amsterdam did acknowledge and commemorate their experience in the "lands of idolatry." Miriam Bodian discusses the prayers said for Men of the Nation who were executed for Judaizing at auto-da-fé's; sometimes these martyrs had family members in Amsterdam, some of whom would later identify themselves as children of a martyr. Some cases of extraordinary martyrs of the Inquisition—individuals who held tight to their faith and challenged the Inquisitors—were honored with poems recalling their courage and piety.[47] But these practices rarely carve out a space for the individual to reflect upon his or her own experience. Especially rare are discussions of an individual's conversion story. This felt absence makes the texts we do possess all the more remarkable.[48]

Cardoso's choice to narrate his life experiences was not only a personal act of self-reflection. Cardoso's Old Christian past marks him as an outsider, and his *Vida* was part of a strategy to gain full acceptance from his new religious community.

As will be seen in greater detail in chapter 4, Cardoso's *Vida* makes the case for the sincerity and solidity of his conversion to Judaism. By describing his rigorously intellectual path to Judaism, Cardoso proves that his conversion is not based on mere opinion or circumstance. His numerous accounts of self-sacrifice on behalf of other Jews both in Portugal and in Northern Europe reveal his courage and commitment to the God of Israel and to his people. Cardoso's *Vida* becomes a lobbying document for his complete acceptance within Amsterdam's clannish and exclusive Sephardic community.

He is well aware of the imbalance of power between himself and his likely reader. To invert this hierarchy, Cardoso turns to the righteousness and selflessness of his deeds, the manifest presence of God's favor in his life, and the ultimate authority of scripture as the defender of the downtrodden and the stranger. His life and its textual record allow Cardoso to find his place of honor among his newfound religious community, the Jews of Amsterdam, who were probably his most likely, if unacknowledged, audience.

Cardoso's text is framed by a theologically charged preface and conclusion. These endpoints lay out the central theological argument of his text: Despite his Old Christian blood, the convert now known as Abraham Pelengrino has an honored place in the House of Israel. This theological framing of his account reflects a great deal of autonomy and control over the crafting of his narrative. We do not encounter the presence of any intermediary who intrudes into the writing or appears as the explicit *Vuesa merced* who is mediating the text. That said, the text partakes of certain narrative practices common to the notarial style associated with the *relación* and the *discurso de la vida*. He begins the body of his narrative by presenting certain basic information: "In order to begin the story of my fate, I am a son by blood of a man named António Cardozo de Macedo, native of Guimarães, a current resident in the city of Ponta Delgada on the Island of São Miguel, a squire and a merchant."[49] He goes on to explain his stay in England, the name of his father's English business associate, where he studied, and the exact date he arrived in England. As seen earlier, Inquisitors were instructed to record the genealogy, places of residence, and names of individuals with whom the accused had any dealings. As noted in the earlier analysis of Montezinos's use of toponyms, dates, and specific names, details served an important role in the *relación* as well. Mentioning the names of the seven Protestant sects he considered before settling on Calvinism, or including the name of the nobleman who cared for him after his conversion, ground his story within the reality of a believable narrative. This becomes especially true in the latter part of his narrative when he refers to certain prominent members of the Sephardic community who conceivably might have been able to discredit his account. By including their identity, he ensures that they become guarantors of his story's validity.

"Las puso con su vida. . .": Transforming Life into Text
in Luis de Carvajal's Mystical Autobiography

The opening lines of Luis de Carvajal's *autobiografía* introduce its basic narrative contours: who the author is, the main purpose of his account, the intended audience, and the structure of the ensuing narrative. The author/autobiographical subject is Luis de Carvajal's inspired alter-ego, Joseph Lumbroso, who was moved by the divine spirit to record "the received mercies and gifts from the hand of the Most High."[50] His stated goal was to make these divine mercies known to those who believe in and wait upon the "santo de los santos." This would appear to refer to other believers in the God of Israel, whether crypto-Jewish or otherwise. The events are recorded in the form of a "brief history" of his life up to his twenty-fifth year. This chronological narrative begins with his birth and continues until shortly before his arrest by the officers of the Inquisition, which, in turn, caused the transformation of the *Vida* from a spiritual autobiography meant to inspire its readers into a catalogue of Luis de Carvajal's (alias Joseph Lumbroso's) sins.

Carvajal says that the text was composed for those who "believe in the Holy of Holies and await His Great Mercies."[51] This is a text written for believers in search of the constant edification and inspiration they need on their soul's precarious journey through the wilderness of the world. Carvajal planned to send the autobiography to his brothers who were living in the religious freedom of an Italian ghetto. This would imply that his intended audience included the Jews of the diaspora, primarily those living in the safety of Italy.[52]

By writing the account in the third person and using the name Joseph Lumbroso, Carvajal distances himself from his autobiographical subject. Joseph Lumbroso becomes the protagonist of this retrospective narrative. This distancing between Carvajal and his autobiographical subject is complicated further by the central role that God plays in the narrative. Joseph is moved by the divine spirit to write his narrative—"awakened by the Divine Spirit." In a move reminiscent of other spiritual autobiographies, Carvajal does not write his life story of his own will; rather, he is compelled by an outside force. In Carvajal's case, that force is God himself instead of a confessor of flesh and blood. Carvajal's agency is also complicated by the central role that God plays in his life. Joseph Lumbroso is not the only protagonist of his *Vida*. Carvajal tells the reader that he has made a record of God's "mercies and gifts along with the story of his life . . . up until his twenty five years of wandering, in order, as a brief history."[53] The narrative tells of God's intimate presence in Joseph's life; on some level the goal of the *Vida* is to prove to its readers that their lives, their *peregrinación*/journey and God's providence are inseparable as well.[54]

The figure of the *peregrino* was metaphorically charged in the early modern Iberian world. Christian authors invoked the pilgrim to describe the path of the individual through the trials and temptations of the world toward salvation.

However, for crypto-Jews and ex-converso Jews in the Western Sephardic diaspora, the *peregrino* would refer to someone who found salvation by returning to the path of Judaism. Often the return to Judaism implied actual dislocations and wanderings in search of a place where Judaism could be practiced. The geographic movements and the travails of the road and sea, however, were secondary to the spiritual journey. Carsten Wilke cites these lines from the ex-converso poet Joao Pinto Delgado who describes the *peregrino* as someone who left the Catholic world in order to be with his "desired companions": "Leaving behind gentile impurity, he came to delight in the pleasure of the congregation of his beloved companions."[55] The journey of the *peregrino* is defined by his leaving a place of impurity in order to find his place in the service of the true God. By invoking his wanderings Carvajal taps into this central motif in Iberian religious discourse and invites his readers to find their own path to salvation.

It is possible that in choosing to narrate his autobiography in the third person, Carvajal is composing an autohagiography with Joseph Lumbroso as its subject. The *autobiografía* warps the penchant for details characteristic of the *relación* and the *discurso de la vida* into a mystically-hued narrative of divine grace, enlightenment, and spiritual audacity. After a brief exhortation to God and a justification for his autobiographic act, Carvajal begins to give the relevant information about his family and place of origin, his schooling, and the reason for his family's move to New Spain. Instead of simply stating these facts, Carvajal begins to weave in his theological meditations into the narrative. For example, the family's decision to go to New Spain, where they had to keep their Judaism hidden, as opposed to the religious freedom of Italy was understood to be an "incomprehensible and just" Divine punishment.[56]

Following the narrative mode of the *relación* and the inquisitorial *discurso*, Carvajal mentions all the places he traveled in New Spain, his various jobs, and the people with whom he has had both brief and extended contact: the "God-fearing" doctor who cured him upon his arrival in Tampico, the traveling priest who sold him a Latin Bible, the Rector of Santiago de Tlaltelolco whom Joseph served as a scribe, the old cripple who shared his Jewish books, the monk whom Joseph converted to Judaism, and many more. While some of these individuals are mentioned by name, most are not. By concealing their names, Carvajal could be protecting their identity in the unfortunate event that his text fell into the wrong hands. However, this precautionary measure cannot fully explain his choice. If he was concerned with protecting other crypto-Jews from persecution, why would he endanger his mother and his sisters by referring to their acts of Judaizing?

As will be explored in more detail in chapter 3 and 4, Carvajal sees divine providence revealing itself at every step of his journey. The individuals Luis encounters—his family, his teachers, his superiors, as well as strangers on the road—are described as messengers of God; Luis/Joseph encounters them at the exact moments that he needs them, and they give him what he needs in order to move on to the next stage of his spiritual quest. Dreams and mystical visions are central to the way that Joseph interprets his life. I believe that on some level, by referring to these individuals in a generic fashion, he can make them figure in his dream-like narrative. Without their names, they are stripped of their personal subjectivity, and their relevance lies in the role they play in the unfolding psycho-spiritual drama that is Joseph's life.

Dreams and mystical visions form an important part of Santa Teresa's *Libro de la Vida*.[57] Her confessor was particularly interested in better understanding her mystical aptitude and her techniques for achieving ecstatic prayer. Ostensibly, by presenting her experiences to her confessor, Santa Teresa becomes a passive subject being studied and observed. Her mystical visions, however, endow Santa Teresa with agency: She should be listened to because her ideas are not her own; they are God's. Her process of conversion, her victorious struggle with the devil, the clarity of her visions, and the efficacy of her prayer all prove the validity of her authority and the authenticity of her calling.

Dreams and their interpretation perform a similar function within Carvajal's text. They endow Carvajal's experience with a divinely sanctioned validity and turn him into a spiritual authority. Instead of telling his life story in order to avoid punishment or curry favor with his superiors, Carvajal hopes to inspire his readers' belief in the God of Israel and strengthen their commitment to the Law of Moses. In most instances of mediated self-writing the subject assumes a subordinate role to the reader for whom he or she is writing: a nun for her confessor, a conquistador for his king, or an accused heretic for an Inquisitor. Carvajal, however, speaks from a position of power. His readers are the other crypto-Jews who need guidance and encouragement; his enlightenment and the force of his experience allow him—as they allow Santa Teresa despite her official inferiority to her confessor—to assume a position of power and give advice, direction and inspiration.

Carvajal, Cardoso, and Montezinos produced texts whose artistry and rhetorical needs pushed them to blend and transform disparate generic practices into idiosyncratic and vibrant narratives. They reached their readers and told their stories by employing a variety of narrative voices. Our exploration of early modern Iberian autobiographic writing thus far reveals that they were not alone in this eclectic mode of composition. While the content of their stories differed from those of their Christian contemporaries, these crypto-Jewish authors participated in the same circulating exchange of rhetoric and language in order to transform their experience into text.

The ensuing chapters study how three individuals crafted their sense of self in conversation with their wider social networks and their more intimate family connections. These autobiographical narratives are deeply rooted in the communal relations of their authors. The most intimate of these develop within the home and the extended family. However, family can also function as an expansive organizing principle, creating connections with individuals normally seen as foreign. Bonds of friendship, trust, and community are formed with those outside the most immediate family circle based on shared beliefs instead of shared bloodlines, marital bonds, or business relationships. I refer to the groups created by these bonds as faith families. They are central to the dynamic of religious awakening and self-fashioning in Carvajal's, Cardoso's, and Montezinos's narratives. The self arises out of an encounter with the other. The authors' sense of who they are and the very texture of their journey in the world is marked by their intimate relationships, both with family members and with those who become "like brothers" through shared faith and sacrifice.

2 "Hermanos en el Señor"

Spiritual and Social Fraternity and
Paternity in Luis de Carvajal the Younger's
Spiritual Autobiography (New Spain, 1595)

LUIS RODRÍGUEZ DE CARVAJAL was born into a New Christian family in 1567 in Benavente, a small Spanish town close to the Portuguese border. According to his own account, he was secretly introduced into his family's crypto-Jewish practice during one Yom Kippur around his thirteenth birthday.[1] While most of his family practiced some form of Jewish ritual in secret, they lived outwardly as good Catholics: Luis went to a Jesuit school in Medina del Campo, and his brother Gaspar—who appears to have been shielded from any knowledge of the family's Judaizing until later in his life—entered a Dominican monastery. Luis's uncle, and namesake, Luis de Carvajal, *el viejo* (the elder), was a decorated conquistador who was rewarded for his services to the crown with the title of Governor of Nuevo Leon, a large frontier territory in the northeastern corner of modern day Mexico.[2] He invited his family to join him as part of the core group of colonists in this new territory. With their economic prospects narrowing in Spain, the family accepted the governor's invitation and followed him to the New World in 1580.

Luis was designated his uncle's heir and worked closely with him upon the family's arrival in Mexico. Luis was very careful to keep his own crypto-Jewish proclivities secret from his devoutly Catholic uncle. When he was not with his uncle, Luis spent much of his time with his father and his older brother Baltasar; they worked mostly as itinerant merchants peddling wares throughout the Mexican countryside.[3]

The Carvajal family's Judaizing eventually came to the attention of the Holy Office. Almost all of the members of the family, including their uncle the governor, were arrested, tried, and reconciled to the Church at the auto-da-fé of 1590 in Mexico City.[4] The governor died soon after his arrest, before serving his sentence of exile for harboring and abetting heresy. Luis, his mother, and sisters all confessed to their crimes and beseeched the mercy of the Mother Church. For their penance, the Carvajal women were assigned to work in a convent. Luis was first assigned to a hospital but was quickly sent to work at the renowned Colegio de

Indios at Santiago de Tlaltelolco, where he taught Latin to an elite group of indigenous men and served as the rector's scribe.[5]

After his first arrest and imprisonment, Luis deepened his commitment to crypto-Jewish practice. This tenacious drive eventually caught up with him, and the Holy Office arrested him a second time in 1595. This time he refused to confess his heresy and rejected the cross. After a year of investigations and countless theological debates with his Inquisitors, Luis de Carvajal, along with his mother and sisters, Isabel and Catalina, were sentenced to death at the auto-da-fé of 1596 in Mexico City.

Most of our knowledge of the Carvajal family comes from the extensive records of their two trials before the Mexican tribunal. In addition to the official transcripts from the court proceedings, we find several texts written by Luis himself. Within the docket of his second trial we find some texts that were written while he was in prison and were transcribed into his official dossier. These include several letters Luis clandestinely wrote to his sisters close to his final sentencing, offering them hope and courage. These mystically charged texts offer an insight into Luis's psychological and religious state throughout this last trial.[6]

As part of the evidence against Luis there was yet another, more extensive text: a spiritual autobiography, the *Vida*. This small leather-bound book was written in the almost microscopic script that Luis mastered as a scribe. It was preserved along with the rest of the testimony relating to Carvajal's prosecution in the Inquisitorial archives, which became part of the Archivo General de la Nación after Mexican independence. While the original book was stolen from the Mexican National Archive in 1932, the eminent historian of colonial Mexico Alfonso Toro had transcribed it a few years prior to this unfortunate theft. The *Vida* begins with Luis's childhood in Spain, discusses his embrace of Judaism, and his exploits throughout Mexico both before and after his first incarceration. From internal evidence in the text it appears that Luis began writing his *Vida* around 1592, after his first arrest. The text ends with events that occurred just a few months before his second arrest.

Luis intended to send the autobiography to his brothers Baltasar and Miguel, who had already escaped to the religious freedom of an Italian ghetto; his goal was to declare the glory of God's providence as it was revealed in his life. Luis, using his Jewish name of Joseph Lumbroso, introduces himself as "one of the wanderers and captives of the West Indies."[7] He states that he was awakened by the divine spirit to record the acts of providential kindness that graced the "twenty-five years of his wanderings," "So that it would be known to all those who believe in the Holy of Holies and who await the compassion that He shows to sinners."[8]

Luis's *Vida* is unique within the early modern period: it is an autobiographical account written by a practicing crypto-Jew while still living in the Iberian world. As discussed previously, while there are a few notable—and fascinating—autobiographies written by former crypto-Jews, they were all penned after the individual crypto-Jew made it to the safety of an open Jewish community. To write down one's Judaizing exploits while still within the grasp of the Inquisitors was an extremely dangerous (and unwise) decision—as made clear by Luis's case. What he saw as a record of his heroic exploits in service of the divine—"Lord of Hosts" (*Señor de los Exercitos*)—was used as "first-class" evidence against him in his trial as a recalcitrant heretic.

The *Vida* serves as a complement and counternarrative to the version of the Carvajal family's experience recorded in the copious transcriptions of their two trials before the Holy Office. Its goal is not to ascertain the full extent of the Carvajal family's heresy. Rather, it is a crafted and focused narrative of one individual's search for religious enlightenment and his struggle against the forces of nature and society. The *Vida* allows the reader to see the events of Luis's life as he chose to present them. The text is written in the third person, utilizing the name of Luis's Jewish persona, Joseph Lumbroso. The Luis/Joseph who is created within this narrative is heroic, self-sacrificing, crafty, and energized by prophetic inspiration.

Carvajal's narrative of personal transformation has generally been approached as a precious documentary resource in the reconstruction of converso religious mentalities or as a documentary complement to the Inquisitorial trial records of the Carvajal family's prosecution. This reconstructive work is essential and has benefited all subsequent research into the Carvajal family and crypto-Judaism in Mexico. However, the *Vida* has much more to offer the careful reader.

Reading the *Vida* through the lens of family, both as a thematic trope and a sociohistorical phenomenon, at once contextualizes the autobiography within its wider Atlantic world and opens up its psychological and religious dynamic. Here, I will focus on the constellation of family relationships and their impact on Carvajal's religious persona as presented in his *Vida*.

A Brief History of the History of the Carvajal Family

The Carvajal family's trial records have provided scholars with almost unprecedented access to the inner and outer workings of this early modern converso family. These rich records have been studied by a varied group of historians for over a century. The first comprehensive study of the Carvajal family was *La familia Carvajal* (1944) by the eminent historian of Colonial Mexico, Alfonso Toro. In *La familia Carvajal*, Toro uses the extensive trial records of the Archivo General de la Nación (AGN) and Luis's own writings, particularly his *Vida* and letters, to reconstruct the events surrounding the Carvajal family's activities in New Spain as well as to contextualize the experience of these conversos within the wider colonial reality of the late sixteenth century.[9] Seymour B. Liebman and Martin A. Cohen in the 1960s and 1970s studied the Carvajal family further, looking at the religious dimension of Luis's crypto-Judaism and the way this case sheds light on the wider story of crypto-Jewish activity in the colonial Americas.[10] In most cases the *Vida* along with the Inquisitorial record of the Carvajal family have been mined in order to reconstruct the historical context of crypto-Judaism in the Americas. Most recently, Miriam Bodian has brought a sharp eye and a nuanced approach to the study of Luis's life and eventual martyrdom in *Dying in the Law of Moses*. In addition to critically synthesizing much of the previous scholarship on Carvajal's career, Bodian offers a thought-provoking and sensitive analysis of the intellectual currents running throughout Luis's crypto-Judaism.[11]

My analysis centers on how Luis conceives of family in socioeconomic and spiritual terms as well as how he crafts the image of his family members—both the bonds of blood and the bonds of faith and dreams—within the narrative contours and spiritual exigencies of his *Vida*. The Inquisitorial testimonies deepen and complicate our appreciation of these social bonds. Many of these very same individuals present themselves before the Inquisitors or are described by others within the pages of the trial records. These different acts of presentation often contradict, subvert, or broaden the image that Luis crafts in his narrative. The *Vida*'s rhetorical goals determine the shape and import of a particular individual within the narrative just as the description of an individual within the context of an inquisitorial interrogation impacts the way that person is described or describes him- or herself. I do not look to either textual resource as an objective record. Rather, I am dealing with the construction of personae and the shaping of images. The counternarratives found in the different trial records will be used to contextualize and problematize the *Vida* and enrich our understanding of Luis's conception of family and the nature of crypto-Jewish family life in the late sixteenth-century Iberian world.[12]

Of Fathers and Uncles

Throughout his narrative, Carvajal develops intense relationships with a range of father-figures while his own father recedes into the background. Each individual supplements and nourishes an important aspect of Carvajal's personality. His interactions with these different figures prove essential to his spiritual trajectory. His most prominent paternal figure and the one who is developed earliest in the *Vida* is his uncle and namesake Luis de Carvajal, *el viejo*.

In many ways this relationship is quite typical of the socioeconomic structures of the early modern Iberian merchant class, among whom it was common for sons to live with their uncles as a means of learning new aspects of a business as well as a means of "thickening" the bonds between the different parts of the merchant family. In other ways, as we will see soon enough, this relationship was most unusual and ultimately untenable for uncle and nephew to maintain.

In his investigation of the social structures of the Portuguese trading diasporas of the early modern period, *A Nation upon the Open Seas*, Davidken Studniki-Gizbert points out the centrality of family bonds in the success of the global trading networks at the heart of converso economic activity. Not only were sons initiated into the family business by their fathers, but there was a widespread practice of nephews spending many years with an uncle in order to learn a different aspect of the family business and to "thicken" the bonds of kinship, trust, and mutual interest within a larger trading network, "Casa Comercial."[13] Studniki-Gizbert points out numerous instances wherein nephews refer to their uncle as their father and vice versa, or cousins refer to each other as brothers. In this sense, the time spent away from one's immediate family helped blur boundaries and allowed for a greater sense of a corporate identity within the family.

Luis and his uncle and namesake seem to follow a similar pattern with certain important differences. Because the governor did not have any children, he chose the teenage Luis to be his appointed successor. In acknowledgment of this new bond, Luis uses his matronym, Carvajal, instead of his father's surname, Rodríguez. During his first few years in New Spain, Luis works closely with his uncle and is trained in the ways of frontier government: He spends much of his time "pacifying" the fierce and nomadic bands of Indians known as the *chichemecos*—that is, beating back these tribes in an attempt to protect the developing silver mines of Taxco. Luis is being groomed to inherit his uncle's title in line with the special patent the governor received from the king.[14]

However, because of their religious differences, Luis experiences his time with his uncle as torture. He refers to his uncle as "blind and miserable."[15] While much of the governor's extended family, including his business partner and father-in-law were committed crypto-Jews, to some degree or another, the governor was a devout Catholic who would never tolerate Judaizing in his territory let alone within his family.[16] Luis had to keep his Judaizing a total secret from his religiously "blind" uncle. A dichotomy develops early on between Luis's inner life—the world of his autobiographical persona, Joseph Lumbroso, which he is able to share with his immediate family and the tight-knit circle of fellow crypto-Jews—and his public identity as the heir to the governor, Luis de Carvajal.

In the beginning of his first inquisitorial interrogation, Luis is asked if he knows the reason for his arrest:

He said: he did not know, although he presumes that this evil originated from the said Governor Luis de Carvajal, his uncle, who is almost a mortal enemy, for certain controversies between him, his parents and his brothers and for all the damage that he inflicted upon them in deceiving them into leaving Spain, for his sake they are poor and lost, or because some enemy has raised a false testimony against him.[17]

Luis points to personal and economic tensions with his uncle as the underlying cause of their enmity. For obvious reasons, he chooses to hide their deep religious differences in this first audience with the Inquisitors. In the *Vida* there is almost no mention of any economic falling out with the governor, outside of the frustration with their less-than paradisiacal living conditions in Pánuco. In his *Vida*, his uncle is an enemy because of his religious fanaticism, but before the Inquisitors Luis recasts their problems as financial squabbles common among family members. This portrayal is in keeping with the general defensive strategy Luis employs at the beginning of his first audience: He denies any possible trace of Judaizing, going so far as to claim to be of Old Christian stock.[18] During his initial audiences he claims that the only reason he would be arrested is the vendetta that his uncle has against him over economic issues.

As his first trial progresses, we get a more complex picture of the rift between the uncle and the rest of the family. Thus, we hear about Doña Guiomar, the governor's estranged wife who lives in Seville; the entire family stayed at her house prior to their move to Mexico. According to initial testimony by Isabel, Luis's older sister, it was during this stay in Guiomar's home before their transatlantic trip that the governor's wife approached Isabel with the mission of trying to convert the governor to his ancestral faith. Later on we hear about the fateful moment when Isabel attempts to proselytize her uncle and is almost killed by his zealous rage.[19] The uncle begins to draw a line between himself and the family. Initially he sees Luis as different from the rest of the family, as a loyal nephew and a pious Christian. While he demotes Baltasar from his position as treasurer because of his Judaizing, he tells Luis, "You are different." This eventually gives way to the full realization of Luis's active Judaizing, and at that point we can see a true break between them.

While Luis attempts to portray his problems with his uncle in economic terms, as the trial continues we see that the economic breakdown—his uncle's decision to disinherit Luis—is a reflection of a religious crisis, one in which faith is stronger than blood. The bond between uncle and nephew from the beginning of their relationship has dissolved. The governor had hoped that his hard-won achievements on the battlefield and his political maneuverings at court, which seemed to offer him a piece of the "conquistador's dream"—a noble reinvention as a new world *hidalgo*—would be passed on to an heir, if not a son then at least his next of kin. Yet, the religious divide ultimately destroyed the bond between the governor and his nephew.

Family Secrets, Shifting Narratives

According to Luis's *Vida*, his induction into his family's crypto-Judaism is almost coincidental with his uncle's invitation for the family to join him in New Spain. At the very beginning of his narrative he tells of his early education in the "rudiments or fundamentals of the Trinity" first with a "relative" and then later at a school in Medina del Campo, where he continually asked God to grant him "the light of his Holy Knowledge."[20] Luis reveals himself to be a deeply religious person even when he is firmly within a Catholic context. It is at this point that he discovers his family's crypto-Jewish secret: "It was on one of the special days, the one that we call "[Day of] Pardons," a holy and solemn day for us, on the tenth day of the seventh moon, and as the truth of God is so clear and pleasant, all his mother, brother, and older sisters and cousin had to do was call his attention to it [in order for him to accept it]."[21] This Yom Kippur revelation roughly correlates to his thirteenth year, and while it is not clear if the family was aware of the rabbinic notion of bar mitzva, a thirteen-year-old in the early modern world would already be assuming the responsibilities of adulthood and thus could be trusted to guard this volatile information.[22] Carvajal is initiated into the practice of secret Judaism by his family members: his mother, brothers, and sisters. His father, curiously, is not mentioned. In fact he plays a very minor role in the *Vida*: He dies within the first few years in New Spain, and his death is merely noted without impacting the narrative flow of Luis's *Vida*; at most Luis refers to him as "pious"—apparently indicating that he was committed to some form of Judaism but this was not a major force in his life.[23]

When Luis does mention his father, it is in the context of his father's decision to take his family to New Spain even though their true desire was to go to Italy "where the true God could be better worshipped." Implicit in Luis's comment is a sense that the move to Mexico, which the father decided upon, was not the best choice for their crypto-Jewish commitments.[24] Francisco Rodríguez de Matos is again shown in less than glowing terms.

After this reference to the father we only hear three more pieces of information about him. After being caught in a terrible storm, Luis and his brother Baltasar emerge unharmed, and when reunited with their family, their "loving" father greeted them with tears and "a thousand thanks and praises to the Lord." After this incident Luis mentions that he goes to Mexico on business with his father and that soon after his father passes away: "God took his father from this life." Luis dispatches his father's death with one line, but goes on at considerable length to describe his own providentially arranged and life-changing purchase of a Latin Bible.

His father's Jewish commitments are evoked one more time in the *Vida* when Luis discusses his sisters' marriage to two converso merchants. Luis stresses the point that his father had resisted the governor's plans to marry his daughters Catalina and Leonor to Old Christians, "soldiers and gentile officers."[25] His father withstood the pressure from his brother-in-law: "While he was alive, he [showed] great fear of the Lord in resisting [his marriage proposals] and upholding His highest command which prohibit it [marriage to gentiles]."[26] Within the entire *Vida* this is the one example of Francisco Rodríguéz's strong leadership within the family. We will discuss these marriages and their wider implications later in chapter 3; at this point however, it is important to appreciate that in the *Vida* Luis's father is a committed crypto-Jew and part of the family's inner circle of faith, but not a driving force in the family's religious life. From the *Vida* it would seem that his father was not an essential player in his religious awakening and thus little space is dedicated to his life and memory.

The minor role his father plays in the *Vida* is at odds with the portrait that emerges from his family's testimony during their first trial. In those proceedings we see Francisco Rodríguez de Matos as the one who teaches Luis and his siblings about Judaism. Francisca Nuñez de Carvajal, the matriarch of the family, claims that it was her husband who taught her about Judaism. An intriguing image of Francisco Rodríguez's secret Judaism comes from his son Gaspar, the Dominican monk. All evidence seems to show that Gaspar discovered his family's Jewish secret only later in his adult life, and even then it came in waves of ambiguous revelations, roundabout comments, obscure hints. During his trial he tells the Inquisitors about a strange series of questions his father posed to him as a means to instigate doubt as to the validity of Christianity in his son. The first exchange occurred while they passed through an Indian village. Apparently in the anonymous, non-Christian setting of this Indian village, his father felt comfortable asking seemingly innocent, yet theologically charged questions such as " 'Why do we keep Sunday and not Saturday?' "[27] Another day, his father shared "that he felt confused when he saw the preachers using the figures of the Old Testament, some for one purpose and others for another."[28]

In another instance the father asked a question that pointed to the ironic incongruity between the absence of all Jews from Spanish territory and their presence in the heart of Rome: "Why does the Pope consent to Jewish communities in Rome?"[29] In all of these cases, Gaspar tells the Inquisitors, he conclusively resolved his father's doubts. However, the last question, which was the most loaded and personal, was never fully resolved: "Why did he become a friar when he knew he could never be one?"[30] Gaspar understood his father to be referring to his converso lineage as an impediment to entering the Dominican order. Gaspar gave the "party-line" explaining that the rules excluding conversos were made "out of fear that they would revert back to something of their breed and caste from which they descended, and this one [Gaspar] was not reverting back to that."[31] Gaspar explained to his father that these rules were in place for other conversos, those who were unstable in their faith, whose Judaism was skin deep, and that Gaspar was not like them. His father left him with a biting observation: "Everyone thinks that about themselves."[32] His father was pushing Gaspar toward the realization that he was not so different from those "other conversos," whose Judaism was still coursing in their veins. Then the conversation was interrupted by the arrival of a stranger, and they never returned to the subject. That Gaspar recalls the details of these conversations several years later could be understood as a testament to their power and the role that his father played in his life.[33]

Gaspar also shared another indication of Francisco Rodríguez's crypto-Jewish commitments with the Inquisitors. In testimony given in connection with the family's first trial, Gaspar describes having discovered that that his father requested a Jewish burial. This sent him into a fit of rage. Seeking out his mother, he proclaimed that his father would be burning in hell,[34] though he did apologize to her later. Despite his horror at his family's crypto-Judaism, it appears that he does not want to either cut off relations with them or turn them in. He preferred to hold on to half-truths and vague observations that allowed him to believe that his family was not filled with heretics. Another tactic that emerges in his testimony is his stated belief that he somehow corrected whatever heretical ideas they might have had, as if all they needed was some loving fraternal enlightenment.

The governor's testimony also portrays Francisco Rodríguez de Matos's Judaizing as having deep roots. The governor says that he was worried about his brother-in-law's orthodoxy since they first discussed the family's move to Nuevo León.[35] The governor tells the Inquisitors that Rodríguez had originally planned to take his family to France where Rodríguez's brother Diego lived. It was clear to the governor that if his brother-in-law managed to leave Spain for the south of France, he, like so many other Portuguese conversos who made that move, would embrace Judaism. "He had heard that the Portuguese go to France to live, or to Flanders or to other remote places in order to evade the Inquisition and live in the Law of Moses."[36] By convincing them to move to Mexico, he prevented his sister and her family from living among "such bad people."[37] He worked hard to bring them to Mexico as a means of saving their Christian souls.

He tells the Inquisitors that once in Mexico, he worried that Rodríguez might have negatively influenced Luis, Baltasar, and the other children: "By chance they have absorbed some of their father's taint, . . . or perhaps, by chance, they were taught a false doctrine."[38] Catalina testifies regarding her sister Isabel that although Isabel claimed that she was taught about Judaism by her dead husband, Gabriel de Herrera, in reality it was their father, Francisco Rodríguez de Matos, who acted as her guide.[39] Catalina tells the Inquisitors that after Isabel's husband died, she was about to enter a convent—she even cut her hair in preparation for her initiation—but her father insisted she join the family in Mexico in order for her to embrace Judaism.[40]

Before the Inquisitors, Luis offers a version of his initiation into his family's crypto-Judaism that differs greatly from the one that he gives in his *Vida*. In his testimony from the first trial, Luis, like his other family members, points to his father as the teacher of the entire family. In this version, Luis tells the Inquisitors that his father waited till after their arrival in Mexico to initiate him into the secret and that he told Luis with whom in the family he could share his newly discovered faith—namely, his mother, Francisca Núñez, his sister Doña Isabel, and his older brother Baltasar. After his father's death Luis confided in this inner circle, and they confirmed his father's message: They were in that Law because his father had told them so and taught them.[41] They went on to discuss religious concepts such as the arrival of the messiah and the true law. In order to deepen their education in Jewish matters, Luis's father introduced him to some of the prominent members of the small, tight-knit group of Mexican crypto-Jews such as the old cripple Machado and, most importantly, the erudite Dr. Manuel Morales. These men became important role models and resources for Luis's and Baltasar's religious practice, especially after their father's death.

As his testimony unfolds, Luis, like Gaspar, tells the Inquisitors about some of his father's rhetorical skills. For example, he discusses how his father overcame Luis's doubts about abandoning Christianity—the only religion he knew.[42] According to Luis, his father was so bold in his belief that he even approached the governor and tried to shake his rock-solid Catholic faith. After this encounter, the governor confided in Luis: "'You know how your father lived in the Law of Moses?' and this one [Luis] responded while crying: 'It is a great evil.' And the named Luis de Carvajal [the governor] told him: 'and for this reason I love you more than your other brothers. You should know that your father wanted to deceive me, trying to persuade me to accept the Law of Moses.'"[43]

Luis deepens the image of his father as the prime mover of the family's religiosity, and for the benefit of the Inquisitors, he gives a picture of himself as remorseful, as well as conflicted about his Judaizing. His uncle sees him as "different" from his other family members; his uncle feels he can trust him, but not the others, because somehow he is truly Christian.

At this point, Luis presents himself to the Inquisitors as remorseful for his religious stumbling, painting his father as an active and compelling dogmatizer who convinced young Luis to embrace the Mosaic heresy. This portrait of his father as the driving force of the family's religious life stands in stark contrast to his limited place within the narrative economy of Luis's *Vida*. He is mentioned a few times and is described as pious but not as a major religious force in the family's life. He dies early on in the narrative, and his death is mentioned in one line. However, Luis's description of acquiring a Latin Bible which follows his father's death takes up considerably more space.

One obvious explanation for these two radically different versions is the fact that before the Inquisitors Luis was trying to control the damage done to the rest of his family. Luis might have decided to place the blame for the family's Judaizing on his dead father, instead of his mother and siblings. Although he is very clear about the extent of the family's heretical practices, he identifies his dead father as the instigator of the heresy.

However, I do not believe that it is so simple. It should be noted that almost all of the other testimonies, including those of the governor, Gaspar, Felipe Nuñez (a trusted soldier of the governor's), and others point to Francisco Rodríguez de Matos as a learned, active, and rather audacious Judaizer, not a pious but passive bystander, as Luis depicts him in his *Vida*. By minimizing his father's role in his religious development, Luis creates more psychic space within the *Vida* to chart his self-propelled religious trajectory. Luis's self-image in the *Vida*, and to a great extent in his second trial testimony, is that of a courageous, divinely inspired servant of God. Holy books are the source of his greatest religious experiences as are those moments of clear divine intervention that occur in his tumultuous life. Luis does not erase the presence and impact of his wider crypto-Judaic circle— his mother, sisters and brothers along with the many fellow conversos are essential to his religious life—but the axis of his spiritual development turns on his deeply personal relationship with God, which, from the beginning of the narrative until the end, is mediated through his study of sacred texts. And so in some way he minimizes the role of his father in order to allow his own self-actualization to unfold more freely, as well as to open up possibilities for alternative paternal relationships for his autobiographical persona, Joseph.

Spiritual Paternity

Luis's uncle would have been the most natural fit for a surrogate father, and, for his part, he does in many ways treat Luis as a son: He gives him his name, he designates him as his heir, and he trains him to take over his governorship. But their radically opposing religious beliefs make an honest and intimate relationship impossible. Despite their biological and socioeconomic bonds, Luis and his uncle do not inhabit the same social space. Luis and his family are part of an extensive converso network whose members, in addition to their family and business connections, share a secret commitment to the Law of Moses. Despite his own converso origin and his marriage to a Portuguese conversa, the governor places himself outside of the religious commitments of this subterranean community. He might have followed many of the economic and marriage practices common within converso circles, but he vociferously rejects their secret commitment to Law of Moses. In fact he is an enemy of those dedicated to the "true worship of God"—that is, Luis's fellow crypto-Jews bonded by faith and often enough by blood.

The first father-figure whom Luis mentions is the *licenciado* Dr. Manuel Morales, who traveled to the New World on the same boat as the Carvajals family. Luis describes him as "an acclaimed doctor, especially in the fear of God our Lord."[44] This doctor cures Luis of a terrible illness soon after arriving in Mexico, and it seems that his ability to provide physical healing is intertwined with his spiritual gifts. In one instance, Luis and his brother meet an old crippled man in Mexico City, referred to as "a Jewish cripple" who was treated by Dr. Morales. Seeing that the poor man's body was beyond hope, Morales decided to insure the health of his soul.[45] He left him a manuscript copy of Deuteronomy and other Old Testament texts, translated into *romanze*. Luis refers to this volume as "a book, or a medicinal compress for the health of the soul."[46] Morales left Mexico before Carvajal's first arrest, but his personal example and the various religious texts he distributed had a lasting impact on the crypto-Jewish circles that Luis was a part of.

While he does not mention him in his *Vida*, we know from Inquisitorial sources that Gregorio López, a saintly and iconoclastic hermit, nurtured Luis's evolving religious sensibilities.[47] Luis refers to him as a better Jew than himself: "He [López] keeps the Law of Moses more perfectly than himself."[48] In Luis's estimation, López may appear as a pious Christian but in actuality he is a devout Judaizer who "believes in one God." Luis proclaims, "if only he [Luis] would be like his shoe."[49] These statements are part of a rambling account Luis gave to the prison spy, Luis Díaz, who was placed in his cell during his second imprisonment. Díaz gained Luis's confidence by expressing genuine interest in Judaism. Luis seems intent on impressing Díaz with the audacity, courage, and piety of the wider crypto-Jewish network of México.[50] For this reason he describes the Judaizing of multiple fellow crypto-Jews and singles out other clergy who secretly practice Judaism. It would appear that in Luis's calculus, revealing Gregorio López as a Judaizer would make an impression on his religiously confused cellmate—and in a way that points to an entire subculture of other seemingly pious Christians who have embraced crypto-Judaism. Luis portrays himself as a student of López and someone whom López would care about. Luis pleads with Díaz to go to López upon his release and "to let him know about the way that he was going to die, because as [Díaz] would surely see, [Luis] was going singing and preaching the Law of Moses, and he would give him [López] notice of the joy that he had in prison, singing and dancing with much rejoicing because he was dying for God, his Lord."[51] Luis wants Díaz to know that he is a disciple of López and that López would be proud of Luis's commitment to martydom. While in many instances in his autobiography and his testimony Luis presents himself as the teacher and the leader of his fellow crypto-Jews, here he presents himself as a devout student of a master Judaizer, someone seen by most as a Christian saint but who in actuality was committed to the Law of Moses. In Luis's telling, López functions as a clear alternative to the harsh Catholicism of his uncle and the empty psychic space left by the absence of his father.

Hermanos en el Señor: Brotherhood, Spiritual and Social

Luis tells us of his close relationship with his brother Baltazsar, with whom he shares his commitment to crypto-Judaism: they travel the countryside peddling their wares in search of an honorable living for their poor widowed mother; along the way they meet other crypto-Jews, with whom they celebrate holidays, encounter new religious texts, and have opportunities to serve the God of Israel freely. At one point Luis describes their bond as interconnected, and elemental as the sea and land.[52] The fraternal love is bound up with their spiritual yearnings, their love for each other is "en el Señor."

Luis's brother Gaspar represents a more complicated view of brotherhood. As was noted earlier, Gaspar was never formally introduced into the family's secret, instead—as was done in many crypto-Jewish families—he was "given" to the church; he became a Dominican monk and he moved to Mexico before his family and lived in a monastery in Mexico City.[53] In the *Vida*, Luis is pained by his brother's spiritual darkness and wants to at least try to "enlighten" him: "They considered it regretful to leave behind their brother, the blind one, a Dominican friar, an educated preacher already [established] in his [monastic] order, and thus with a strong and loving spirit, both brothers [Luis and Baltasar] went to see him in his monastery which was located next to the inquisitorial prison."[54] The religious divide between Luis and Baltasar and their devoutly Catholic brother Gaspar does not (at least at first) negate their family bond. It is this fraternal bond that impels Luis to place himself at risk and to help save his brother from spiritual error. Is it an over-reading of Luis's matter of fact account to suggest that the location of his brother's convent "next to the inquisitorial prison" would serve to highlight Luis's bravery and selflessness? He is willing to enter the lion's den to save his brother.[55]

Luis initiates a Socratic style theological discussion by beginning with some simple questions about the nature of the Ten Commandments. At least in his own telling, Luis is victorious. However, what is of interest in this exchange (which takes up almost two full pages out of the entire 33-page text) are the ways that Gaspar is included and excluded. Gaspar is referred to as "the blind monk . . . the unfortunate one . . . sad" but also as "his older brother."[56] Gaspar's description of the Law of Moses as something that is "good to read it but not to follow it" is slammed as blasphemy by Luis.[57] Their theological differences are intimate inversions of each other. It is not so much that they believe in radically different religious positions, but that they each have radically different understandings of many of the same religious truths: neither deny the importance of the Bible—they disagree about what the verses mean; neither of the two brothers deny the existence of God or eternal salvation; however, they disagree about whether it is the "Law of Moses" or the "Law of Jesus" that achieves this goal. The distance between them is at once minor and unbridgeable. Their fraternal connection is what draws them together, but it heightens the pain of their theological disagreement.

When Luis invokes the support of Christian proof texts for his position on the eternality of the Law, he refers to "your preachers" and "your crucified one."[58] As if to say, "Yours, but not ours!" In Luis's telling, at the end of the argument, Gaspar is dumbfounded; he is convinced by Luis's arguments but cannot accept the truth; he pleads with Luis and Baltasar "let's not talk about this any more."[59] No longer able to engage in dialogue, Gaspar shuts down their engagement and concludes by setting himself off from his brothers: "Blessed be God who took me out from among you all."[60] In essence Gaspar is disavowing his connection to his family; it is as though God marked him from the womb and saved him from his family and the stain of heresy.[61] He is bound up with the *Sagrada Familia*, part of the eternal drama of the Christian mysteries. Gaspar does not need his brothers of flesh and blood, he has his monastic brothers in Christ. It seems that at this point the sense of dispossession and alienation is mutual. In response to Gaspar's rejection of their religious ideas, Luis and Baltasar rejoice in their lot: Both brothers replied, one from each side, "Glory to our God and Lord who has not left us in the blindness and perdition of this miserable one."[62] They respond "in stereo" by praising God for their lot and decrying their brother's sorry state. They praise "Nuestro Dios"; does Gaspar have the same God? These dividing lines are harsh but allow for easy mirroring: both sides call the other blind and "lost," sitting in darkness.

Luis tries one more time to reach out to his brother. He suggests that they take a few days to study and then meet again. Luis's bibliocentricism plays a major role in this encounter.[63] The Bible is the common denominator between the two and he proposes that through reason they should be able to arrive at the "truth" together: "whoever will be convinced by the truth should stay with it."[64] When they meet again, Gaspar tells his brother that he no longer wants to engage in these discussions: he excused himself by saying that his law forbade him from inquiring into it or debating it.[65] Instead of the primacy of the text and the guiding light of human reason, Gaspar holds fast to *auctoritas* and the handed-down dogmas of his religious order—there is no place for them to meet.

Luis's bond with Baltasar was informed and strengthened by their shared religious passion and shared experiences in pursuit of the Judaic truth. With Gaspar we can see that the bonds of brotherhood are severed because their theological differences are too deep. Their bonds of fraternal love and obligation are attenuated by this religious difference, and what might be more accurately seen as a discursive chasm. Gaspar's affiliation with his monastic order, his commitment to his spiritual brothers, prevents him from engaging the very ideas that Luis and Baltasar put forward. Baltasar and Luis come away saddened by their inability to reach their brother; in the zero-sum game of exclusive religious truth Gaspar's "blindness" will insure his damnation.

In retelling the story of this exchange, Luis is presenting himself as a dedicated brother as well as a successful "dogmatizer," actively seeking to win people over to heresy.[66] He is able to express and defend the truth of Judaism, reducing a devout monk to silence.[67] Beyond this heroic self-fashioning, Luis's relationship with his brothers reveals the ways that family ties, especially among conversos, can bind together individuals with radically different religious orientations. However, those differences can and do come between them. The diversity of opinion and commitments in one household is surprising and was hard for contemporaries to fully appreciate. In their interrogation of Gaspar, for example, the Inquisitors are puzzled that he would suspect some of his family members more than others. They ask him: why would he have differing levels of suspicion regarding the brothers, born and raised behind the same doors by the same parents?[68] His answer simply points to the difference in age, indoctrination and his own success in keeping some of his sisters "Christian." However, the Inquisitors surprise is understandable: how could brothers, raised by the same parents, be so different? In these tangled relationships we can appreciate the complexity of blood and faith, of the ways that belief marks the intimate connections between members of the same family and how those very same family bonds color and shape belief and religious commitment.

From Stranger to Brother in Faith: Fray Francisco Ruiz de Luna—Renegade Monk, Inquisitorial Spy, and Old Christian Judaizing Martyr

In the prisons of the Inquisition Luis experiences some of his most transformative experiences. As described in his *Vida*, prison is a site of prophetic dreams where Solomon, Jeremiah, and Job reveal divine secrets to him through parables.[69] Luis presents himself as a noble servant of the Divine, willing to suffer and sacrifice for his faith in the dark depths of the Inquisition's secret prisons. It is also a site of friendship and communion of a most surprising sort.[70] The Inquisitors place a monk who was arrested for minor religious infractions into Luis's cell. The monk, Fray Francisco Ruiz de Luna, was ordered to not reveal his religious title to Luis in the hope that he will be able to spy on him and provide the Inquisitors with more evidence of his heresy.[71] Early on, however, the wayward monk and the Judaizing heretic discover a unique bond in their shared captivity.

From their earliest moments together, Luis describes an easy and amicable relationship: after the two prisoners began to speak for a while, he was gladdened by the company.[72] They are both happy to have social contact, to share a conversation as a respite from the dark loneliness of their imprisonment. But as all things in Luis' *Vida*, the arrival of this monk is no mere coincidence, neither is it really about the poorly executed plans of the Inquisitors, but rather it is all part of a divine plan. Luis prefaces the arrival of Fray Francisco into his cell with a lament over being cut off from his holy books while in prison. He desires above all else to be able to pray and study the Bible. Sure enough, while Luis is denied access to books, this monk requests and promptly receives a breviary with which to pray. To Luis this is a great salvation; now, he is able to access the Psalms included as part of the Catholic prayer book and pour out his soul to the God of Israel. Luis describes his deep joy at seeing the prison warden enter their cell with the breviary: "With the highest delight and joy in seeing that the Lord, his God, sent him, through that command, what he so desired, which was to have a means through which to recite the Psalms as was his custom."[73] At first, however, Luis was unable to fully express his Judaism because of the presence of his "compañero," the monk. However, through Divine intervention the monk was "enlightened and converted to the true God."[74] Luis describes how they engaged in theological discussions and how after a few days the monk began to see the truth of the Law of Moses. Their relationship was transformed from simply one of prison camaraderie born of boredom and loneliness into a spiritual bond. In the course of a few days Luis went from hiding his Judaism to celebrating the God of Israel with the lapsed monk: "They would rejoice and console each other and would sing hymns and praises to the Lord. . . ."[75] They would dance and praise God for having enlightened the monk and allowing them both to share in the divine service.

They also bonded over sacred texts. Fray Francisco lent Luis his breviary, allowing him to "poach"[76] passages from the Hebrew Bible out of the Catholic text for his own Judaizing ends. Luis describes them spending hours in their cells discussing "sagradas historias."[77] During one such exchange, the monk was hungrily drinking in Luis's words when he declares: "What would I have given to have been enlightened by the truth of God outside of this prison, to have encountered it [the divine truth] while in the monasteries, which generally have open libraries filled with the sacred Scriptures and many other good books."[78] This bizarre offhand comment made by Francisco—his desire to have been a Judaizer in a monastery so at least he could spend his time reading the Hebrew Bible—plants a seed in Luis's mind. He asks, "are those books open to all?"[79] Luis is struck by the idea of having access to vast libraries of religious works and echoes his friend's sentiment and declares: "Oh how I wish I was in one of those. . . ."[80] Eventually this wish comes true, but even at this moment in the narrative, the two cellmates share the same dream of free access to religious texts.

In addition to prayer and study of the Bible, Luis and Fray Francisco share in another more primal religious act. Despite their hunger, the two Judaizers discard the pork products in their meager rations and bury them in the dirt floor of their cells as a "sacrifice."[81] Luis describes how they would suffer great hunger by passing up on this "forbidden food." These shared acts of devotion and sacrifice, as in the case of Luis and his brother Baltasar, serve to bring the two inmates together and transform the monk from a "good stranger" into "a confessant of the true God and His holy law" who eventually will wear "the martyr's crown" (corona de martir).[82] Luis is amazed at this transformation because of Fray Francisco's Old Christian background. He repeatedly mentions the fact that Fray Francisco took to the Law of Moses as if he were raised by Judaizing parents: "It was engraved on the soul of this good foreigner the divine truth as if he was raised in it all of his life and was taught it by pious parents."[83] Fray Francisco's embrace of the "truth," his bravery and sacrifice is miraculous—the divine truth has been inscribed on his soul, without the usual dialectic between nature and nurture. The case of this renegade monk who ends his life at an *auto da fé* as an obdurate Judaizer is a sharp counterpoint to Luis's brother Gaspar.[84] Despite their shared blood and despite Luis's best attempts to reach out to him and "show him the truth," Gaspar remains "other" to Luis; their fraternity is undone because of their different religious commitments. In the case of Fray Francisco, otherness is overcome by shared faith and sacrifice.

A powerful example of the role of sacrifice and the forging of a spiritual family can be seen in Luis's narrative of Fray Francisco's eventual martyrdom. Fray Francisco is sentenced to the galleys after his first inquisitorial trial. While on board he reportedly desecrated a crucifix and was re-arrested by the Holy Office. During his second trial, Francisco declared himself a devout Judaizer. He also lied to the Inquisitors in order to protect Luis. He testified that Luis taught him about Judaism before Luis's confession and reconciliation to the Church, thus saving Luis from being arrested as a false "reconciliado."[85] Luis praises the monk for his bravery and integrity: "Joseph's companion confessed the truth of the God of Israel before the tyrants with such a courageous spirit that has never been seen in someone of a foreign nation."[86]

According to the *Vida*, Francisco tells the Inquisitors to their faces that only the God of Israel is true and all other gods are frauds and tricks of the Devil. He audaciously claims that the "king and the inquisitorial dogs" know this but their hearts are hardened to the truth like the heart of Pharaoh.[87] It is not only that Francisco is pious, passionate, and brave; his commitment to Judaism is remarkable because of the way that it breaks with his ethnic past. He is of an "estraña nación," an Old Christian, but becomes a crypto-Jewish martyr. Through his sacrifice he gains communion with Luis and his people.[88]

Fray Pedro de Oroz, a Christian Father Figure
Who Enables Luis's Jewish Rebirth

We have already discussed the minor role that Luis's father plays in the *Vida*. In his place, Luis has a wide range of alternative father-figures, most notably his uncle and Dr. Morales. These two represent two extremes—his uncle is a zealous Catholic, intolerant of any Judaizing proclivities, whereas Morales is the paragon of crypto-Jewish piety and heroism. In addition, after his first trial, Luis encounters a third figure who has a profound effect on his religious development and whose kindness leaves a lasting impression on his entire family.

As part of his penance after his first trial, Luis was assigned to work at a hospital and its adjacent church.[89] Luis missed his beloved sisters and mother who were assigned to a different locale. He was also deeply troubled by his job as a custodian which included taking care of the statues of the saints in the church.[90] The idea of tending to the "House of the Idols" drove Luis to tears—while mopping the floor Luis would cry his woe.[91] After a year at this job, he gained permission to rejoin his mother and sister and was placed under the watch of Fray Pedro de Oroz, the rector of the Colegio de Santiago de Tlaltelolco.[92] At Tlaltelolco Luis taught Latin to the Indian students and was a scribe for Fray Pedro. It was during these years, 1591–94, that Luis managed to gain access to and copy a vast amount of religious literature essential to his crypto-Jewish self-discovery. The accessibility of Bibles and exegetical and philosophical commentaries allowed Luis to learn more about the Old Testament and deepen his understanding of the practical and theological underpinnings of his devotion to the Law of Moses.[93] Fray Pedro's confidence in the sincerity and efficacy of the Carvajals' penitence afforded the *reconciliados* a great degree of liberty, which they used to clandestinely reconnect to their crypto-Jewish practices. They developed close friendships with the leading crypto-Jews of Mexico City and the surrounding countryside, spent the Sabbath with them in prayer, and celebrated the festivals of Passover and the Day of Atonement.

Luis first describes Fray Pedro with great tenderness and respect for his piety: "An elderly monk, a man of great virtue. . . . [He] loved [Joseph] and with a special love, he loved not only Joseph but also all of his people. And since the bloodthirsty wolves took away their goods and property and they [Luis's family] were left impoverished, this one from his very own plate and table would give to them for all the days of his life."[94] The fact that Fray Pedro is a devout Catholic does not color Luis's positive description. Fray Pedro is a man of "virtue" and generosity despite his Catholicism. Compared to the "bloodthirsty wolves" of the Inquisition who have left them destitute, Fray Pedro shares his own food with the Carvajals. His love is "strange" or "special," and it extends to Luis's "people," presumably Luis's family.[95]

As Fray Pedro's scribe, Luis works very closely with him; this allows them to bond over their shared intellectual passions. Luis is given the special privilege of having his own key to the library to facilitate his copying of various manuscripts. As is often the case in the *Vida*, this favor is framed as a sign of divine providence; it is an act of mercy, straight from God's generous hand.[96] Luis points out that none of his other companions in the monastery were given this privilege.[97] The theological framing of their relationship notwithstanding, in Luis's narrative he and Fray Pedro have a shared passion for books. Just four months after Luis's arrival at the monastery, Fray Pedro purchases Nicolas de Lyra's glosses on the Pentateuch. Luis describes Fray Pedro's excitement and desire to share the good news with Luis: "and when they brought them [the books] he himself [Oroz] came bringing good tidings and Joseph responded, 'O what precious things have we brought to our school!'"[98] Both master and disciple revel in their good fortune to have access to such erudite texts.

At the same time, however, the books in the monastery's library mean something different to each of these curious intellectuals. For Fray Pedro they are edifying Christian texts, part of the expanding orbit of post-Renaissance Christian literature. For Luis they are a rich source of biblical and rabbinic materials for him to mine for his own Judaizing purposes. He reads Nicolas de Lyra in order to copy out the passages from rabbinic and medieval Jewish sources that Lyra cites as part of his commentary. He reads Oleastre to seek out bits of rabbinic literature and even discovers the ideas of Maimonides: "In this book the Lord revealed for him the holy thirteen principles and fundamentals of our faith and religion, something not known of or heard of in these lands of captivity."[99] Luis reads these texts clandestinely, sneaking away to make his own copies of biblical passages and craft anthologies of Jewish literature for future use—what he refers to as his "nourishment for the soul."[100] It is clear from Luis's *Vida* that he believed the rector would be displeased if he found him "Judaizing" the library. He describes how he would work on his own texts at night when everyone else was asleep or between classes. His fear of being found out by Fray Pedro is captured in one passage in the *Vida* where he describes an instance when he was about to enter the library, but felt a premonition from God to wait because Fray Pedro was approaching. Although Fray Pedro shares Luis's joy and passion for sacred books, they clearly see the books in radically different ways, and Luis must betray the trust of his benefactor in order to follow his true convictions.

Perhaps Luis's most audacious betrayal of Fray Pedro's largesse occurs a few years later when he sets out to collect alms in order to pay off his penance. Through intensive lobbying and bribery on the part of his brother-in-law Jorge de Almeida, Luis and his family were granted a release from the restrictive terms of their penance in exchange for a large sum of money that they were meant to collect through alms. In order to help Luis gain his freedom, Fray Pedro not only releases him from his duties at the monastery, but arranges for Luis to receive fifty letters commending him to all the monasteries in the province: "He again favored Joseph as he did previously."[101] This act of kindness and concern on the part of Fray Pedro enables Luis to free himself from the limitations of his penance. Through his travels he makes the most of the hospitality of the monasteries while at the same time reaching out to Judaizers throughout the countryside and celebrating Jewish rituals with them.

We can assume that Fray Pedro believed that he was showing Christian charity toward a sincere *reconciliado*. Luis, however, uses this trust in order to collect the money that will enable him and his family to leave New Spain and eventually travel to the religious freedom of an Italian Jewish community. This subterfuge is in line with Luis's crypto-Jewish activity—he lives outwardly as a pious Christian while he secretly subverts Christian texts and practices in the course of his Judaizing. Within the inquisitorial context, Luis has no other choice but to hide his true intentions from Fray Pedro, and in the *Vida* there is not the slightest hint of remorse or concern. In fact Luis treats the entire relationship with Fray Pedro, from his initial request to bring Luis to Tlaltelolco to his ongoing kindness and granting of special privileges to Luis, as orchestrated by the hand of God. In the theological frame of Luis's *Vida*, Fray Pedro is an instrument of Providence. However, there are fissures in that orthodox narrative, cracks in the providential view that allow Luis to relate to Fray Pedro with tenderness. And in those moments we see one of the remarkable ways that this impassioned crypto-Jew, who was so committed to his "heresy" that he was willing to risk it all for the God of Israel and the Law of Moses, was able to connect with this kindly priest who nurtured and cared for him and his family both physically and spiritually.

This relationship points to the complexities of crypto-Jewish identity formation. Luis's crypto-Judaism is ultimately very Christian—he crafts a Judaism out of Christian texts and reworked Christian concepts. His religious bond with other crypto-Jews has to do with a shared belief and a shared rejection of Christianity. But Judaism and Christianity cannot be so neatly separated—one flows from the other—both have evolved in a conscious and subconscious dialectic with each other.[102] Thus Luis is able to appreciate the humanity and kindness of Fray Pedro and share in his joy over the arrival of a particular book; but at the same time, Luis exploits his kindness and uses his books toward very different ends.

Gaspar the Dominican monk is Luis's brother in blood, but because of their religious differences they become estranged from each other. Both brothers feel blessed to have been saved from the other's fate: Gaspar is thankful that he was never tainted with Judaism, while Luis praises God for having enlightened him with the Mosaic truth. His cellmate, the renegade monk, is a stranger who becomes part of his people through faith, devotion, and sacrifice. With Pedro de Oroz we find a more ambiguous relationship. He is a father-figure, whose benevolence nurtures Luis's body and soul but who ultimately is not part of his spiritual quest.

In the next chapter we will analyze the dynamic between Luis's social bonds and his religious self-fashioning as it plays out in his relationships with women, with a primary focus on his relationship with his mother and sisters. These intimate bonds play an essential role in Luis's religious leadership. Luis's interactions with his sisters take place primarily within the domestic sphere, and this context informs the nature of these relationships. Luis's social bonds are solidified by the primacy of text and direct access to divine inspiration as the engine for religious activity. Yet the gender dynamic between Luis and these women also has a profound impact on the way he conceives of his place within his family drama and in turn how he shapes his spiritual self-portrait in the *Vida*.

3   A Prophetic Matrix

Motherhood, Sorority, and a Reimagined Sagrada Familia

Luis's MOTHER AND sisters are central players in his own story of spiritual enlightenment. The relationships he develops with them offer a window into understanding Luis's complex acts of self-fashioning, but also deepens our understanding of the nature of family in the wider context of Mexican crypto-Judaism. It is impossible to consider the role of his sisters without including Mariana's and Leonor's husbands who become fully integrated into the Carvajal family and their travails. These marriages give us an insight into converso social practices and the relationship between socioeconomic and religious concerns. They also illuminate the power and limitations of social cohesion as well as the more ephemeral but intense spiritual bonds between individuals. For this reason, as we turn toward the strong females in Luis's life, we will also explore his relationship with his brothers-in-law, and their role within the Carvajal family.

One trend in historiography locates the center of crypto-Jewish religiosity within the domestic sphere and identifies women as the main agents of religious activity and community-building.[1] Under the eye of the Inquisitors, conversos wishing to continue their dedication to Judaism had to avoid practicing Jewish rites in public; therefore, the privacy of the home was the preferred space for crypto-Jewish religious activity. From their roles in the preparation of food to the conduct of intimate prayer circles, crypto-Jewish women were central to the underground practice and maintenance of Judaism. While not diminishing the importance of domesticity and women's leadership within the crypto-Jewish context, our study of the Carvajal family offers a counterpoint to this scholarly tendency.

In the Carvajal family we encounter a crypto-Judaism in which family is essential, but the domestic sphere—and domestic activities such as cooking, cleaning, and so on—are not at the center of religious life.[2] Rather, in the case of the Carvajals and their wider converso network, prayer, fasting, and direct engagement with sacred texts, as well as active rejection of Catholic symbols and theology, are the mainstays of religious activity. In Luis's spiritual autobiography and his letters penned in prison, as well as the extensive trial records of the family's two encounters with the Holy Office, we see a dynamic wherein the impetus and energy for their commitment to crypto-Judaism is shared among multiple family members and members of the wider converso network, male and female.

Luis de Carvajal's relationship to text and textuality shapes this social-spiritual dynamic. Sacred texts serve as the fuel for Luis's religious quest: they guide his understanding of Jewish rituals and beliefs, they inspire the prayers he composes and teaches to his sisters, and they fill the tiny notebooks brimming with inspirational religious texts he shares with his family. But Luis's relationship to text goes beyond their utility and inspirational power. Luis relates to his and his family's experience as part of a grand divine narrative. The vicissitudes and small salvations that his family experiences are part of a providential story that needs to be deciphered. His religious leadership is informed by the sacred texts he encounters, but perhaps more importantly, he refracts his and his family's experience through a providential lens. He believes that this narrative will inspire his fellow crypto-Jews, most notably his family, to see themselves as part of a divine plan, and thus, despite all of the danger and hardship they experience, they can be sure that they are on the path of righteousness.

In his *Vida* Luis is the main interpreter of these texts and the prophetic narrator of their experience; thus, he assumes a central role in the family's crypto-Jewish activities. His drive to fashion himself as the family's spiritual guide overshadows and distorts the religious passion and heroism of some of his relatives as recorded in other sources. The various recorded testimonies allow us to consider alternative narratives and the choices that Luis makes in crafting his story.

In the following section, I will focus on some of the central female protagonists within Luis de Carvajal's religious and social network. There is a complex interplay between how these individuals are portrayed in the varied inquisitorial testimonies and the personae they assume within Luis's *Vida*. This tension informs the discussion of Luis's mother, Francisca Rodríguez de Carvajal, his sisters Catalina and Leonor and their husbands, his younger unmarried sisters Mariana and Ana, and his older sister Isabel.

Francisca Nuñez de Carvajal: Saintly Martyr, Inspired Matriarch

First we will focus on Luis' relationship with his mother as refracted through his autobiographical narrative and his trial records. This relationship is one of the central currents running through Luis's self-fashioning and his transformation of his family's experiences into a divine drama of struggle, sacrifice, and enlightenment.

The *Vida* opens with an exhortation to the God of Israel and praise for his providence, which has guided Luis/Joseph through twenty-five years of wandering. After his initial exhortation he begins with his youth and quickly moves on to tell of his initiation into the family secret. As discussed in the previous chapter, Luis writes that on a Yom Kippur around his twelfth or thirteenth year, his mother, sisters, an older brother, and a cousin introduce him to the truth of their family's crypto-Jewish identity[3] As noted earlier, at this seminal point in his religious awakening his father is absent, and it is his mother who assumes a position of leadership.

In the previous chapter, we saw how the absence of his father inspires a quest for spiritual fathers and teachers such as the well-versed Dr. Morales, the eccentric Christian saint, Gregorio López, and even the kind and learned Pedro de Oroz, the rector of the monastery where Luis eventually works after his first imprisonment. But it is important to see the role that his mother plays in his spiritual development, well beyond his initiation. Throughout the *Vida* she is described as saintly and pious. When his sisters are engaged to two new Christian merchants, the event is described as almost miraculous. Not only was it celebrated by the inner circle of the family but their non-converso neighbors, "foreign and gentile women," come to congratulate the family and turn to the matriarch with amazement over the great turn in fortune brought about by these nuptials.[4] "Giving the good word to the blessed mother, many of the gentile women said to her: 'My lady what a great prayer you offered' to which she responds, 'as Saint Sarah said, "it is not all up to the merits of Man—which are always few or nonexistent, but rather Divine Mercy.'"[5] While Sarah the biblical character never utters these exact words, this description echoes the sentiments of wonder and amazement expressed by the biblical Sarah after the birth of Isaac. This is one of the many ways that Carvajal weaves the strands of his family's experience in a biblicist mode, shaping their individual personae into the cast of a providential drama.

This biblicizing of his mother within the *Vida* becomes more established after their first imprisonment. During her arrest, Luis describes her as "the blessed mother, who although she was wounded by such a savage blow from such a cruel enemy, donned her cloak with gentleness and crying [over] her trials while praising God for them, she was taken by those cursed ministers, the butchers of our lives, to that most dark prison."[6] Despite the cruelty of her fate, she bears her burden with faith in the divine and acceptance of His judgments. Luis uses the term *mansedumbre*, which refers to the docile nature of sheep, to describe his mother's attitude to her persecutors because she walks faithfully, as sheep do, to the slaughter of the wolf-like clutches of the Inquisitors. In other scenes, the Inquisitors are described as "murderous wolves"; here they are "verdugos," butchers, executioners.[7]

One Friday morning when Luis hears his mother being taken from her cell, he realizes that she is being taken to the torture chamber, and through a crack in the door he hears her suffering. Luis gives a graphic account of his mother's torture. Luis tells the reader that he felt more pain and bitterness on that day than during all of his imprisonment. As he heard his mother's screams he prostrated himself on the ground. Presumably Luis was praying for his mother, pleading with God to show mercy, or was he simply overcome with emotion as he heard his mother's suffering?

Then, however, Luis's profound sense of helplessness and sorrow gives way to a prophetic vision. Falling into a deep slumber as he lies at the foot of the door, listening to the horrific sounds of his mother's torture, he receives a clear message of divine consolation: A devout man appears to Luis with a beautiful "batata" asking him to smell it. Luis concurs that the yam smells good, and the man then breaks it in half and reveals the meaning of this vision: "Your mother who was whole before she was imprisoned and broken by torment was like a good smelling fruit with the good scent of patience [*olor de paciencia*] before the Lord, but now that she is broken with torments she gives an even greater scent of patience before the Lord."[8] Her image as a devout and brave martyr is confirmed in this dream. The dream's imagery echoes the biblical phrase for a sacrifice accepted with divine favor—his mother's suffering and sacrifice make her deeds sweeter to the Lord.

In a later scene, during a moment of turmoil involving a possible encounter with the Inquisition, his mother receives a dream that reveals that the threat the family feared would prove to be a false alarm and that God would protect them again.[9] With this dream, Luis points the image of his mother in a new direction. She is not only a saintly martyr, but she, like her son, has become enlightened and touched with prophecy.

We do not know what Francisca Carvajal de Rodríguez thought of her torture. We do not know if she interpreted it as a divine gift, or if she felt closer to her God after leaving the torture chamber. The matriarch of the Carvajal family becomes a central character in Luis de Carvajal/Joseph Lumbroso's narrative of spiritual resistance, religious heroism, and divine grace. He fashions his mother's persona accordingly, representing her as a saintly matriarch, suffering for her children and her faith. Serving as an inspiration to Joseph, she would have been a heroic model for the intended readers of the *Vida*.

Love and Marriage: Ties That Bind

We begin our analysis of the relationship between Luis, his sisters and the wider crypto-Jewish network with a formative moment in their lives that had a lasting impact on the entire Carvajal family—namely, the marriage of Carvajal's sisters, Catalina de la Cueva and Leonor de Andrada to Antonio Diaz de Cáceres and Jorge de Almeida, respectively. I include this exploration of the personalities of Luis's brothers-in-law and their complex relationships with the rest of the family in this section because they enter into the Carvajal family network through their marriage to Catalina and Leonor. Marriage is an essential element of converso socioeconomic and religious activity. Women in the pre-modern world so rarely wrote about their experiences and thus we must look to more mediated and indirect records of their lives such as text describing their interactions with their husbands and other family members as a way to investigate their attitudes, activities, and self-perceptions. Almeida and Díaz de Cáceres's story, and the textual trail they left behind, will open up new ways of understanding their marriages and the socio-psychological dynamic of the wider Carvajal family.

We have already discussed the providential frame and heavy biblical imagery Luis uses to describe this event, especially as it relates to his mother. However, these nuptials had a profound impact on the wider Carvajal family network and illustrate how socioeconomic concerns are inextricably intertwined with religious commitments. As discussed earlier, Francisco Rodríguez de Matos, the deceased patriarch of Luis's family, plays a rather minor role in his family's religious life in the *Vida*. However, in one area, he does actively fight to preserve his family's crypto-Judaism, consistently rebuffing his brother-in-law's marriage proposals for his daughters. The governor wanted to introduce them to eligible Old Christian soldiers, an option that in Luis's telling was clearly anathema to his father's crypto-Jewish commitments.

Marriage was not a matter of the heart; it was a method for solidifying a family's interests, mostly social and economic. The governor's desire to marry his nieces to upstanding Old Christian soldiers was a means for this conquistador with a checkered converso past to integrate himself more fully into the Old Christian establishment. His niece's marriage to other members of the class of conquistadores and land owners would signal his full arrival into Old Christian society, while also serving as a bulwark against the family's converso past and his wife's active Judaizing. Perhaps he also felt that marrying off his young nieces to Old Christians would inevitably crush any Judaizing tendencies they might have and thus protect him from further scandal. It is possible, of course, that the governor might have believed, or wanted to believe, that his extended family were actually good Christians who, like himself, welcomed the opportunity for burying their converso past.

In the *Vida*, Francisco Rodríguez's opposition to the governor's potential grooms is presented as an act of religious resistance—a deep commitment to passing on the family's crypto-Jewish life. It also reflects a different view of socioeconomic success. Francisco Rodriguez was interested in perpetuating and expanding his family's mercantile activity by marrying his daughters to other commercially oriented New Christians, while his brother-in-law saw his future among the ranks of the New World landed gentry, men like him, who came to the Americas and through the sword were able to remake themselves into a new nobility.

These New World hidalgos were former warriors who were rewarded with land and in many cases forced Indian labor.[10] Carvajal was certainly on that path:

He was not only a rich man, but also a decorated warrior whom the king rewarded for his services with a *nearly* noble title in that Carvajal now had the right to pass his governorship down to an heir. Moreover, in addition to being a successful conquistador in Mexico, he had previously engaged in slave trafficking in Africa and trade in the Caribbean, activities that were quite common for young men with his Portuguese converso background.[11] While he eventually married the daughter of his business partner, Miguel Nuñez, a Portuguese converso based in Seville, he later saw the governorship as an opportunity to erase his converso past and become a new man, free of the stigmas attached to New Christians. It would be in his interest to do everything possible to further solidify his image as a landed Old Christian gentleman. His nieces' marriage to Old Christian soldiers, as opposed to Portuguese merchants, would go a long way in that direction.

On the most basic level, the argument between Francisco Rodríguez and his brother-in-law can be understood in social, economic, and ethnic terms. The governor wanted his family to follow a path that would solidify their place among the Old Christian elite, while Rodríguez wanted his daughters to marry within the wider converso social network. The religious element was also a factor. The governor, whose crypto-Jewish wife stayed behind in Seville instead of joining her husband in the New World, wanted his nieces to move away from the converso orbit with its proclivity for crypto-Jewish activity, and thus distance himself and his wider family from suspicions of heresy. Their father, who was apparently a Judaizer, wanted his daughters to continue living their lives according to the Law of Moses.

When we turn our attention to Catalina's and Leonor's grooms it is similarly difficult to divorce their Jewish commitments (whatever they might have been) from their own socio-economic and ethnic concerns. These two grooms exemplify the murky and complex relationship of religious tendencies, socioeconomic realities, and personal idiosyncrasies. Almeida and Cáceres, both of Portuguese converso origin, were successful merchants who were moving to include mining as part of their portfolio of business ventures.[12] Why would they want to join the Carvajal family, given their penury? Were they interested in gaining the connections and protection of the governor, as they moved into mining in Taxco? Were they looking to be part of a crypto-Jewish family who would not only keep their heretical secret but also allow them to practice Judaism? In the *Vida*, Luis portrays his brothers-in-law as saviors sent by God: "Suddenly they heard bells and trumpets at their door, the cause of which was the arrival at their house of two grooms whom the Lord sent to the God-fearing orphans of His Nation."[13] Almeida and Díaz de Cáceres were sent by the Lord who does not forget orphans and widows! Luis seeks to infuse the story with providence by invoking the leitmotif of divine concern for the orphan. Luis describes the grooms as "His believers and of His People"; they were believers in the God of Israel and were part of the people of Israel, "su pueblo."[14] In Luis's telling, they were both reli-giously committed to Judaism and were ethnically connected to the wider crypto-Jewish network.

Leaving the trumpets aside, Luis's family's salvation takes an unmistakably economic form. Almeida and Díaz de Cáceres move them family out of the mos-quito infested Pánuco home where the Carvajal *doncellas* wore threadbare dresses and walked around shoeless to a new home and new life of prominence and ease in Mexico City. Luis describes his first encounter with his sisters after their wed-ding, when they moved to the capital: "He saw the orphan sisters who were sup-ported by the Lord; in place of their torn skirts, they were covered in velvet, gold jewels, and silks in their husband's houses. And there too, accommodated and supported, were the other widows and orphans supported by the Lord."[15] Drawn to the physical manifestation of his sisters' new status, Luis sees the providential nature of their marriages being borne out in the complete transformation of their poverty into luxury and elegance. His descriptions echo the sentiment of the psalmists when he writes: "The stone which the builders rejected has become the corner stone."[16] The brothers-in-law provide not only for their brides, but also for the wider family, the widow and orphans. Francisca Carvajal, the widowed ma-triarch along with the younger sisters, Mariana and Ana, and Miguelico, the youngest son, move in with their new in-laws. Díaz de Cáceres and Almeida either approach this as an act of generosity or simply an expansive view of who is in-cluded in one's family unit. Luis, however, turns it into another expression of di-vine care, they "were supported by the Lord." In Luis's telling, the brothers-in-law are not only "servants" of God, but emissaries of God, on a mission to take care of these pious young ladies.

When Isabel, the oldest sister, is first arrested in 1589, Almeida provides funds for her maintenance.[17] He stays on in Mexico throughout the trial, even interven-ing with the sentencing of his wife and in-laws and it is only when the Holy Of-fice comes to arrest him that he flees.[18] He sneaks out of Mexico City to his mines in Taxco and tries to put his finances in order, all the while eluding the grasp of the Inquisitors.[19] Continuing this game of cat and mouse with the inquisitorial officers, Almeida returns to Mexico City where he finds a secret hiding place from which he is able to handle some of his affairs and weigh his options.[20] Sensing his imminent arrest, he leaves Mexico for Madrid where he hopes to work his con-nections at court and reduce or commute the sentence of his wife and her family. From both Luis's portrait of Almeida and the inquisitorial record, it is clear that he is deeply committed to his wife, Leonor, and he treats her mother and siblings as his own.

Almeida's solidarity with the wider Carvajal family is intertwined with both financial and religious concerns. Concurrent with his efforts to commute their sentences and remove their *sanbenitos*, Almeida tries to get Luis to collect the debts owed him and liquidate his assets,[21] as indicated in a letter Almeida sent to Luis from Madrid. Soon after the family's second arrest, this letter was intercepted by the Holy Office and preserved as part of Luis' testimony.[22] It discusses the last few arrangements left to be made before the family can leave New Spain and betrays Almeida's frustration and anxiety with the slow pace of this operation. The fact that this letter came too late for Luis to read lends it a certain pathos and poignancy; the many leagues of ocean separating them and the irregularity of ships' crossings make communication difficult, but especially at this sensitive moment.[23] Almeida wishes he heard back from Carvajal earlier. He chastises Carvajal for continuing his contact with Ruy Fernandez, a converso merchant in Havana whom Almeida grew to distrust. Almeida blames the delay in resolving their status to this error. Almeida reserves his harshest condemnation for one of his former associates, his uncle Tomás de Fonseca. He instructs Luis to "have no agreements with him, rather with all rigor collect what he owes me and destroy him, and when he cannot pay back what he has stolen from me let him lose it [all] and let lice eat him in jail."[24]

Again we see how deep bonds of blood and years of economic dealings can be the basis for the greatest betrayal and enmity, as well as the strongest loyalty and generosity.[25] It is notable that his wrath does not stop with this uncle, but extends to Fonseca's children as well: "And as the Lord lives, if I desire to return to that land it is in order to avenge myself on that thief; because I am not coming, I will do whatever I can from here so that neither he nor his sons born of a whore will rest easy, nor his daughters born of his mistress can use my wealth to marry."[26] So at the same time that Almeida goes to extremes to protect his in-laws, he wants to not only cut off his relationship with his uncle, but wishes to bring the wrath of heaven upon his cousins whom he regards as "children of a whore." Within Almeida's socioeconomic logic and sense of ethics, his uncle's financial deception renders his entire lineage unfit and outside the purview of his "family." We have a vision of a socioeconomic network wherein ethnic, cultural, or even blood relationships are not inviolable. Blood may be thicker than water, but that thickness can be dissolved through neglect and betrayal.

Almeida is deeply concerned for his wife and her sisters, writing that Mariana's and Ana's "illnesses weigh on me, as they should."[27] He beseeches God's care and protection for them and for his wife, "whose hands I kiss a thousand times."[28] His sisters-in-law are not *cuñadas*—they are "queridas hermanas" and indeed he acts like an older brother in seeking their welfare along with that of his wife and child.

Almeida's relations with the men in his family orbit are more strained. In the same letter he also mentions that he has not been in communication with his own brother Hector de Fonseca; he places the blame on his brother for not writing. This comes in the same paragraph where he tells Luis about Baltasar and Miguelico's arrival in Rome, a place where they would be safe from the Inquisition's grasp and free to live open Jewish lives.[29] Almeida even includes greetings for Gaspar, though they are laced with some bitterness over Gaspar's not having written to him for four years.[30] It turns out that Fray Gaspar was planning to join his family on their return voyage to Europe. This appears to indicate either that he believed in their reconciliation to the Church or that he put his lot in with his family despite the religious chasm separating them. That Gaspar is still an active player within his family highlights how religion, while a powerful "thickener" of social relations, is not the only determining factor. This letter is a quotidian indicator of the depth and idiosyncratic nature of family bonds. Some blood relatives are disowned and marked as enemies, others are simply forgotten, and then other relationships, based on a mix of financial and sentimental bonds, are rock solid.

Before we conclude the discussion of Jorge de Almeida and the shifting construction of family bonds, I want to consider a bizarre detail that predates the family's first arrest. According to testimony from Mariana de Carvajal, Almeida voiced his desire to take the family out of New Spain and to move to a Jewish community where he could marry Mariana, his wife's younger sister. Reflecting an extreme "biblicism"—however muddled—Almeida believed that once he was living in a Jewish community, he would not only be permitted to have a second wife, but also be able to emulate the biblical Jacob and marry two sisters.[31] This plan led to violent arguments within the family. Mariana was already betrothed to Jorge de León, the brother of their close family friend, Gonzalo Pérez Ferro. Ferro was insulted and launched a bitter protest. In an argument with his brother and sister-in-law, Díaz de Caceres got so upset that he slapped Leonor, and in another instance he stabbed Almeida. Two engagements were broken off, and plenty of bad blood was sowed.[32] While it was certainly against Catholic notions of a proper marriage, did the family see in it some far-off ideal, or was it just a vaguely rationalized sexual proclivity? This episode is not recorded or alluded to in the *Vida*, which is not a surprise. It would be hard to weave this into Luis's wider providential narrative and in particular into the image of Almeida as a fraternal savior.

Díaz de Cáceres had a more complicated relationship with the wider Carvajal family than his brother-in-law, Jorge de Almeida. He left the family behind at the exact moment that he realized that the Inquisitors were coming for him. He ran to Acapulco and quickly managed to outfit a ship and set sail for the Philippines. Díaz de Cáceres's trials and tribulations, his imprisonments, swashbuckling escapes, and fortunes lost and remade in the East Indies is discussed at length by Martin A. Cohen and Alfonso Toro.[33] While Díaz de Cáceres was certainly interested in saving his own skin, his flight was not necessarily an act of betrayal. Practically speaking, the Carvajal family would gain very little from Díaz de Caceres's arrest, and the money he made on his journey would serve them well after their release from prison. As would be expected, in the *Vida* Luis frames Díaz de Cáceres's Asian adventure as part of a wider providential plan: "Joseph's other brother-in-law, understanding that he [Joseph] and his mother and his sisters were imprisoned departed for China from where in order to help his wife and daughter that he left behind the Lord brought him [back to Mexico] with no shortage of miracles."[34] In Luis's retelling, this journey to East Asia and back was part of a divine plan for Díaz de Cáceres to help his wife and child.

As in the case of Almeida, Luis chooses to leave out some of Díaz de Cáceres's more unsavory behaviors. Upon his return almost two years later, in the fall of 1592, he was caught in multiple legal and financial complications, which forced him to stay in Acapulco for several months. Even after he resolved these issues, however, he continued to distance himself from his wife and her family. He refused to live with her until a priest intervened and Catalina was reconciled to the Church.[35] Díaz de Cáceres was adamant about not wanting to appear as a crypto-Jew or even associate with crypto-Jews. This was probably more about self-preservation than Catholic piety. During her second trial Francisca Nuñez de Carvajal told the Inquisitors that her son-in-law acted this way out of fear of being arrested.[36] Toward the end of his second trial Luis describes his brother-in-law as someone who was deeply committed to Judaism in his heart but who was extremely apprehensive about getting caught. For this reason he rarely joined in any of the family's rituals. This only intensified after his return from East Asia. Luis describes his total break with the family's religious life: "He would never communicate with us and before us all he acted like the best Christian on Earth."[37] His fear of arrest forced him to go out of his way to appear as a devout Christian.

For obvious reasons both Almeida and Díaz de Cáceres are concerned with their family's public image. After Isabel's first arrest, they are described as speaking harshly toward the rest of the Carvajals: "They had a nightmare of a time with the aforementioned in-laws because they called this one [Luis] and his mother 'confesos' saying that because of them and the imprisonment [of Isabel] they lose their good standing in society."[38] That these two conversos would call their wider family, with whom they themselves celebrated crypto-Jewish rituals, "confesos" may be unseemly and hypocritical, but understandable: With a sister-in-law arrested by the Inquisition, not only were their lives and property at risk, but their "honra" was at stake, and their standing in society was in jeopardy. They publicly lived like Catholics, taking care of their business on Saturdays, insisting on eating pork products, eating lunch on "el día grande"(Yom Quipur). These public "desecrations" of Judaic practices do not necessarily negate their commitment to the Law of Moses in their hearts nor did they immediately indicate a break with the rest of the family. However, they do indicate a fault line in the family that was to grow more severe especially during the family's period of penance following their first imprisonment.[39]

Over time, Díaz de Cáceres's concern with appearing like a staunch Catholic developed a dark side. As his younger sisters-in-law, Ana and Mariana, developed different mental and physical illnesses and their behavior became erratic. Their mental instability loosened their inhibitions and they felt freer to express their disdain for Catholicism and their commitment to Judaism. Mariana reportedly threw statues of Catholic saints out the window; she would walk around the house stark naked, even in front of guests.[40] This was all happening after the family's first arrest and reconciliation with the Church; they would be carefully watched for signs of a Judaizing relapse. Díaz de Cáceres insisted on restraining Mariana, tying her to the bedpost and at times beating her. Citing testimony in the investigation into Díaz de Cáceres, Cohen recounts that tensions were so high regarding Mariana's illness that at one point Díaz de Cáceres slapped his mother-in-law and his sister-in-law Leonor; at another point he threw them down a flight of stairs.[41] Eventually Francisca decided to take her younger daughters and move out of Díaz de Cáceres's home. In the *Vida*, Luis recounts with great pathos the details of his sisters' illnesses and the effect on the wider family. However, he never mentions Diaz de Cáceres's violent reaction to Mariana and Ana. Luis tells the reader throughout the *Vida* that his goal is to point out God's providence: "My intention is only to write down the immense blessings and mercies that the Lord, the God of Israel did for Joseph and his people."[42] He does not purport to record the entire family's history in what is a documentation of God's kindness. Díaz de Cáceres enters into the narrative to the extent that he is part of the story of God's unfolding love and care. This clear restatement of the *Vida*'s purpose actually occurs in a section about Díaz de Cáceres, in which Luis says that he cannot relate the ups and downs of his brother-in-law's journey. What is essential is the connection between those tribulations and the fact that thanks to divine providence he was able to return and help his wife.[43] Díaz de Cáceres might have maltreated his sisters, and possibly did not always live an exemplary crypto-Jewish life, but in the *Vida*, his acts of concern for his wife and child are what stand out and are worthy of memorializing. The miraculous nature of his multiple escapes from danger in the Philippines and Macao are a testament that his return to Mexico is part of the greater narrative of the family's deliverance.

Audacity in the Archives: Isabel Rodríguez de Andrada

The case of Isabel, the oldest child of the Rodríguez-Carvajal family, illustrates the complex interplay between the inquisitorial trial records and Luis's *Vida*. Luis ignored Díaz de Cáceres's shortcomings in his portrayal of his brother-in-law because he sought to craft a narrative of inspiration, whereby the hand of God is made evident in the lives of those who risk everything to serve the one and true God. A similar selectivity obtains in the case of Isabel. In the *Vida* she plays a rather marginal leadership role within the family's religious life, yet when we look at her own testimony and that of others relating to her case, we encounter an active Judaizer and dogmatist who takes great risks for her faith and is a religious leader in her own right. This gap points to the role Isabel plays within the inner logic and rhetorical mission of the *Vida* and within the wider constellation of her family and community.

In her testimony Isabel described her Jewish commitment in great detail. A committed Jewess already in Spain,[44] she listed the practices and fundamental beliefs that constitute her Judaism, as well as taking the further step to clarify their difference from Catholicism. She was arrested because she miscalculated the openness of Felipe Nuñez, one of the governor's trusted assistants, to the Judaic truth. Nuñez was scandalized when Isabel spoke to him about the Law of Moses and eventually reported her dogmatizing to the Inquisition.[45] Earlier she attempted to enlighten her uncle. This confrontation almost cost her life. Upon hearing her blasphemy, he became incensed and shocked. He told the Inquisitors that "without bearing another word I gave her a blow [*bofetón*] that threw her to the floor."[46] His rage was such that he covered his ears and warned Isabel that he would kill her if she did not abandon Judaism.[47] The image of Isabel that emerges from the first trial is of a devout crypto-Jew who was knowledgeable and confident enough to engage others in religious discussions. She was also brave enough to confront her powerful and violent uncle on this volatile issue.[48]

Isabel's commitment to Jewish practice continued after her reconciliation to the Church. The transcript of her second trial attests to the depth of her Judaizing activism. Emily Cairns Colbert's analysis of this transcript uncovers the multifaceted nature of Isabel's religiosity and the contours of her leadership. It shows, for example, that Isabel led her sisters and other crypto-Jews in Judaizing rituals: fasting, praying, keeping the Sabbath, and avoiding forbidden foods. One year when Luis was away it was Isabel who organized Passover celebrations for the women of her family and other members of their crypto-Jewish circle: "In the house of the aforementioned Doña Ysabel they observed and celebrated the feast [*pascua*] of the lamb on Friday in maintenance and observance of the Law of Moses and as part of the ritual they ate unleavened bread as well as roasted and stewed hens and they observed as a memorial to God liberating His people Israel from the captivity of Egypt."[49]As this description demonstrates, the women involved not only observed such rituals, but also understood the religious meaning behind them. Moreover, according to Colbert, other women present at this ceremony saw Isabel as their leader, and in referring to Isabel as the biblical Sarah, they cast her as someone responsible for their eventual redemption.[50]

At one point in the trial Luis explained why he wrote a particular letter to Isabel and not to any of the other sisters: "He said that it [the letter] was for the said Doña Isabel because she knows how to read, because the others cannot read fluidly and even though it says on the paper that it was sent to all of them he does not know to what end that was done because as he said the others do not know how to read."[51] These selected sources give the clear impression of a woman who was not only personally devout and intellectually capable, but intent on spreading the Mosaic truth, regardless of the danger of such activity.[52] And yet, in the *Vida* she is featured only twice, once in Luis description of his initiation and again when he discusses the family's first arrest, at which point he represents Isabel's failed attempt at converting Felipe Nuñez as the catalyst for their arrest: "His widowed sister [Isabel], . . . was accused by a heretic, but of our Nation, whom a year ago she attempted to teach the divine truth."[53] This brief reference to Isabel alludes to her zeal and dedication to "the divine truth" and to teaching it to a fellow converso, even one estranged from Judaism like Nuñez. But the direct connection between this zeal and the arrest of the entire family certainly leaves Isabel in a bad light. Most puzzling is that throughout the rest of the *Vida* her deeds do not register at all.

The elision of Isabel's leadership in the *Vida* points to one of its fundamental rhetorical aims. Luis states that it is a chronicle of divine providence and crypto-Jewish heroism meant to inspire the Jews of the diaspora. It is also a textual space for Luis to fashion his religious self-image and make sense of his experience. The *Vida* focuses on Luis's leadership and his prophetic calling, which enable him to guide his family and the wider crypto-Jewish circle. He continues to develop that self-image in his second trial and through the letters he sends his sisters and mother. Luis easily includes his teachers and his students; he can discuss his saintly mother and his pious but rather passive younger sisters.[54] Isabel, with her strong personality and activism, however, proves a challenge to Luis's self-perceived role in the family. Could it be that ultimately it is too difficult for Luis to share the stage with a peer?

In the next section we will look at Luis' relationship with his younger sisters as developed in the *Vida*—sisters whom he portrays as the passive recipients of divine grace and Luis's own guidance. However, a more subtle reading reveals that within the frame of this general image there is room to discern their religious self-expression and agency.

Joseph and His Sisters

After the family's first trial Luis's place within the family dynamic shifted in a significant way. His older brother, Baltasar, escaped New Spain along with the youngest brother, Miguelico. His brother-in-law Jorge de Almeida stayed on in Mexico for close to a year after their sentencing at the auto-da-fé of February 24 and then remained in limited contact with the family during his years in Madrid. Antonio Díaz de Cáceres returned from his Asian travels in 1593 but remained distant from his wife and the rest of the family for some time.[55] Even after his reunification with them, he was staunchly committed to distancing himself from any Judaizing activities. We hear relatively little from Gaspar except that he was planning to join his family on their trip back to Europe prior to their second arrest. This would indicate some degree of reconciliation between the Dominican friar and his family. However Gaspar does not appear to be an active daily presence; he is almost entirely absent from the documents covering the years after their first arrest, namely, the *Vida* and the records of the second trial. Francisco Rodríguez de Matos, Luis's father, died several years before their first arrest and the governor died while still in prison after his sentencing. To a great extent Luis was the only male relative living in Mexico during the years following the first trial. Within the early modern Iberian context, a son in Luis's position would be expected to take over the leadership of the family. Within Luis's *Vida* as well as the relevant trial records we find a clear image of Luis/Joseph as the family's spiritual leader and the one who works hardest to secure their release from their Mexican captivity. We will now examine Luis's relationship with his sisters and the way that relationship is refracted through the *Vida*.

In most of the *Vida*, the sisters are presented as pious but relatively passive. They are the objects of divine grace but rarely the initiators of religious practice. It must be stressed that this image is quite at odds with what much of the inquisitorial trial records show about their Judaizing activism and religious agency. However, there are some notable exceptions.

Mariana, one of the unmarried younger sisters, is the subject of one of Luis's many stories of peril and deliverance. We are told that because she was "particularly an enemy of idols and idolatry," she desired to spend the Sabbath at the house of "another sister of the Israelite nation who is fearful of the Lord" in order to avoid the Holy Week procession that passed by her home.[56] Hoping to spend the day in divine service, she took with her one of the devotional anthologies that Luis compiled. On her way she was lost in joy and praise to God for being able to spend the Sabbath far away from the religious processions of Holy Week. Amidst that reverie she lost that special book—she refers to it as a textual treasure, "tesoro muy estimado"—somewhere along the way. Her heart stopped, she searched frantically but never recovered the book. Mariana returned home distraught, certain that the book would be found and that the entire family would be arrested for their relapse to Judaism and would meet their end at an auto-da-fé.[57] As in so many other points in the narrative, at the moment that they assume all is lost, providence surprises them. The constable comes knocking on their door, not to arrest them, but rather to deliver two baskets of bread—restitution to his customers from a local baker who was caught cheating on the size of his rolls.

This vignette casts Luis's sister as devout and engaged in her Judaism. Her disdain for "idolatry" and her decision to spend the Sabbath with her "sister," a fellow crypto-Jew who lived far away from the religious processions at the center of town, reflect a deeply personal religiosity. Her Judaism has a strong textual dimension, since the Sabbath for Mariana is not only about refraining from work but also has to do with prayer and devotional readings; why else would she bring this precious book of prayers? While Mariana exhibits essential signs of agency, the main thrust of the story depicts her as acted upon: she loses the book, she cannot find it, and all the family can do is wait for their cruel and bitter end. It is Luis's providential narrative that turns the story into one of deliverance by connecting the lost booklet to the arrival of the basket of bread with their echoes of biblical miracles.[58]

The next scene where we encounter Luis's two unmarried sisters deals with their illnesses. Thematically both cases are linked by the centrality of language and its disruption. When Ana became afflicted with a throat disease, her cure involved subjecting her to painful and destructive lacerations to the throat, which made it impossible for others to understand her. Her older sister Leonor was the only one who could communicate with her. "And even then, the suffering patient did not lack divine comfort and support because the Lord subsequently opened up her sister's mind [the one married to Jorge de Almeida] so that she could understand everything that she would say. And in this way the doctor and the surgeon and all of the rest would use her [Leonor] as the interpreter to understand the sickly one who was healed by the infinite mercy of the Lord."[59] Ana was not abandoned; Leonor became an agent of God's healing. God "opened up her understanding," and she was able to understand Ana's needs. Leonor was not only a kind and dedicated sister, but was blessed in her ability to decipher her sister's words.

While Ana was suffering from her throat disease, Mariana became increasingly unstable. Luis points out that this "locura" endangers the entire family and not only Mariana. She throws statues of the saints out on to the street in front of passing Christians (the "idolators"). She speaks incessantly and often incoherently; when she does make sense, her statements reveal her Judaizing commitments. Luis describes her statements as so dangerous that only God could save the family from their implications. However, Luis finds something to admire in the unrestrained expression of religious truth: Day and night she does not stop talking, and mixed in with some crackpot statements, she says many revealed truths.[60] Do the monks and other devout Catholics who come to visit her appreciate the meaning of these revealed truths? Her insanity has allowed her to access a certain religious truth, and she is emboldened to share it with the world around her, without fear. For a moment we can sense that Luis desires her madness—it enables her to touch the prophetic and live externally the way he lives internally.

Leonor receives a divine gift to be able to communicate beyond normal language with her recuperating sister. Mariana, suffering from her madness, is freed from the imposed silence—the silence that the family relies upon to keep their secret safe—and can express the unspoken in public.

Keeping their secret while at the same time sharing their spiritual truth is a constant challenge for this clandestine community of Mexican conversos. Eventually the Carvajal family along with the wider Mexican crypto-Jewish network is arrested because of the lack of discretion of a fellow crypto-Jew. On the very day that his penitential garb (*sanbenito*) was removed, Luis went to the house of his good friend and fellow Judaizer Manuel de Lucena. That night Lucena tried unsuccessfully to convince his guest Domingo Gómez Navarro of the truth of the Law of Moses. Gómez Navarro was so scandalized that he denounced both Lucena and Carvajal to the Holy Office.[61] Because the secret was not guarded tightly enough, the entire network was caught.

While secrecy was essential to their survival, this studied self-repression instilled a sense of shame. When Luis reflects upon his experience during the first trial, he describes his shame at not being able to express his true beliefs to the Inquisitors. Throughout the trial records there are references to individuals who do not perform more Jewish rites out of fear, preferring to keep their Judaism in their heart; they are referred to as "judíos de corazón," "Jews of the heart." For Mariana the internal and external are seamless. Her outbursts threaten the family's security, and they are not in line with the basic premises of a religious system that is dependent on secrecy and policing of borders. However, in her mad indiscretions we can sense Luis's admiration of her ability to speak "revealed truths" directly to all.[62]

As mentioned earlier, after their first trial Luis was the only active male presence among the Carvajal women. While Luis portrays himself as a spiritual guide and committed brother and son before their first arrest, his self-image as the family's spiritual guide and physical guardian comes fully into focus after they are sentenced at the auto-da-fé and they begin their penance. Luis was placed to work as a custodian in the Hospital del los Convalecientes de San Hipólito in Mexico City while his mother and sisters lived together near the monastery in Santiago de Tlaltelolco, a short distance away.[63] Eventually Luis was allowed to live with his family and was placed as a teacher and scribe at the Tlaltelolco monastery. Upon his arrival, he was shocked to see that his family had abandoned their previous crypto-Jewish practices: "Arriving into the company of his mother and sisters he discovered that because of the great terrors that the enemies placed upon them and through the bad advice of some friends, they bought and consumed food which is prohibited by the Law of God; Joseph put this to an end."[64] Luis does not focus on the family's abandonment of Sabbath observance, or Jewish prayer, but instead (like the Inquisitors), emphasizes their consumption of forbidden foods. In his retelling, his mother's and sisters' Catholic "relapse" is inspired by their fear of being re-arrested as well as the "bad advice" of certain friends. This last detail points to the absence of Luis's leadership in their lives: while he was separated from them soon after their sentencing, they fell under the sway of others who led them astray. But all was not lost: "By the grace of God, they placed before themselves the example of the saints who allowed themselves to be torn apart through cruel torture before eating foods forbidden by the Lord. Nor would they pretend to eat them. And since their hearts were with their God and Lord, even though they did these things out of fear, very little was needed to stop them because with great tears and awe they converted to the their God and Lord and they got rid of all these vile things and food, which was for their good."[65] Their abandonment of crypto-Judaism was out of fear and thus, in Luis's telling, all that was needed was a firm reminder of the truth. He uses the examples of the martyrs who sacrificed everything to keep the covenant alive. Again we see the power of text in their religious lives. By "placing before them the examples of the (martyred) saints" they easily "converted" back to their Jewish commitments.

Luis continues his leadership of the family in secular matters as well. Once they receive word that they can raise funds to lift their penitence—namely the wearing of the *sanbenito* and the travel restrictions that barred them from leaving New Spain—Luis takes the initiative, traveling around the countryside, staying in monasteries, and connecting with other crypto-Jews while collecting the necessary funds. He not only cares for his family members' souls but also watches out for their material needs.

Throughout the rest of the *Vida*, as well as in the varied inquisitorial testimonies from the second trial and even the letters that Luis surreptitiously sent to his sisters during their imprisonment, we find Luis portrayed as the main religious guide for his family and the wider Mexican crypto-Jewish network. In order to better demonstrate the complex dynamic between Luis and his sisters, I have chosen to focus on one testimony, that of Leonor during her second trial. Leonor's testimony is evocative of the intense relationship she had with her brother and his outsized influence on the family. Her words must be treated carefully and put in context. Her main interest in recounting her experiences to the Inquisitors was to gain as much exoneration from the tribunal as possible. Identifying her older, charismatic, and learned brother as the instigator of her relapse into heretical depravity played into contemporary attitudes about the frailty of women and their susceptibility to demonic persuasion.[66] However, I believe that her testimony should not be reduced to this stratagem. This image of Luis as spiritual leader and teacher is echoed throughout his *Vida* and can be found in other testimonies given by family members and fellow conversos.[67] It would be logical for Leonor to use that image in her own defense, but she did not have to fabricate it in order to do so. More importantly for our purposes, her testimony illustrates the fascinating interplay between Luis's self-fashioning in the *Vida* and how the people in his inner circle perceived him. It also reflects how Luis saw his sisters, as well as the subtle but profound ways that they inspired and shaped his own religious journey.

Leonor begins her testimony against Luis on her hands and knees, begging the Inquisitors for forgiveness. She points to Luis as the inspiration for her relapse to Judaism. She tells the Inquisitors: "And the truth is that about a year ago, more or less, her brother, Luis de Carvajal, said to her and asked her if she had distanced herself from the Law of Moses; and she responded that indeed she had. The aforementioned Luis de Carvajal, her brother, told her: do not do this, nor should you believe in the Law of Jesus Christ, because it is laughable, you should only believe in the Law of Moses."[68] Luis proactively reaches out to his sister and pushes her to shake off her allegiance to Catholicism; by simply asking her about her religious allegiance, he begins its destabilization. He mocks Catholicism—"es cosa de burla"—in an attempt to undercut whatever attachment she had developed during the years of their penance. She goes on to describe the content of that "true faith."[69] She begins with a list of practices that Luis instructed her to perform and then moves on to religious ideas she was meant to believe: "Fast on Mondays, Wednesdays and Thursdays from sun-up to sun-down; keep the Sabbath; she should avoid all pork products; fast on the "Great Day" (Yom Kippur); believe in only one God; realize that the sacraments and mysteries of the Church are like nothing (cosas de aire) and that it is only through the Law of Moses that she can hope for redemption."[70] Throughout this testimony she mentions that she was reverting back to how she was before her first arrest and penance.[71] She would like the Inquisitors to believe that if it was not for Luis's persuasion, she would have remained a good, reconciled daughter of the Church. She says this explicitly: "And this one [Leonor] due to the persuasion of the aforementioned, her brother, Luis de Carvajal, about a year from when this discussion [with her brother] happened, this one [Leonor] decided to leave the Law of Jesus Christ and turn toward the said Law of Moses."[72] Luis strengthens her resolve when he clarifies the finer points of Jewish eschatology: "The true Messiah who will come is [in actuality] the one whom the Christians refer to as the Antichrist, the one who will gather in the people of Israel who [now] wander dispersed and will take them out of captivity and the prisons and take them to Mount Sinai where he will give them palms and crowns for having kept the Law of Moses."[73] Notwithstanding her apparent confusion of Zion with Sinai, Leonor reveals her grasp of some of the fundamental differences between Judaism and Christianity. The same figure whom Catholics deem the Antichrist is the true savior of the Jews. We get a sense of Luis's messianic rhetoric and how it might have enticed his family to stay firm in their devotion to the true law that would promise them great rewards at the end of days. This messianism can also work as an implicit counternarrative to the Christian view that the Jews' exile was proof of God's rejection: God has sent the Jews into exile but he will also redeem all those who withstood the test of exile, stayed faithful to the Law of Moses, and did not succumb to the temptations of the Church.[74]

Luis not only successfully inculcated basic religious concepts in his sisters and mother, but also effectively taught the details of devotional life and ritual. Leonor is able to recite from memory thirteen religious poems along with a Hispanized version of the Shema prayer. She acknowledges joining in with her sisters as Luis read these prayers, especially on the Sabbath. Her mother was present but unable to follow along with the recitation of these assorted prayers.[75] That Francisca de Carvajal was not familiar with them would indicate that they were not handed down orally; rather, Luis most probably generated these texts either from his own poachings of biblical material in the monastery or from other crypto-Jews with whom he was connected. Leonor mentions that some of the prayers were "the Psalms of David in Spanish which he selected out of the Bible that was in the school at Santiago de Tlaltelolco," while others seem to be poems that Luis composed himself.[76] That Leonor was able to remember these long prayers by heart points to the regularity of this ritual. Her description of the singing reflects the centrality of Luis's guidance: "the aforementioned Luis de Carvajal would sing [the songs] to this one [Leonor] and to her mother . . . [and] her sisters."[77] In another instance she describes how she and her sisters "would respond because they also knew them [the songs] by heart."[78] Leonor's testimony sketches the basic contours of the religious persona that Luis crafted for himself in his *Vida*—that of a charismatic and talented spiritual guide whose inspiration is drawn directly from his encounter with biblical texts.

The relationship between Leonor and Luis was a dynamic one. Luis might have inspired her return to Judaism and he might have been the family's ritual and spiritual guide, but Leonor's piety has also inspired Luis. He was so moved by the intensity of her self-mortifications that he wrote a book dedicated to these "acts of penitence" that he meant to send to their brothers living as open Jews in Italy or as he refers to them, "to his brothers who are Judaizing outside of the reigns of His Majesty."[79] Throughout the autobiography we see how Luis transforms his experiences into a textual testament to divine providence and to the spiritual courage of his fellow crypto-Jews. This falls in line with the stated purpose of his *Vida*—to provide inspiration and encouragement to his fellow Jews. The book is not simply a religiously-tinged picaresque; rather, it becomes a medium for meditation and devotional reading. Leonor herself seeks out the book: "And this one [Leonor] would take the aforementioned book some times to read it and the aforementioned Doña Isabel, her sister, would do the same thing."[80] Luis's text shapes Leonor's individual acts of piety into a coherent narrative and forms them into a spiritual mirror where she can find an ideal image of herself. To a great extent this book becomes a liturgy, a text that she can return to and read as an act of devotion.

This is not unlike the reading of "lives of the saints" or the reading of Saint Teresa of Ávila's *Libro de la vida* by other nuns, who sought inspiration from these works. Electa Arenal and Stacey Schlau have shown how confessors in Mexican convents would often require the nuns under their direction to record their mystical experiences for a variety of ends, one of which was to keep them as spiritual records that could be used to edify others. Thus, the religious community would be nurtured by the written record of their "sister's" experience. In a curious parallel, the Carvajal family reads Luis's book to see their own lives transformed into a providential narrative. That Leonor would sometimes read this text about herself indicates the power of this practice for self-edification.

Luis's goal was partially to build up Leonor's faith in the efficacy and righteousness of her commitment to Judaism. He weaves her acts of piety into the family's narrative of redemption: "Through her merits, God performed miracles for them."[81] Both before the arrest and even once in prison, Luis continued to encourage Leonor and his other sisters. He would send them notes wrapped in fruit shells praising their saintliness: "He would call her [Leonor] 'saintly' and 'blessed martyr' and she was the one whom he recognized as a great servant of the Lord. And in this way the aforementioned Luis de Carvajal would encourage them through small pieces of paper that he would send to their cells wrapped in plantain [skins]."[82] The goal of this praise before and after their arrest was basically the same: to strengthen her resolve to remain true to the Law of Moses despite the dangers she faced. After their arrest the focus switched from their imminent redemption to the glories of a blessed martyrdom, with Luis saying "that she should be strong in order to endure martyrdom for God, and sending her blessings because soon she would enjoy the [Heavenly] Glory because he held her up as a saint and celebrated her as one."[83] Even from his prison cell Luis tries to reach his sisters and encourage their continued adherence to the Law of Moses. These letters reflect Luis's self-image as the family's leader and his concern for his sisters. But they also implicitly reveal the deep need that Luis has for his sisters: Would his religious quest matter if he were truly alone? If his passion and sacrifice was not shared by anyone else, would they have any value?

Luis desired to share his religious experience with others, with his family of flesh and blood, with his family built out of social and economic connections, and most powerfully with his family of fellow believers in the Law of Moses, those who partook of his dreams and visions. I end this chapter with a tragic encounter that was possible only because of this hunger for community and this belief in the possibility of strangers becoming intimates, of an apparent enemy being transformed by the naked power of the truth.

Betrayal

As was commonly done in the Mexican inquisitorial prisons, a wayward cleric named Luis Díaz was placed in Carvajal's cell to function as a spy.[84] Because of

Carvajal's success in turning the monk Ruiz de Luna into a sincere and heroic crypto-Jew during his first trial, he might have been predisposed to believe in Díaz's openness to crypto-Judaism. Carvajal's desire to connect with Díaz might also suggest his own loneliness and desire (inspired by his earlier prison experience) to share his spiritual life with a fellow believer. Thus, he not only quickly tells Díaz about his own religiosity, but he goes on to recount, with great detail and excitement, the courageous deeds and spiritual activities of his wider crypto-Jewish network. His goal is to convince this cleric who seems to have lost his way with Catholicism not only that the Law of Moses is the true law, but that there is a vibrant community of the faithful whom he could join. This community is more than a group of like-minded individuals—they are like a family; in embracing the Law of Moses, Díaz would also be part of that family of enlightened believers.

Díaz picks up on the deep bonds between the crypto-Jews and uses it as a way to get more information about this large and interconnected network. He tells Carvajal that he wants to know who the Judaizers are in order to "get to know them and love them like brothers."[85] Later on he uses similar terminology when he asks Carvajal, "Would you tell me who are your brothers?"[86] Díaz is able to push Carvajal for more information because he says he wants to meet his "brothers." He gives the impression of desiring to be a part of the spiritual brotherhood that is so essential to Carvajal's religious world. He perceptively hits Luis where he is vulnerable. When Luis realizes that Díaz is a spy he is despondent, but not only because of the damage Luis has done to the people he loves, but because of Díaz's deception and betrayal. Díaz records Carvajal's lament: "Where was my good sense when I bared my soul [breast] to you?"[87] He realizes that he let himself be tricked by this deception: He revealed his heart—literally uncovered his breast; he allowed himself to be vulnerable to someone who called himself a brother; and he was taken advantage of.[88] At the same moment that Carvajal believed that he was welcoming another stranger into the fold, of inviting in another searcher into his spiritual family, he endangered the entire community.

At a much later stage of the trial, after Carvajal realizes the extent of the information that the Inquisitors had regarding the wider network and after undergoing torture and sensing the continual threat of more,[89] Luis stopped describing only his own Judaizing exploits and began to describe the Judaizing of his wider circle in great detail. Almost without any direct prodding of the Inquisitors, he continually returned to the audiences, sometimes even requesting them in order to inform on the heretical activities of his friends and family members. It may be that Luis's deep fear of torture led him to give such a complete accounting so as to avoid the rack, however perhaps something else was at play. I believe that as Luis understood that his end was near he wanted the inquisitors to know how bold, committed, and widespread crypto-Judaism was in New Spain. Carvajal was *Judaizing* his confession: Instead of being a remorseful accounting of his depravity it became a record of his community's defiance. His centrality to this community was an essential component to his own self-image, and this self-image was further solidified throughout the trial. During the entire second trial he never backed down from his commitment to Judaism; nor did he ever refer to fellow Judaizers as sinners. Instead, he described people throughout Mexico praying to the one true God, keeping Passover, fasting, and studying the Law of Moses. He also demonstrated the variety of religious attitudes—of those who were Judaizers in their heart (*judíos de corazón*), of those who taught even their youngest children about the Law of Moses, and of those who were devout Judaizers married to spouses who were either indifferent or rabidly anti-Jewish. With his death awaiting him, Luis had no other outlets besides the Inquisitors who would continually meet with him. The walls of the prisons of the Holy Office became his world. His resistance to the Inquisitors and his commitment to Judaism were ultimately pyrrhic, but in some perverse way, by testifying against his fellow Judaizers he was able to resist the Inquisitors' triumphalism by portraying the force and extent of New Spain's underground Jewish network.

Conclusion

Luis de Carvajal crafts a narrative of spiritual enlightenment and heroic sacrifice guided by the boundless hand of providence. But from its very beginning, the *Vida* is not a tale of one man's soul and its solitary journey to the divine truth, but rather a story intimately bound up with networks of family and fellow spiritual travelers. As I have noted earlier, Natalie Zemon Davis asserts that early modern autobiographical writing is distinguished not by the author's subjective independence, but rather by his or her "embeddedness" within given social realities.[90] The author's unfolding of self is mediated through the disparate relationships that make the autobiographer who he or she is. Mothers, fathers, siblings, teachers, masters, and servants are essential to shaping the autobiographer's self-portrait. Luis's autobiography is informed by the networks of trade, kinship, and culture developed by converso families in the early modern Atlantic world. No one single element was the determining factor in maintaining these networks; business or blood ties often overcame religious differences, and vice versa. By looking closely at how these relationships were transformed within Luis's narrative, we see that they were not only essential to the socioeconomic mechanics of these transatlantic networks, but were also the stuff of dreams, of psychological unfolding and spiritual transformation.

4 Writing His Way into the Jewish People

Faith, Blood, and Community in Manuel Cardoso de Macedo's Vida del buenaventurado Abraham Pelengrino

> Wherever you go, there shall I go, and wherever you will sleep, I will sleep, your people are my people and your God my God.
>
> Ruth 1:16

THE THREE AUTOBIOGRAPHICAL texts analyzed in this book highlight the centrality of family to crypto-Jewish activity in the early modern Sephardic Atlantic. The texts reflect the individual authors' attempt at crafting narratives of spiritual community—of a sacred family composed of fathers and mothers and brothers and sisters who are bonded not only by blood or socio-economic ties but by their religious commitments and sacrifices. These relationships are an essential piece of the personal story of religious transformation at the heart of these autobiographies. The texts reflect a tension between the authors' sense of spiritual autonomy and their deep imbrication within a vibrant and complex social network.

In all three cases, social ties and a sense of ethnic belonging complicate and deepen the experience of spiritual transformation. Bonds of blood go only so far to secure a sense of religious identity and a place within the faith community: In all cases either the author or his close companions transcend racial and ethnic origins to become part of God's covenant with his chosen people. In Luis de Carvajal's autobiography Jewish lineage and being part of the wider converso "Nation" was not the essential marker of piety. As shown in the previous chapter, blood relatives could often be deniers of the truth of the Law of Moses and even turn into mortal enemies, and Old Christians could easily become great servants of the Lord of Hosts. While Carvajal is aware of family bonds and the power of the wider converso network that he was a part of, in telling his story of spiritual enlightenment, he works hard to weave together a congregation of believers in the Law of Moses regardless of their bloodlines. Antonio de Montezinos, as we will see in the next chapter, managed to see not only the humanity but the secret Jewishness of his Indian porters. Their racial otherness was bridged through experiences of mutual sacrifice and a shared vision of the messianic future. The Hebreo-Indians he encounters in the Andes became his teachers, and he in turn became their emissary. Montezinos's tale of spiritual enlightenment and his own open embrace of Judaism would have been impossible without the guidance of these Indians.

For Manuel Cardoso de Macedo, blood is inescapable. His Old Christian lineage and the particularly virulent anti-Jewish sentiments of his forefathers weigh heavily on him, and he is concerned that this legacy will make his integration into the Jewish people difficult. I contend that his *Vida* is a means for this Old Christian to write his way into the Jewish community by showcasing his purity of intention and his self-sacrifice on behalf of the converso families who take him in as one of their own. Early on in his narrative Cardoso rejects his family of flesh and blood and replaces it with individuals who both materially and spiritually support his religious transformations and become his surrogate parents and siblings. This chapter examines this process of identity transformation by tracing Cardoso's self-fashioning in the pages of his spiritual autobiography, the *Vida del buenaventurado Abraham Pelengrino.*

Catholic, Protestant, and Jew:
The Many Lives of Abraham Pelengrino,
alias Manuel Cardoso de Macedo (1585–1652)

Manuel Cardoso de Macedo led a life of physical journeys and inner transformations. He was born into a fervently Catholic Old Christian, family in the Azores. While living in England in the early 1600s the young Manuel discovered the radical ideas of the Reformation and became a devout Calvinist. On a return visit to the Azores, his "Lutheran" heresy—as all Protestant beliefs were termed by the Inquisition—was discovered, and he was arrested by the local bishop and sent to the jails of the Lisbon Inquisition. After months of theological debates with the Inquisitors, Cardoso was still firmly committed to his Protestantism until he met a fellow prisoner, a converso who was under investigation for secretly practicing Judaism. This encounter opened the door to his most daring and all-consuming religious adventure. He realized that the truest way to fulfill the word of God was through the faithful adherence to the Mosaic Law, and he resolved to join the Jewish people. After his release from prison, Manuel clandestinely left Portugal and joined the Sephardic community of Hamburg, eventually settling in Amsterdam.

Within the safety of the Amsterdam Jewish community, Cardoso recorded this religious narrative in his *Vida del buenaventurado Abraham Pelengrino.*[1] The *Vida* is a unique document: an autobiography written by an Old Christian convert to Judaism in the early modern period. While there are some notable cases of Christians converting to Judaism in medieval or early modern Europe, there are almost no autobiographic reflections written by these individuals about their experience.[2]

Cardoso's manuscript was preserved in the Ets Hayyim Library of Amsterdam. B. N. Teensma prepared an annotated edition with a Dutch translation (1976), and Yosef Kaplan included Cardoso in his 1977 study of Old Christian converts to Judaism.[3] H. P. Salomon uncovered valuable information about Cardoso's relationship with the Dias Milão family in his *Portrait of a New Christian*. Outside of these important contributions there has been scant scholarly interest in Cardoso's life story and its implications for understanding the complex religious world of the Western Sephardim or the phenomenon of Christian conversion to Judaism in the early modern period.

The *Vida del buenaventurado Abraham Pelengrino* presents the reader with a portrait of a young man's journey in search of the divine truth. Manuel Cardoso de Macedo charts his transformation from an Old Christian to a devout Jew with many riveting stops along the way. Cardoso casts himself as an independent seeker who is willing to endure great suffering in order to live by his beliefs and become part of his new Jewish faith community. Interlaced throughout this narrative is a profound unease about his place within the Jewish nation. Right at the beginning of the narrative, Cardoso asks: How could someone who descended from so many generations of vicious Jew-haters find a place beneath the wings of the divine presence? The spiritual transformations at the heart of his *Vida* are deeply intertwined with his relationship to his Old Christian legacy and are most strikingly represented by his difficult relationship with his father. As he rejects Catholicism, he also loosens his bonds to his family; in place of these biological relationships, Cardoso consistently finds father-figures and fellow spiritual travelers who take him in, support him materially and spiritually, and in so doing, help fuel his religious quest.

Like Luis de Carvajal, Manuel Cardoso presents himself as an intrepid, resourceful, and inspired religious adventurer. Both of their autobiographies also reveal the extent to which these very personal religious quests were inextricably linked to wider family networks, with their attendant socioeconomic and affective dynamics, and the family-like relationships each individual developed with a variety of like-minded religious searchers. A major difference between these two spiritual autobiographies lies in the fact that while Carvajal was part of a vibrant converso family and was initiated as a young adult into his family's crypto-Judaism, Cardoso had no blood connection to the people of Israel, and for this reason he employed the *Vida* to make a case for his worthiness, not only as a sincere and pious servant of the God of Israel but as a committed member of the people of Israel.

This chapter will look at the impact of his family relationships on the telling of his story. It will focus in particular on his contentious relationship with his father as well as the alternative fathers and brothers and sisters with whom he shares a spiritual bond. Cardoso's intense and formative relationships with these individuals point to a dynamic Atlantic world, where cross-cultural and multinational trade networks facilitate the exchange of ideas and the possibility of personal transformation. As a microhistory, Cardoso's narrative illuminates its wider socioeconomic and cultural matrix. Read from this angle, the *Vida* deepens our understanding of the nature of early modern social bonds that cross ethnic, national, and religious lines. This context, however, does not subsume the individual features of Cardoso's life and its textual representation or reduce it to a proof text.

While my main focus is the text of the *Vida*, I also make use of the proceedings from Cardoso's two trials before the Lisbon Inquisition.[4] Until this point these sources have been utilized to establish certain facts in the biography of Cardoso or of the Dias Milão family with whom he had a relationship with in Portugal. However, the Inquisitorial *procesos* have much more to offer. When read in conjunction with the *Vida*, they provide a suggestive counterpoint to Cardoso's self-presentation in his autobiography. The repentant and almost sheepish heretic who appears in the trial records is barely recognizable as the same person as the brash Protestant and budding crypto-Jew we encounter in the *Vida*. There are obvious and sound reasons for this gap. What is of interest is not which version is most "truthful" in a positivist sense, but rather what are the differing strategies of self-fashioning employed in these versions and what can the gaps and fissures between these alternative narratives tell us about Cardoso's own process of conversion.

The Weight of Blood

The conversions and spiritual awakenings recorded in Manuel Cardoso de Macedo's *Vida* never occur when he is alone. Each religious transformation is the product of a powerful encounter, not only with a religious text or idea but with a religious person. These interactions challenge Cardoso's beliefs and drive his investigation into new religious possibilities. Cardoso's willingness to rethink his religious identity is connected not only to the ideas that he encounters for the first time, but also to the social bonds he forms with these new spiritual comrades, who teach him, as well as support him and provide him with a safe space in an alien environment. These new bonds, in turn are informed by his fraught relationship with his father and the religious legacy that Cardoso feels he has inherited. As he forges a new religious identity and creates a new religious community, his past and what it represents are constantly present. As an Old Christian, Cardoso's move toward Protestant heresy and later toward the "dead" Law of Moses is a clear rejection of his former life and his family relationships. As distant as that past may be, it is inescapably with him in his present.

Cardoso's Old Christian origins weigh heavily upon his newfound religious identity. He begins his *Vida* by declaring his thanks to God for the miraculous way He brought Cardoso to His service and "His knowledge."[5] This act of divine grace and wondrous providence is all the more miraculous because Cardoso is "of a people so seperate from the Jewish people, of gentile blood, dispised in His eyes, as it says in Malahy chapter 1, verses 2 & 3. 'And Jacob I loved, and Esau I abhored.'"[6] In the Bible Jacob's twin brother Esau is often portrayed as a violent and dangerous menace to his brother. While Jacob is described as a "simple (or perfect) man, a dweller of tents," Esau by contrast is a "man who knows hunting, a man of the field" (Genesis 25:27). Later on Isaac tells his son Esau, "By your sword ye shall live" (Genesis 27:40). These violent images led the rabbis of the Talmud to map Esau and his descendants onto the existential enemies of the Jewish people: Esau was typologically equated with the Roman Empire. Later this typology extended to the spiritual heir of Rome's earthly dominion, the Catholic Church. This biblical quotation from Malachi and many others like it were used in rabbinic Judaism not to refer exclusively to the two sons of Isaac and Rebecca, but rather to describe their progeny: the Jews and the Romans and later the nations of Christendom.[7]

Cardoso applies this typology to his own ancestry in the stark terms of the beloved and the despised; he is the descendant of a people "estranged from Him," and he carries the blood of those who are ontologically despised in God's eyes. He is unworthy of God's grace and guidance because not only does he come from the blood of the typological Jewish enemy, Esau, but his very family and nation, the Portuguese, were the most virulent enemies of the Jews: "Being of a lineage that is such an enemy of His people, to such an extreme that he [the father] declared that there wasn't enough fire in his hand to finish them [the Jews] off."[8] His legacy, passed down through blood, is one of genocidal fury against the people of God, and yet Cardoso, by an act of divine "compassion" is brought close to the God of Israel.

This sentiment is echoed toward the end of his account: "I give praise to the God of Israel for the mercies which he did for me in bringing me to His knowledge through such extraordinary measures, so that I have a continuous obligation to praise Him for taking me out from among my brothers and giving me a place among His People."[9] Again, Cardoso conjures up the weight of his national, religious, and familial legacy and is thankful that despite his past he is still accorded a place among God's people.

Cardoso's obsession with his own blood comes out of a conceptual inversion of *limpieza de sangre*; instead of Jewish blood being the carrier of a stained legacy, predisposing an individual to sin, it is Old Christian blood, free of any Jewish intermingling, which is seen as the most toxic and prone to corruption. Cardoso seems to use the ontological underpinnings of *limpieza* to "carnalize" rabbinic typologies. The rabbis use biblical figures and stories to talk about their contemporary political situation, while Cardoso uses these typological personae as a guide to the ontological nature of his own nation.

Jerome Friedman charts out the racial nature of the regime of *limpieza*.[10] He quotes Fray Prudencio de Sandoval, the biographer of Carlos V, who wrote in 1604: "Who can deny that in the descendants of the Jews there persists and endures the evil inclination of their ancient ingratitude and lack of understanding, just as in Negros [there persists] the inseparability of their blackness. For if the latter should unite themselves a thousand times with white women, the children are born with the dark color of the father."[11] The psychological, moral, and physical characteristics of the parents are passed down in an irreducible form, and the children must live with the consequences. The contamination of converso blood was so potent a threat that one Portuguese author urged that Old Christian children not be "suckled by Jewish vileness because that milk, being of infected persons, can only engender perverse inclinations."[12] It is easy to see how this biologically understood fear of Jewish contamination could be inverted and applied to Catholics by someone like Cardoso, who was raised within the cultural context of Iberian Catholicism.

Cardoso's ontology of his tainted gentile blood also appears to be informed by the rhetoric of racial superiority common among the ex-marranos of Amsterdam. Yosef Kaplan points out the not-so-subtle ways these former New Christians, once discriminated against because of their blood, turned the tables on their oppressors by appropriating the notions of "pure blood" for themselves. Isaac Orobio de Castro, a leading polemicist of the Amsterdam community, went so far as to distinguish between the born Jews who were given the "honroso nombre" and proselytes who despite their sincere efforts could never attain the same level of honor. Commenting on Orobio de Castro's choice of terminology Kaplan writes: "In fact, is there not in Orobio's words a kind of Jewish version of the Iberian principle of separatism, which distinguished between 'Old Christians,' who were also *puros* and *lindos*, and the 'New Christians' . . . ? Did Orobio not distinguish here between 'Old Jews' and 'New Jews'? And is not the term *honourable name*, which he used in the context of the distinction, one of the characteristic signs of the social discourse that was consolidated in Spain at the time of the *limpieza de sangre!*"[13] Cardoso would have been exposed to the idea of a blood-based, irreducible marker of spiritual aptitude both in his Portuguese upbringing and within the walls of the Jewish community he chose as his new spiritual home. It is no wonder that it was of such concern to him.[14]

Blood/lineage/roots (*sepa*) is such a powerful force that Cardoso resorts to an elaborate theory of transmigration of souls to explain his miraculous conversion: "I believe that my soul belongs to a wicked Jew (Israelite), a desecrator of the Divine Law. The Blessed Lord, through His mercies dealt kindly with this soul, placing it in this filthy vessel, far away from His paths so that in that state he would turn away from his evil deeds."[15] Cardoso's gentile body is the "impure vessel" that provides the appropriate vehicle for an errant Israelite soul to return to God's path. Here Cardoso echoes a kabbalistic concept of the convert as the carrier of a Jewish soul that was reincarnated as a merciful punishment for his past deeds; by coming back to the world, the soul has an opportunity to right the wrongs of its previous life.[16] This system of spiritual rehabilitation is the only way that Cardoso can explain how he broke free from his family's Catholicism and embraced his newfound Judaism: Cardoso does not share the same spiritual inheritance of his family; his body is Old Christian, but his soul is Jewish. In this schema, his conversion, then, is not a radical break with his inherited past, but rather a long overdue homecoming for his "original" self.

The impure state of his earthly "vessel," however, remains a challenge to his eventual conversion, and he again acknowledges God's mercy in placing the errant Israelite soul into his body and in guiding his path toward Judaism: "And in this way He has kept me in the observance of His Law so that in this way I will be able to reach the Divine light."[17] It is through God's grace that Cardoso's Jewish soul pierces through his impure body to reach the "divine light." Cardoso sees himself as at once bound by and free of his family's Old Christian legacy. Cardoso does not set out to present a unified account of his spiritual transformations; rather, his is an eclectic and untidy self-portrait in which blood vies with spirit in a dialectic of free choice, determinism, and divine grace.

The narrative firmly establishes Cardoso as a righteous convert. He begins the *Vida* with the issue that, in his eyes, compromises his claim to that status—namely, his gentile blood. He first appeals to the metaphysical in order to silence the claim of his Christian past on his Jewish present. After all, who can argue with the ways of providence? Cardoso envelops his story with appeals to the divine: He begins with the exposition on the transmigration of souls and God's beneficent guidance and ends by invoking God's promise of love and acceptance to the outcasts and the strangers by citing Isaiah (56:6–8). However, the bulk of the *Vida* is dedicated to Cardoso's courageous and sincere journey, *peregrinage*, toward enlightenment. The *Vida* that purports in its forward to tell of the divine mercies bestowed upon the humble convert quickly leaves the metaphysical sphere to describe the immanent causes and worldly encounters that drive its protagonist's search for religious truth.

An Azorean Catholic in Queen Elizabeth's Court

> Until now I took your grace for a Portuguese, but I now take you as an Englishman.[18]

> [Be careful] that this lad does not stay close to a seaport because of the communication that he maintains with the English . . . and because of the affection that he feels for that people.[19]

Cardoso describes his arrival in England, his introduction to the study of the Bible, and his first break with the religion of his fathers in the following matter-of-fact passage: "I did not find the sect of my parents to be good, and seeing the variety of religions that existed, I did not feel it proper to choose any of them until I could learn more about them and choose which one suited me best."[20] It seems that distance from his parents gives the fourteen-year-old Cardoso the psychological freedom to begin reconsidering his parents' religion. Cardoso's process of differentiation from his parents is aided and informed by the Protestant milieu in which he finds himself. He says that after attaining a basic understanding of English, he is introduced to the text of the Bible: "Scripture was the first thing that they placed in my hand after the ABC."[21]

The emphasis on study of the Bible gave him the strength, courage, and tools to judge the religion of his fathers on his own. Beginning to figure out his own identity, he decides to methodically investigate the different religious systems. He describes going to London where he was able to buy "seven books about seven religions." He settles on Calvinism, which he deemed "closest to reason." Catholicism was the religion he inherited from his parents, and in rejecting the Mother Church there is a rejection of his parents and the very act of passively receiving a religious faith. His quest for a new religious truth is wrapped up in his awakening sense of autonomy and independence, and this is why he describes Calvinism as a personal choice arrived at after careful investigation. Reason, as presented here, undoes the ties that bind him to his Catholic past and drives his path of independent inquiry.

Throughout his narrative, Cardoso de Macedo presents himself as a religious searcher who utilizes reason and a careful reading of scripture to guide him. Catholicism is rejected because it fails the test of reason. However, can the decision be so completely abstracted from his own social and psychological situation? The undefined "reason" that Cardoso de Macedo so fearlessly applies to his religious beliefs covers up what seems to be the strongest force in his rejection of Catholicism: the drive to differentiate himself from his father's shadow and simultaneously be accepted and integrated into his new peer group. As I will show in the subsequent analysis, Cardoso's break with Catholicism is never independent from his break with his family or the warm embrace of his Protestant friends and protectors.

In his inquisitorial testimony Cardoso presents himself as a passive agent whose heresy was situational. He was sent by his father to Topsham near Exeter, where he lived with a Mestre Escot, an innkeeper whom his father knew. [22] Within a year he mastered English so well that Escot introduced him to the Bible. In addition to exposing him to the Bible in English translation, Escot and the others around him taught the teenager all about the countless ways that the Catholics went about "blind" and in "error." He explains to the Inquisitors that he went to the Protestant churches and prayed like a Protestant because that was what everyone around him did. Instead of discussing his critical inquiry into the varieties of Protestant sects and his rationally guided scrutiny of the Bible, as he does in his *Vida*, Cardoso presents himself as young and vulnerable and dependent on his master. [23] He tells the Inquisitors that he served as a servant, a "criado," and went along with what his master and the people around him were doing. He became a "Lutheran" out of osmosis and inertia, not as a result of a zealous intellectual search. And for this reason, he admits his heresy and asks for forgiveness at his first hearing, claiming his youth as the reason for his straying from the Catholic truth. [24]

This portrayal is best suited to his defense strategy; his best hope of receiving a light sentence depends on convincing the judges that he was young, impressionable, and under duress. In contrast, the persona that Cardoso crafts in the *Vida* is idealistic, independent, and driven to discover the truth at any cost. What these two narratives share is the centrality of the wider Protestant social context for his religious transformation. To the Inquisitors he paints himself as weak-willed and describes Escot and the wider society as coercive; in the *Vida* his passion and intellectual curiosity are encouraged and energized by the various teachers, friends, and religious sponsors who become his new religious community.

In the *Vida* Cardoso describes the social benefits he received upon his conversion. As a young foreigner the allure of belonging and being cared for must have been great. After his conversion, he tells us that "the locals [the natives of that land] were very pleased with me as they saw me continue in their Church and with the ways that I demonstrated my zealousness in their religion, and in that way I was respected by them." [25] As a new and exotic convert, Cardoso became something of a celebrity: his conversation was sought out and he was welcomed into the homes of nobility. He tells of one "Great Lord" who treated Cardoso as a member of his own family: "with his sons and daughters he was like a brother, without any distinction between them." [26] Later another nobleman introduced Cardoso to Queen Elizabeth, who awarded him a stipend "So that with this I will be connected with greater firmness in their religion." [27] As Cardoso divorces himself from his parents' Catholicism, he finds surrogate parents and family who support him in his new religious life. [28] His first act of true independence—his rejection of Catholicism and discovery of Calvinism—is quickly followed by a recreation of familiar structures that mitigate the vertigo of his conversion.

His turn toward Protestant faith is a rejection and breaking off of connections to his family and the Mother Church. He works hard to transform himself into his new persona by integrating into the culture and social life of Protestant England, distancing himself from other Iberian expatriates and hiding his apostasy when back in the Azores.

When confronted with other Catholics in England, Cardoso brazenly declares his new religious allegiance. He describes an encounter with the Spanish ambassador who was curious as to why this fine Portuguese lad never observed Mass at his residence like all the other Iberian expatriates in London. Cardoso curtly rebuffs his inquiry: "Your Excellency can concern himself with his own servants, but not with me."[29] He is clearly drawing the line between himself in his new religious and social identity and the circle of Iberian Catholics associated with the ambassador. For the ambasador, Iberianess is synonymous with Catholicism, and thus Cardoso should be a regular at his residence. But as Cardoso makes clear in his response, he is not part of " 'His Excellency's' " retinue; Cardoso's apostacy literally places himself "outside" of that Iberian circle.

This attitude is best expressed in the comment made by a certain Joao Castro who met Cardoso in Topsham and seems to have traveled back with Cardoso on his last journey to the Azores. Their conversation was recorded in Castro's testimony against Cardoso preserved in the dossier of Cardoso's first trial before the Lisbon Holy Office. After Cardoso spoke about the errors of the Catholics and the truth of Cavinism, Joao told him: "Until now I took your grace for a Portuguese, but I now take you as an Englishman."[30] To his fellow Azorean, Cardoso appears outwardly in all ways as a Portuguese: his speech, presumably his dress, the fact that they are both going home to the Azores—all point to his Portuguese identity. Perhaps after spending so much time among English "heretics," Castro hoped to find some comfort in conversation with a fellow Portuguese traveler. In their conversation, he quickly realizes that Cardoso has "gone native"—he is no longer Portuguese, despite his origin and accent. His Calvinism transforms him into an Englishman. Cardoso seems to confirm this assessment by telling him that he planned to move permanently to England and begin a new life there.[31] Cardoso also understands that he cannot be both Portuguese and a Calvinist.

Traveling between these two poles of his emerging identity—England and the Azores—perhaps Cardoso was seduced by the liminality and anonymity of the ship and loosened his tongue, letting slip his Calvinist secret. Whatever the reason for Cardoso's openness aboard the ship, upon his arrival in his native São Miguel in the Azores, he was extremely circumspect about his Calvinism. Around his family Cardoso kept his beliefs secret and presented himself as a full-fledged Catholic. He recounts how he traveled back home to visit three times without his father sensing that anything had changed. Without the communal support he enjoyed in England, Cardoso's Calvinism had to go underground. Cardoso confessed to Joao that while he would "die for his religion," when he returned home to the Azores, he only went to church out of compulsion.[32] Back with his family he lived like a crypto-Protestant.

The conversations that Cardoso had with Castro triggered his arrest. Upon arrival in Angra, Joao discharged his conscience by reporting to his local bishop and recounting Cardoso's brazen declarations of heresy. This testimony offers a portrait of the young Cardoso from the perspective of a contemporary, as well as sheds light on many of the interactions both in England and the Azores that Cardoso recounts in his *Vida*.[33] Castro describes the scandalous declarations that Cardoso freely dispensed: The Pope is no better than any other man; priests should not be celibate; there is no reason to refrain from eating meat on Fridays— the basic Protestant litany. Castro also tells us that Cardoso displayed knowledge of the Old and New Testaments and "English" books. According to this witness, Cardoso was planning to live permanently in England and to get married there. He was coming back only to get money from his father. This would be Cardoso's last trip back home.[34] He was placing himself firmly within the orbit of his new religious and social world. The support of his different English benefactors—those who treated him "like a son"—seemed to have provided him with the stability and connections to enable him not only to practice his religion but to solidify his position within English society.

This plan to make a final break from his family after this trip could also explain why he would not confront his father directly and thus risk losing his financial support or worse. That he can deceive his father both religiously and financially reflects a pragmatic side to Cardoso that will serve him well during his time as a crypto-Jew in Portugal, but it also reflects his deep rejection not only of his father's faith but also of any paternal relationship between them.

There are a number of possible factors informing Cardoso's rejection of his father at this point in time. Cardoso views his father, as will be seen shortly, as a violently zealous Catholic and an overbearing paternal figure. It would be logical that with several hundred miles of ocean between then, the adolescent Manuel would be free enough to entertain a life outside of his father's shadow and perhaps to rebel and differentiate himself in the way that would have the most impact on his father: apostasy. In the charged Counter-Reformation context in which Cardoso grew up, to reject the family business would not make the same impression as rejecting the Mother Church. Ephraim Shoham has recently shown that in medieval times, there was a high incidence of conversion narratives involving adolescents. There is something about the instability of that stage of life that leads to thoughts of transformation, of rejection of the old in order for the young adult to emerge.[35] Through conversion to a foreign religion the usual psychosocial drama of adolescent differentiation receives the halo of divine sanction and encouragement. The lines are drawn unequivocally because in the pre-modern world there is no room for the child to return to the world of the parents once the child has apostatized. This is not a rejection that can allow for a mature re-embrace of the family; it is a radical break.

An additional clue to why Cardoso felt impelled to go so far in his rejection of his father and the Church appears in the genealogical information compiled about Manuel's family and included at the beginning of the proceedings of his first trial.[36] "Manuel is an illegitimate child born to an unwed mother."[37] Breatiz, the mother, who had passed away when Cardoso was young, had been "a single woman who lived off of washing laundry in Ponta Delgada." While Cardoso's paternal side consists of a long line of merchants, his mother's side is clearly more humble.[38] After his mother's death, Manuel was raised as a full son of Antonio Cardoso, even carrying both of Antonio's family names: Cardoso for his father's family, and Macedo for his mother's. However, could it be that his illegitimate status came out in some way in his father's treatment or in his own self-image? We do not know enough about how his father related to his other children. It is also important to note that "fijos naturais" in the Iberian world were common enough among both noble and humble families for this stigma to not carry the same weight it did in other cultural contexts. Nonetheless, it is possible that this distinction in his status positioned Cardoso to see himself as already outside of his intimate family circle even before his youthful religious experiments.[39]

Cardoso kept his Calvinism hidden from his father even after the latter confronted his son and directly asked him if he had strayed from the teachings of "their Holy Faith." Cardoso understood that for his father their shared faith was essential to their bond, and so he was unable to tell his father directly of his Calvinism. This uncharacteristic circumspection points to the fear his father instilled in him. According to his narrative, after his arrest Cardoso fearlessly proclaimed his Calvinism to the local bishop and the Inquisitors in Lisbon. But to have done so directly to his father's face may have been too emotionally difficult or downright suicidal, considering his father's fervent Catholicism.

His father's warning about the severity of apostasy highlights the violent power of blood and faith and can explain why Cardoso would be careful to keep his religious commitments secret: "Son, have you said something against our Holy Faith? Because there is an Inquisitorial official here to arrest you. If he would be here because you were a theif, a murderer or highwayman I would save you, giving you my own horse and money and if I would not have it I would carry you on my back, because this is what fathers do for sons, and sons for parents. However, for something pertaining to the Faith, I would go myself seven leagues on foot to get the wood to burn you."[40] His father sets up a clear distinction between the sacred and the profane; bloodlines are stronger than any worldly obligation, but obligations to God suspend all other attachments. If his son were a renegade from the law he would give anything to help him—but if his son has broken faith with the Church then his obligation as a child of the Church outweighs his paternal bond. The love and dedication he would show his son in a time of need would be reversed; he would zealously punish his son's apostasy with no regard for their shared blood.[41]

His father unwittingly confirms Cardoso's earlier undoing of his Old Christian past: While it is in his blood and while he was nurtured by the teachings of the Mother Church since his youth, his Catholicism and the ties that bind him to his parents' world can be severed and Cardoso can become an "other"—a new person with new commitments and ideals.

While his father confronts him openly about his heresy, Manuel dissimulates and masks his true beliefs. In England he is able to break away from his father's grip, but back home Cardoso is unable to directly tell his father about his new beliefs. His fear of or reverence for his father is such that he hides his religious commitment. He offers his father a mask, made up of his old self, which thinly hides his new identity. He responds to his father's zealotry with an equivocal, almost sarcastic response: "May God repay Your Mercies for this goodwill."[42] It is hard to imagine that Cardoso considered his father's commitment to walk seven leagues to fetch the wood to burn his own heretical son a reflection of his "goodwill." In Cardoso's equivocal reply, he uses the language of respect and piety to mask his true intentions.

In the *Vida*, Cardoso rarely resorts to masking his religious commitment. He generally presents himself as a fiery convert—openly declaring his religious allegiance, even to potential enemies such as the Spanish ambassador and his Inquisitors. However, there are exceptions to this general trend: Cardoso tells his reader that he hides his Protestantism from his father during his trips back to the Azores, and later while in prison he hides both his brief but radical agnosticism and his budding Judaism from his Inquisitors. I would propose that his masking of religious conviction, while possibly reflecting a certain lack of zeal, reveals how charged his religious choice is; he could not reveal it without destroying his relationship with his family and bringing on the homicidal piety of his father. His need to conceal his faith is indicative of the psychic weight that his conversions carried.

The ecclesiastical authorities apprehended Cardoso before he left the Azores. In the *Vida*'s telling, the local bishop wanted to clarify the matter of his rumored apostasy and hoped to avoid prosecuting the son of a respected family. He hoped that Cardoso would simply confess and ask for absolution, which he would easily receive. He assures Cardoso that "we know from what stock you come from."[43] To the bishop, Cardoso's Old Christian stock (*gerasão*) would guarantee a fundamental core of Catholic piety. Any tainting of that piety was probably only superficial and could be easily corrected. Cardoso's neophyte zeal, however, complicated the bishop's job: "I responded like an impetuous kid: 'I am a Calvinist, and a Calvinist I will die, except if there would be someone who could convince me with reasons which would conform with my understanding.' "[44] Cardoso has rendered his *gerasão* irrelevant to his present religious state. He proclaims himself free of the claims of his family's legacy. If the bishop wishes to bring him back to the fold, he must use the universal language of reason, not the parochial language of family, blood, and faith.

This temerity, which eventually landed him in the prisons of the Lisbon Inquisition, is indicative of a new model for religious faith and identity—one that is driven by reason instead of tradition, which Cardoso embraces in his self-portrait. Reason has undone his ties to Catholicism and only reason will bring him back to it. The heavy weight of his Old Christian legacy that he bemoans at the beginning of the *Vida* comes undone by his own critical investigations. In discussions with his Inquisitors Cardoso states that "if I distanced myself from the religion of my fathers it was because of the abominations of the Papist religion."[45] In Cardoso's self-portrait, it is his own critical thinking that brought him to reject the "religion of my fathers" and become a different person: "I am a Calvinist and a Calvinist I am going to die!"[46]

We find almost no echoes of this heroic self-image within the records of his first trial. He answers only as much as he needs to. He neither challenges the Inquisitors to a theological duel, nor shows any temerity. In contrast to his account in the *Vida*, we also do not see any explicit entreaty on the part of the Inquisitors that this Old Christian from a nice family simply confess and go home. Instead he quickly recounts his errors and begs for forgiveness. With his initial confession received, the Inquisitors continue their interrogation with two goals in mind: to ascertain information about other Portuguese heretics living in England and to make sure that Cardoso has not tried to spread Calvinism in the Azores either through conversation or distributing heretical pamphlets. His time in prison is not filled with the Inquisitors varied attempts to bring him back to the Mother Church; on the contrary he asks to return with very little prompting. It is hard to square this image with his own self-portrait.

Cardoso presents himself in the *Vida* as a deeply committed Calvinist during his time with the Lisbon Inquisitors. Their counterarguments against his Protestant heresy are not convincing, and so with their polemical arsenal depleted, the Inquisitors resort to an alternative approach in hopes of reconnecting this errant child of the church to his roots. Thus, after the months of solitary confinement in a dank prison cell to which they committed him, the Inquisitors decide to move Cardoso to the house of a respectable and honored man whose good Christian example would inspire Cardoso: "There you will be touched by the Holy Spirit, so that you will turn toward the milk of the Church that you suckled [as a child]."[47] Here, the Church is not just a matter of theological choice; it is a connection as primal as that between mother and child. Cardoso's *Vida* describes how hard he worked to undo the claims of that upbringing on his present self—the primary mover of that transformation is what he calls "reason." The Church, unable to beat him at the use of reason, attempts to reconnect him with his former (pre-rational) self.

The plan never has a chance to take off. Before he was actually moved to the home of this upstanding family, he was placed in a holding cell with an accused Judaizer, Henrique Dias Milão, a New Christian who vehemently denied being a crypto-Jew to the Inquisitors despite the evidence they had proving a long history of active Judaizing.[48] It was through him that Cardoso first came into contact with a written account of Judaism. When Cardoso began to read the practices cataloged in the "booklet of his crimes," he was shocked to find out that there were still people in the world who actually kept the laws of the Bible: "There were people who kept that religion, because all that was [recorded] there was in accordance with Scripture."[49] He spent the entire night reading the pamphlet and considering its implications on his own religious life. The next morning he found himself again at a religious crossroads, unsure of his next step: "I awoke without any form of religion, wiping out all of the Scriptures, not believing any of them, and seeing it all as a fable. In the end I was turned into a libertine."[50]

His new-found agnosticism allows him to cynically dissimulate a change of heart to the Inquisitors. He appeals to their mercy and forgiveness. He claims to have been possessed by a devil and likens himself to a drunk who when seduced by wine becomes somebody else only to wake up in the morning and not remember any of the previous evening's disastrous exploits. Cardoso fed the Inquisitors exactly what they were hoping to hear and they joyously welcomed him back to the fold. He was asked to repent his sins and was penanced at the auto-da-fé of April 5, 1609. In addition to the *sambenito* he was obliged to wear, Cardoso was sent to the Escolas Gerais, a reform school for penitent heretics for rehabilitative instruction in the Christian faith.

His claim of being possessed is not just an expedient solution to his juridical situation; it also reflects his present spiritual state. For several years he was a dedicated and passionate Calvinist whose convictions appeared solidly grounded in reason and scripture. In one night the entire edifice of his faith crumbled to the ground. Indeed, he was now like a man waking up from a drunken stupor, unable to make sense of what at one time seemed so witty and intelligent but now in the sober light of morning just sounds like gibberish. His past life became "other" to himself, and it was at this point that he used his former heresy to mask his present radical agnosticism and budding discovery of Judaism.

He fools the Inquisitors by speaking their language equivocally. His Calvinism may seem like the foolish "words of a drunk," but not because he sees the shining truth of Catholicism. His Protestantism has been replaced with a vertiginous skepticism that will soon bring him to the embrace of the perfidious "dead law" of Moses; this is hardly the upright Catholic future the Inquisitors desire for him. He mocks the Holy Office's "open arms" by skillfully performing the role of sincere penitent with the sole purpose of saving his life, which at this point is certainly not worth sacrificing for his discarded Calvinism.

He lies about his faith because he has lost it. As has been already pointed out, Cardoso rarely presents himself as being expedient with his faith. When he is firmly committed to a religion, he is almost always honest about it. He dissimulates about his faith in only two instances: once with his father, and then when he becomes part of the Portuguese marrano underground. Whereas fear and reverence are most probably the cause of his dissimulation with his father, in the latter case he masks his actual religious commitment in the attempt to save the lives of his fellow crypto-Jews. Apart from these two notable exceptions, Cardoso presents himself as a courageous believer. His bravery and willingness to endure suffering for his beliefs are essential to the *Vida's* implicit rhetorical goal of proving Cardoso's well-deserved place among God's people.

In the trial record we do not see any sudden shift in his testimony along these lines. There is also no mention of his being placed in Dias Milão's cell—not that this would necessarily make it into the record. What is interesting is that the role of the remorseful penitent that Cardoso describes in this section of the *Vida*, a persona he claims to adopt only after his crisis of faith, is how he appears throughout his first trial. From the very beginning he recounts his heretical beliefs and rejection of Catholic practice, but only as part of a confession leading to his petition for mercy and his desire to return to the Church. In the trial records there are no theological debates with the Inquisitors. The only bold proclamations of his Calvinism come from testimony of others who met him in England. These are two irreconcilable images that point to the very different rhetorical contexts of his prison testimony and of his *Vida*. Cardoso writes the *Vida* as a retrospective, and in that retelling he crafts his present self-image.

Cardoso's discovery of Judaism calls into question his once solid belief in Calvinism. He is profoundly confused and enters a brief period of radical agnosticism, and it is during this time that Cardoso is able to feign remorse for his heretical "nonsense," plead disingenuously for the Holy Office's mercy, and ultimately save his life.[51] As he confesses in his *Vida*: "Following this I decided to go to the [Inquisitors'] table and retract [un-say myself] in order to not die."[52] This "un-telling" of his past life was possible only because of the spiritual emptiness and lack of conviction he now felt.[53]

From *Libertino* to Old Christian Marrano

Cardoso was not paralyzed by his agnosticism. Upon his release from prison, he was placed in the Escolas Gerais, the reform school set up for inquisitorial penitents in the Santa Marinha neighborhood of Lisbon, where his Inquisitors hoped that he would be shepherded back to the flock of the faithful. All penitents who were not sentenced to death or the galleys were placed in these schools. After several months they would be allowed to leave but had to reside in the nearby Santa Marinha neighborhood so that inquisitorial officials could check up on them and ensure their full reintegration. Cardoso was successful at convincing the officials of his piety, and he was soon released.[54]

Prisons are often the best schools for criminality, and this "reform school" was no exception.[55] In the *Vida* Cardoso describes how he made use of the high percentage of conversos there to deepen his understanding of Judaism: "And with my conscience never being at peace, I would approach certain individuals who would appear to me [as possible crypto-Jews], and I would ask them: 'Why did they arrest you?' And when they would say to me that they were arrested for being a Jew, I would continue to ask them if it was so. If they would say 'yes' I would try to extrapolate from [what they told me] what I saw fit.[56] Cardoso points to two essential characteristics of how he understood his religious transformation. His search to understand Judaism is self-directed. He decides which conversos to approach as potential sources, and he is the one who carefully extracts the information that he finds relevant for his own religious quest: "I would try to extrapolate from [what they told me] what I saw fit." At the same time, Cardoso bonds with his informants. Most strikingly in this passage, we see how he begins to transform himself into not only a Jew but a crypto-Jew. In order to get the information he wants, Cardoso must act like a marrano, even before becoming a Jew. He practices stealth and dissimulation in order to reconstruct the religious world of which he received an earth-shattering glimpse in the jail of the Inquisition a few weeks back. His choice to learn more about Judaism leads him along a path where he not only encounters a new social circle, that of the New Christians, but also must adopt the subversive practices characteristic of crypto-Judaism because of inquisitorial surveillance.

After two months in the reform school, Cardoso is released and moves in with the children of his former cellmate, Henryque Dias Milão. Cardoso refers to Milão, who was sentenced to death for his Judaizing practices, as his "comp[anheiro]o." Cardoso decides to stay with Milão's children because he wants to learn more about Jewish ritual and belief. Thus, he went with "the goal of keeping the Sabbath and going little by little taking notice of the Law of Moses, because it appeared to me to be the true [law], of which I did not have any knowledge because in my father's house it was said that the Jews adored a heiffer [*toura*, a female *touro*].[57] He has discovered the true nature of Judaism only recently because growing up in his father's house, the only knowledge of Judaism he had was a (perhaps humorous) refrain claiming that the Jews adore the "toura," not the Torah.[58] Again, Cardoso cites his family legacy as the primary obstacle on his path to religious truth.

It is thanks to his cellmate and then later on the inmates at the school that Cardoso comes to see the truth of Judaism.

As seen previously in Cardoso's conversion to Calvinism, the human and social dimension is central to his spiritual transformation. Not only does Cardoso gravitate toward the Jews for religious knowledge; he also begins to identify himself with them: "I was acquiring affection for the Men of the Nation, and [I began to] take upon myself their troubles as my own."[59] His move toward Judaism, while grounded in intellectual rigor, is intimately tied up with his empathy for the Jews, his taking their "troubles as his own."[60] This expression of empathy reflects his (desired) identification with both the God and the people of Israel and his willingness to share in their destiny.

In his *Vida* Cardoso includes several examples of his self-sacrifice for his fellow Jews. Each of these instances form pivotal moments in his spiritual *peregrinação*; they signify movement toward a fuller integration into the Jewish community and a more complete transformation into his new religious identity. Within the rhetorical economy of the narrative, they serve to prove his loyalty to both the Jewish people and to the God of Israel.

We should not forget that the narrative frame and stated justification for Cardoso's *Vida* is the desire to recount the miracles and mercies of divine providence as they unfolded in Cardoso's experience.[61] These acts of initiative and bravery are no exception. Instead of diminishing their value, inscribing them into the narrative of God's grace confers upon them a divine seal of approval, assuring the reader (and the author) of the righteousness of his path.

Under Cover of Night: Escape from Lisbon

> I began feeling affection for the people of the Nation, and I began to take on their struggles as my own.

Cardoso's involvement in the failed attempt to help a group of New Christians escape from Portugal forms an essential part of his narrative of sacrifice and heroism on behalf of fellow Jews in the *Vida*. This episode also leads to his second arrest and imprisonment by the Lisbon Inquisition. The proceedings of his second trial before the Lisbon Holy Office provide details about this case, which supplement and problematize the narrative Cardoso crafts in his *Vida*.[62] The trial records also deepen our appreciation of Cardoso's relationship with the Dias Milão family and the ways he seems to insert himself into the fabric of the family despite their different ethnic and cultural backgrounds. Before analyzing Cardoso's treatment of this episode in his *Vida*, I will focus on the trial record in order to better understand this social dynamic and to foreground his autobiographical narrative of the same event.

In the beginning of the trial record, we find the testimony of two witnesses who saw a group of "reconciled" heretics boarding a skiff on the Tagus River in front of the Madre de Deus church. The witnesses claim that they recognized one of the passengers as the daughter of Enrique Dias Milão, who was burnt at the last auto-da-fé. Antonio Dalmeida, head of the Lisbon customs house, and his friend Bernardo Gomes saw the suspicious get-away from the steps of the church and called to have the passengers apprehended before they could reach the ship that would take them to the "lands of heresy."[63] These passengers were Cardoso and Isabel Henriques Milão and her "Indian" maid, Victoria Dias,[64] whom he was accompanying to Antwerpt in an elaborate plan of escape that involved their boarding a small skiff and rowing downstream to an English ship waiting near the Belem neighborhood and ready to depart from the mouth of the harbor.[65] At his trial, Cardoso admitted to contracting the captain and his boat to take these New Christians out of Lisbon,[66] while also arguing that he and the other passengers were innocent—that they were not guilty of moving to lands of heresy because Antwerp was a Catholic city. He tells the Inquisitors that he had no ill intent because he did not think that he or the other passengers needed to receive explicit permission "from this table" to leave Lisbon once their penance was finished. He assures the Inquisitors that since his sentencing, he has been a good Catholic and asks them to verify this with the priests and officials who periodically visited him after his release.

In his testimony, Cardoso puts the brunt of the responsibility for the escape on his own shoulders. After many rounds of questioning, the only member of the Dias Milão family whom Cardoso identifies as being involved in the escape is Guiomar Gomes, the mother of Ana Enriquez Milão and of Fernao Lopes Milão. Lopes Milão is not directly implicated in the case, but he is close to Cardoso. After their time in the reform school, Cardoso had moved in with Lopes Milão and his mother Guiomar Gomes and became their servant in exchange for room and board.[67] Two officials from the school for penitents describe Cardoso as acting like Lopes Milao's servant already during their time at the school. Jorge da Costa and Antonio Ruiz describe him setting the table and bringing their food, among other services. These two officials simply report the details of this relationship and seem not to have been surprised or concerned that this Old Christian was becoming so close with a family of penitent Judaizers.

Cardoso refers to his relationship with Lopes Milão as part of the background behind Guiomar Gomes's request that he accompany her daughter to Antwerp.[68] He is at once indebted to them and trustworthy enough for Gomes to entrust the safety of her daughter to Cardoso.[69] He also mentions Ana Enriques Milão, Isabel's aunt who was living in Antwerp and who requested that her young sons, Anrique and Gonzalo, be brought to her. From the testimony it would seem that Cardoso was responsible for arranging the logistics of the escape and for protecting the younger Dias Milão on the journey.[70]

These accounts paint a picture of an intricate web of blood relationships and the way that Cardoso inserts himself into this family dynamic. He is an outsider who is brought close out of a mixture of necessity and trust. From the outside it appears that Cardoso's relationship with the Dias Milão family is based on his vulnerability and need: He is a young man, on his own and recently released from jail, who could use a place to sleep and some food until he finds his way. The Dias Milão family takes him in and in exchange Cardoso becomes their "criado," domestic servant. Surprisingly, the Inquisitors are not too concerned over how or why Cardoso became close to this particular family. They are more upset that he has sought out other penitents instead of upstanding Christians.[71] The Inquisitors do not recall any connection between the now-deceased Dias Milão's and Cardoso which might explain the relationship between the former Protestant heretic and the family of the convicted Judaizer. And in general there is very little concern on the part of the Inquisitors over any possible Judaizing by Cardoso. His Old Christian status and his past "Lutheranism" throw off the Inquisitors from the scent of his Judaizing.

When the testimonies from the second trial are read in tandem with Cardoso's narrative of his encounter with the Dias Milão family in the *Vida*, we can see that Cardoso follows a path in Lisbon that is similar to the one he took in England. In both situations his religious transformation brings him into contact with local members of his new faith: In England not only does he embrace Calvinism, but he is also embraced by Calvinists; in Lisbon, the same dynamic occurs with Judaism. In both cases he weaves himself into the fabric of his new co-religionists' social networks at the same time as he commits himself more fully to the tenets of the new faith. Insofar as his commitment to a new religious trajectory leaves him socioeconomically vulnerable—how will he support himself, who will protect him, with whom will he share his new path?—his embrace of these surrogate families serves a double purpose of socioeconomic and religious support.

While the trial witnesses perceive his relationship with the Dias Milão family as one of economic dependency on their largess, in actuality the situation appears to have been more complex and mutually beneficial. For, in this particular episode we can see how Cardoso's Old Christian status served as a cover for their escape. The Inquisitors did not suspect him of Judaizing and were more likely to give an Old Christian the benefit of the doubt in a trial. In addition, his facility with English allowed him to more easily arrange the boat for the "getaway." And so it was not only the Dias Milão family who helped Cardoso throughout this chapter of his life; he was able to bring valuable assets to the relationship as well.

His claim in the *Vida* that he was able to protect the other members of the group and that it was only he who bore the brunt of the investigation is partially supported by the trial record: He gave out the names of only a few people and apparently kept the identities of many more secret. The fact that the Dias Milão family took him in upon his arrival in Hamburg is a clear sign that they saw him as a trustworthy and loyal friend, despite his testimony implicating Guiomar Gomes. That said, the trial transcripts do not record every exchange between Cardoso and the Inquisitors, and so his claims that he was singled out for special indignation by the authorities cannot be verified. What is clear is that the Inquisitors are suspicious of Cardoso and believe he has more information that he is not sharing: Why else would they hold him for so long?

Before the Inquisitors Cardoso is cautious and strategic, admitting as much as he can without disclosing too much information. His claim in the *Vida* that he did not give up a single name is not exactly true. However, he was able to stick to his claim that he was the one behind the plot, with Guiomar Gomes having the original idea. He also consistently stood by his argument that he did not think he or the others were doing anything wrong and that they were simply traveling to another Catholic city, Antwerp. The Inquisitors accuse him of hiding information and protecting someone but he does not give up any other names.[72] His claim of having been beaten and singled out for harsh treatment because of their frustration with his silence is not recorded in the trial records. But this is not surprising. That Cardoso transforms this episode into a dramatic account of his bravery and self-sacrifice for the sake of fellow Judaizers is to be expected, and I believe that with the trial record as background we can better appreciate his narrative choices and how they reflect his retrospective fashioning of his religious persona on the eve of his official arrival under the wings of the *Shechina*.

In the *Vida* Cardoso portrays himself as heroically shielding his marrano comrades from the Inquisitorial "pouncing lions."[73] In his telling, thanks to the careful manipulation of his interrogators and his ability not to let loose any secrets, Cardoso managed both to get the other members of his group out of prison within thirty-two days and to keep the identity of the other marranos involved in the plot secret. After the other members of his group were released, the Inquisitors decided to keep Cardoso in prison for some time longer. According to Cardoso, they desired to punish him out of frustration for not being able to prosecute any of the other suspects: "They took revenge on [me] for not being able to condemn anyone, because they were not able to understand the truth [of the plot], and they were unable to deal badly with them, because in my mouth was everything. They kept me imprisoned until another auto[-da-fé], without ever being able to extract one word from me. Thus I left free and clear."[74]

Cardoso's skilled silence and courage save the day. The Inquisitors whose expertise it is to pry open the secrets of the heart cannot even get "one word" out of Cardoso, the Old Christian crypto-Jew.[75]

This episode showcases the strength of Cardoso's commitment to his newly adopted people. It is significant on a performative level as well. This consummate act of deception completes Cardoso's transformation into a marrano. Cardoso uses his inherited Catholicism, the very stain he has tried so hard to wipe away, as the ultimate marrano mask. His Old Christian status clouds the Inquisitors' suspicion, and he is able to manipulate them to the point of winning his comrades' freedom. His Catholicism is now merely a mask that he assumes at will as part of his newly constructed identity.

From Lisbon to Hamburg to Danzig: Temporary Havens

Another account of Cardoso's self-sacrifice occurs in the penultimate chapter of his *Vida*. After his release from prison he goes to live with another crypto-Jewish family, the Rodrigues Pinheiro family of Celorico. He spends almost ten months there until a friend is arrested by the Holy Office and Cardoso decides to flee Portugal before he is implicated in a wider investigation. He arrives in Hamburg and is welcomed by members of the Dias Milão family who had already established themselves in this Baltic port. As part of his formal conversion he is circumcised and takes on the Jewish name Abraham Pelengrino.[76]

Some days later he moves to Danzig where he works in the business of Mosseh Abensur, a son of Henrique Dias Milão. A small riot breaks out against the Abensur family because of a blood libel related to the death of their mulatto servant. Fearing the mob, Mosseh Abensur decides to flee Danzig and abandon his property and merchandise.[77] According to the *Vida*, he urges Cardoso to do the same, but Cardoso decides to stay in order to try to protect the immense holdings of the Abensur family: "I told him that he should go and that I would stay."[78] Cardoso's loyalty and courage come at a high price. In the upheaval, Cardoso is thrown in prison where he is housed with five "murderous thieves." His short time in prison, even for a veteran of the Inquisition's jails, is a harrowing experience: "And thus I would take one month before the Inquisition than one day in that prison. Every day I was distressed by my suffering, and I no longer felt death because I was so sick of life and worn out through my travails."[79] He leaves prison physically broken and struck with leprosy and makes his way to Hamburg, where he is taken in and cared for by members of the small Portuguese Jewish community.

He looks at his sufferings as a divine test of his true commitment to Judaism. He writes: "I considered that He gave me these [troubles] in order to prove whether or not I was committed to His Law."[80] This theodistic sense-making reflects his anxiety about his conversion and his newly acquired status as a Jew. The transformation of identity is complex and never results in a total metamorphosis. The residue of the convert's past life remains, and its presence provokes anxiety about the solidity of his identity. This anxiety is never fully quieted for Cardoso. In this instance he is able to point to his own sacrifice on behalf of the family who took him under their wing as proof of his commitment to Judaism and the Jewish people. Despite his origins, his journey toward Judaism was providentially arranged and carries with it divine sanction.

He works hard in his *Vida* to prove his allegiance to his fellow Jews. However, he has an easier time explaining his direct relationship with the God of Israel. God guides his steps and leads him toward true spiritual enlightenment—even if he sometimes sends him travail and hardship as a means of merciful punishment. It is ultimately God who welcomes him into his covenant. Cardoso ends his narrative with verses from Isaiah (56:6–8) that call out to the "children of the strangers," the outcasts of society, who find their way to God's law:

> And children of the strangers, those who join unto A[donay], in order to serve Him and in order to love the name of A[donay], in order to be His servants, guarding the Sabbath from profaning it, holding fast to my covenant, Lo I will bring them to my holy mountain, and I will rejoice with them in my house of prayer. . . . For my house will be called a house of prayer; so says A[donay] God, to all of the nations, the oppressed of Israel will be gathered, I will still gather unto Him his oppressed ones.[81]

At the beginning of his *Vida* Cardoso confronts the weight of his Old Christian legacy and expresses anxiety about the spiritual and ethnic limitations of his "blood and lineage."[82] By the end of his story, however, he expresses the hope that divine truth is universally accessible and not determined by blood. He enlists his acts of heroism and sacrifice in hopes of securing his place amongst the Jews. He writes the *Vida* while living in Amsterdam surrounded by the people to whose God he has sacrificed so much to serve. However, he is alone, unmarried, reliant on others for his economic stability. As a convert, he has no biological family upon which to depend. The community takes care of him, but he is kept on the margins as reflected by his position as the beadle (*shamash*) in the synagogue. This is a long way off for the son of a prosperous and respected merchant. Alone without any deep social connections within the Naçao, Cardoso calls out to God; he looks for his place within God's house, within the family of the pious. Now at the end of his story, with all his rhetorical self-fashioning exhausted, he places his trust in God's promise to the wayward converts. Abraham Pelengrino has a place in God's house because it is a "house of prayer for all nations"—even Portuguese Old Christians.[83]

The previous pages have sought to analyze the means by which Manuel Cardoso de Macedo became Abraham Pelengrino. I wanted to trace the relationship between Cardoso's many selves and the others he encounters and is inspired by. I contend that his conversions were not only the result of rarefied intellectual inquiry; rather, each religious shift was connected to his encounter with people, whether they be Catholics, Protestants, or Jews, who challenged, inspired, and supported him in his religious quest, and each step toward his new religious state forced him to reevaluate his relationship to his past, his family, and his very own blood.

Cardoso's religious journey was fueled by text and by a dialectical confrontation between himself and both the new religious cultures he encountered and his own family legacy. In his move toward Calvinism Cardoso was inspired by the "reasonableness" of Protestant theology and the kindness of his English hosts, at the same time that as a teenager living far away from his authoritarian family, he was enthralled with the power of his new-found freedom. This act of absolute freedom, however, forced the adolescent neophyte to face his family's presence in his life and decide how best to navigate it. His initial response was to lead the double life of a fiery Calvinist in London and a crypto-Calvinist when returned to visit the Azores. A similar complex of competing drives was at the heart of his discovery of Judaism. His integration into the Jewish people was disturbed by his Old Christian past. This legacy remained a source of anxiety for Cardoso many years after he had converted; on a fundamental level the entire *Vida* is a narrative attempt to find and secure his place within the people of Israel and wipe clean the stain of his Old Christian blood. The anxiety and shame that mark the beginning of his autobiography give way to the prophetic assurance of hope and belonging to the outcasts and strangers, himself included, with which he concludes.

5 "All of Us Are Brothers"

Race, Faith, and the Limits of Brotherhood in the Relación *of Antonio de Montezinos, alias Aharon Levi (1644)*

THE CASE OF Antonio de Montezinos's *Relación* raises questions and explores themes that differ from those of Carvajal's and Cardoso's texts. In both Carvajal and Cardoso we encounter individuals whose spiritual development is deeply connected to their relationships with members of their families and with the various surrogate family members they encounter along their spiritual journey. In the case of Carvajal and Cardoso we also have the interplay between their carefully crafted self-portraits and the jumble of conflicting and alternative narrative voices and perspectives found in each individual's Inquisitorial dossier. This expanded textual network deepens our appreciation of the texture of their varied relationships. In the case of Antonio de Montezinos we know almost nothing about his family, with the exception of a brief reference to his father's name and Menasseh ben Israel's reference to his origins in Villaflor, Portugal.[1] In place of the intricate web of family and trusted outsiders which structures the life stories of Carvajal and Cardoso we find Montezinos telling a story of his own spiritual development and his embrace of a vigorous, messianically tinged Jewish identity, which is inspired by his encounter with individuals who at first seem deeply other and foreign only to be revealed as Montezinos's Jewish brothers. Our previous cases involved the forging of spiritual bonds between strangers and fellow travelers; each subject found alternative fathers and spiritual brothers to replace or supplement their brothers and parents of flesh and blood with whom they did not share the same dreams and commitments. Montezinos forges bonds of brotherhood with the Reubenites and their Amerindian allies despite any obvious blood or spiritual connection. This pact uses the nomenclature of family to fashion a bond which is at once tribal and universalistic.

In this chapter I will focus on how the idea of family, specifically the notion of brotherhood, is developed within Montezinos's narrative. I will also make reference to Menasseh ben Israel's *Mikveh Israel/Esperanza de Israel*, especially as it pertains to the early modern discourse surrounding the origins of the Native Americans and the question of universal brotherhood. I will be looking at the text as a document formed out of the encounter between the Old and New Worlds, deeply concerned with issues of race, religion, and the boundaries of belonging. Montezinos's text grapples with the layers of oppression at the heart of European colonization of the Americas and proposes a particular vision of justice and redemption.

This story is both about and for the agents of that redemption and is concerned throughout with questions of identity, of Montezinos's own and that of his indigenous interlocutors. Montezinos's encounter and its transformation into the narrative of the *Relación* are energized by the notion of brotherhood—of the possibility of sharing a history and a sense of destiny with individuals who appear to be quintessentially other. I will explore the limits, possibilities, and dynamics of brotherhood as it unfolds in the *Relación*. One of the central questions this chapter will address is what can thinking about this text through the prism of family reveal about the nature of its messianism and its engagement with race and identity?

Antonio de Montezinos and His *Relación*

The text that came to be known as the *Relación de Aharon Levi, alias Antonio de Montezinos* was originally an oral deposition given by the Portuguese converso Antonio de Montezinos before a council of eminent leaders of Amsterdam's Spanish and Portuguese Jewish community in 1644.[2] The *Relación* tells the story of Montezinos's travels in New Granada, roughly today's Colombia, from 1639 until the summer of 1644. While crossing the Andes, Montezinos had a laconic conversation with a group of Indian porters in his hire.[3] Sometime later, while imprisoned by the Inquisition in Cartagena in 1639 on suspicion of Judaizing, he had an uncanny epiphany: The Indians he met in the mountains must have been Jews. Unable to shake this notion, he resolved that upon his release from jail he would find the "Jewish" Indians and unravel the mystery of their true identity. Montezinos was released and found the leader of the Indian porters, Francisco, who eventually led him to the remote kingdom of the lost Israelite tribe of Reuben deep in the Andes. The Reubenites entrusted Montezinos with a message for the Jews of the global diaspora about the approaching messianic redemption.[4]

In 1644, Montezinos left the Americas for Amsterdam, where he shared his account with leaders of the Sephardic community. His story created quite a stir, particularly among some of the Christian millenarians then living in Amsterdam. Montezinos's narrative circulated orally for five years until it was published in 1649 as part of a treatise espousing the Israelite origin of the American Indians entitled *Iewes in America*. The author of this curious book, the English theologian Thomas Thorowgood, knew about Montezinos's account from one of his fellow English millenarians, John Dury, who temporarily resided in Amsterdam around the time of Montezinos's arrival. Dury requested a copy of the *Relación* from his acquaintance Rabbi Menasseh ben Israel in Amsterdam. Menasseh was present at Montezinos's deposition and was able to supply Dury with a copy of the *Relación* in 1649. Thorowgood then used the version of the *Relación* that Menasseh provided as the main proof text for his *Iewes in America* where he argued for the Jewish origins of the Native Americans.[5]

Menasseh was actively engaged in discussions with Christian theologians regarding the Messiah's arrival, the place of the Jews within that scenario, and the methods that could be employed to bring about this end.[6] Montezinos's account had profound ramifications for these questions, and its proper interpretation became a contentious issue between Menasseh and his Christian counterparts. Menasseh strongly disagreed with many of Thorowgood's assertions and felt that he was misreading Montezinos's account. After a flurry of letters discussing the issue with Christian and Jewish theologians, Menasseh decided to compose a book that would correct these misinterpretations and clarify his own position regarding the messianic advent, the lost tribes, and their identification with the American Indians.[7] This essay turned into Menasseh's *Esperanza de Israel* of 1650, which was subsequently translated into Latin, English, Dutch, French, and Hebrew. Menasseh also used Montezinos's *Relación* as his central proof text, printing it in full at the beginning of his treatise. In this embedded form it gained its greatest notoriety.

The printed version of the *Relación* focuses on what is arguably the most unusual and thus interesting aspect of Montezinos's life: his discovery of the Reubenites. The text reveals little information about Montezinos's life before or after this central event. We are told only of his name in Hebrew, "Aharon Levi," and that in another time in Spain he was known as Antonio de Montezinos.[8] Even his birthplace of Villaflor, a small Portuguese town close to the Spanish border, is left out. His religious orientation is uncertain prior to this encounter with the Indians: Was he a devout Catholic, an actively Judaizing converso, a complete agnostic, or somewhere in between? We can infer that at least externally, Montezinos would have presented himself as a practicing Catholic. According to his account, he was arrested by the Inquisition at Cartagena but he does not say why.[9] He recounts that while in prison he regularly recited a series of classic Jewish prayers, albeit in a bastardized form. These two details suggest Montezinos's crypto-Jewish proclivities.

Rabbi Menasseh offers a few more biographical details in the body of his *Esperanza*. He informs his readers that he repeatedly spoke with Montezinos during the latter's stay in Amsterdam in 1644. According to Menasseh, Montezinos swore "in my presence and in the presence of many people of quality . . . that everything that he said was the truth."[10] Menasseh uses the *Relación* as his central proof text for his own theories regarding the origin of the American Indians and the signs pointing to an imminent Messianic redemption. The importance of the *Relación* to Menasseh's larger project explains why he goes out of his way to defend Montezinos's reliability and credibility as a witness. Menasseh tells the reader: "Overall, what I give most credence to is the report which our Montezinos, a Portuguese by nation and a Jew by religion, born in a town in Portugal called Villaflor, the son of honored and well known parents."[11] Montezinos' national, religious, and familial identity ensures his credibility to the rabbi and his Sephardic audience. Menasseh mentions Montezinos's imprisonment by the Inquisition as something that "happens to many other of those born in Portugal, descendants of those forcibly converted by the King Don Manuel."[12] According to Menasseh, Montezinos can be believed because he shares the common trauma of the ex-conversos of the Amsterdam community, descendants of those who were forcibly converted, including Menasseh and most of his generation.

Montezinos's credibility, however, is not based solely on his ethno-religious identity. Menasseh describes him as "a good person, without any ambition." That is, his tale can be believed because it brought no material gain to its teller. He came to Amsterdam only to bring to his fellow Jews the "joyous tidings." Once in Amsterdam, he refused to profit in any way from his experience in South America and his tale of meeting a lost tribe of Israel.[13] After staying six months, Montezinos returned to the New World, living the last two years of his life within the open Jewish community of Pernambuco in Northern Brazil. Menasseh tells the reader that Montezinos attested to the truth of his story until his very last day.[14]

Montezinos's arrest by the Inquisition in Cartagena is the only event mentioned in his *Relación* that can be corroborated with external evidence.[15] The records of this inquisitorial tribunal are incomplete, but reference to a certain "Antonio de Montessinos, a native of Villaflor in the Kingdom of Portugal" can be found in the description of cases. The document states that a certain Montessinos was arrested in Cartagena in September of 1639. The authorities suspected that this individual was in fact the same Montezinos who was wanted on charges of Judaizing. He was released on February 19, 1641, owing to a lack of credible evidence identifying him with the inquisitors' suspect. In the *Relación* there is no mention of the charges against him or the circumstances of his release; however, it is reasonable to assume that official document is referring to our Montezinos.

Montezinos's imprisonment coincided with the widespread anti-converso crackdown that followed the discovery of the "Gran Complicidad" (Great Conspiracy) of 1639. On the eve of Portugal's rebellion from Spanish rule in 1640, Spanish colonial authorities came to believe that Portuguese conversos living in the Americas were conspiring with Spain's enemies to take control of Spain's American colonies, with their precious silver mines and vital trade routes. The conspiracy was largely a fiction, but it unleashed a wellspring of anti-Portuguese, anti-converso sentiment among Spanish authorities throughout the Indies. It also served to alert the Inquisition to the dangers posed by Portuguese conversos resident in the Indies, and in turn triggered a wave of arrests and dozens of trials, both in Mexico and Peru, as well as in New Granada.[16] Regardless of his actual religious commitment or his role in seditious activity, the mere fact that Montezinos was a New Christian of Portuguese origin would have made him an easy target of inquisitorial persecution during this period.

Text and Context: The Mediated Voice of Early Modern Autobiography

For most of its history, the text of Montezinos's *Relación* has been seen as insepa-rable from Menasseh's *Esperanza*. Scholars have read it as a curious documentary addition to the Israelite Indian theory or more often, as Cecil Roth puts it, the ravings of a "wild-eyed Marrano."[17] It has been mined for its positivist historio-graphic value but the text offers much more. The *Relación* deserves to be read not merely as an appendix to Menasseh's *Esperanza* but as an independent text.[18] Montezinos's record of his travels in South America is an autobiographical nar-rative that engages the generic practices and intellectual concerns of its historical moment. That it originated as an oral deposition and was published six years later (and after Montezinos's death) complicates but does not obviate Montezinos's au-tobiographic voice.

There are severe limitations to any textual history of Antonio de Montezi-nos's *Relación*. The chief issue is that of a "clean" authorship. The text, as it has been preserved in print, is based on Montezinos's oral testimony. It was recorded in the third person in the style of juridical depositions and almost nothing is known of its textual life before it found its way into Thorowgood's treatise almost six years later. As such, it is difficult to say that Antonio de Montezinos actually "wrote" the text of his *Relación*.

Margarita Zamora's conception of Columbus's diaries as composed by a "cor-porate author"—an amalgam of authors, editors, and readers of the "Columbian texts" including Columbus himself, his son Fernando, his friend and longtime champion of Indian rights, Fray Bartolomé de Las Casas, and the courtier who secured the funding for his voyages, Luis de Santángel, just to mention a few—could be applied to Montezinos's text, which is a transformation of an oral ac-count into a written document by the men who listened to it and the secretaries who recorded it.[19] The subsequent publications and translations of the *Esperanza* and consequently of the *Relación* further also contribute to the texts corporate entity.

As discussed in chapter 2, in the early modern period acts of self-writing were often complicated affairs involving a network of interested parties: the main sub-ject who would recount his or her experience; the reader who asked, or demanded, that the account be given; and the actual or potential readers of the account. Often, as in the case of juridical depositions, the text was fixed in writing by a third party who recorded the oral statements of the subject. Even beyond the issue of transcription, the mere fact that a superior often solicited these texts created a highly mediated form of literary expression. This mediation is a central feature of the suggestive and engaging narratives of the *discurso de la vida* with which each inquisitorial interrogation began, of the confessional accounts of nuns and other religious persons, and of the ubiquitous *relación*.[20] As opposed to the egocentric self-reflection of modern autobiography in which "I am the matter of my book," early modern autobiographic writing is a means to an end. Moreover, an implicit or explicit audience that demanded the writing in the first place is often addressed.

The author was first and foremost a reporter, needing to present his or her case to their reader. While containing instances of unguarded self-reflection and emotional vulnerability, these autobiographic texts were primarily constructed in order to effect a particular end: to prove the subject's innocence, to receive reward for service and loyalty, to prove his or her piety or orthodoxy, and so on. This does not mean that these texts were purely cynical and calculated acts of manipulation. Rather, the readers' demands and expectations had an impact on the framing and shaping of the narrative and affected the way that the author would tell his or her story. It could be said that the "interestedness" of their narratives actually gave many self-writers the structure necessary to engage in self-expression and introspection.[21]

The *Relación* clearly presents itself as a report. It is ostensibly interested in bringing the message of the Reubenites to their Jewish brethren in the diaspora. On another level, however, it is a vehicle for Montezinos's Jewish self-fashioning. Montezinos begins his story as a comfortable converso of unclear Jewish commitment, but by the end of his narrative, he is transformed into a messenger of the imminent redemption. The *Relación* indirectly lobbies its audience, the representatives of the Amsterdam Jewish community, to accept Montezinos as a sincerely repentant ex-converso, and more importantly, as a messianic hero.

The *Relación* addresses a range of audiences and is in dialogue with a broad spectrum of issues: the arrival of the Messiah, the political fate of the Spanish Empire, the location of the lost tribes, the anthropology of the Native Americans, and the personal trajectory of the converso traveler, Antonio de Montezinos.

The *Relación* and the Israelite Indian Theory

Montezinos was not the first European to identify the American Indians with the Lost Tribes of Israel.[22] Since Columbus encountered the "marvelous" West Indies at the end of the fifteenth century, European intellectuals worked hard at placing these new territories and new peoples within their operative cartographic and anthropological categories. For many Europeans, especially intellectuals and other writers who had never ventured to the New World, the natives of the Americas could not simply be Caribs, Taínos, Aztecs, or Incas; they had to be Carthaginians, Atlanteans, Israelites, or any number of other ancient ethnic groups. That is, their origins were located within the classical or biblical world that formed the basis of the early modern European episteme.[23] European thinkers in the early modern period populated the Americas with a host of lost peoples from the ancient past in order to the turn the terra incognita of the New World into the terra cognita of the Old.

The question of the origins of the Amerindians was widely discussed by Northern European and Iberian intellectuals during the sixteenth and seventeenth centuries. It was an issue of particular importance to Spanish political theorists and messianic Catholic and Protestant theologians in the years leading up to and following the composition of Montezinos' *Relación*. Bartolomé de Las Casas, José de Acosta, Gregorio García, Diego Durán, Juan de Torquemada, to name just a few, all dealt with the question of the Indians' Israelite origin explicitly. While the theory was rarely supported by any of these authors, they all discussed it with utter seriousness.

Beyond these scholarly treatises, the vastness and unintelligibility of the New World inspired an elastic and often fantastical epistemology among many of the conquistadors. Columbus was certain that he was nearing the terrestrial paradise; Bernal Díaz del Castillo could not help but think of the valley of Mexico as the land described in the famous chivalric romance known as the *Amadís*; countless explorers went searching for the cities of El Dorado and the kingdom of the Amazons. The need to translate the newness of the Americas—its terrifying and marvelous nature and cultures—into something known and domesticated encouraged Europeans to apply Western terms and concepts to the new American reality. The wider discussion regarding the Indians' ethnic origin no doubt gave Montezinos the license to suspect a connection between himself and the Indians he encountered.

In addition to offering yet another interpretation of the Jewish origins of the Amerinidians, the *Relación* also addressed another issue of central concern to both Christians and Jews: the arrival of the Messiah. According to the biblical prophecies and later Jewish and Christian authorities, the reappearance of the lost tribes of Israel was a prerequisite for the ultimate redemptive process. Montezinos's *Relación* appeared at a time of heightened messianic speculation among both Christians and Jews.[24] Theologians were looking for the signs heralding the end of days, and the exotic Indies were the perfect source of signs ready to be interpreted. Montezinos's account became an active participant in these pan-European discussions. The *Relación* was first published within Thorowgood's millenarian tract arguing for the Jewish origin of the New England Indians, and

Menasseh's *Esperanza* was dedicated to interpreting Montezinos's report in light of contemporary global politics and the messianic prophesies of the Bible. Hopes for the Messiah's arrival were not necessarily the domain of all-out quacks in the sixteenth and seventeenth centuries. While Montezinos's assertion was somewhat extraordinary, it easily fit within the contemporary parameters of educated and reasonable discourse.

Montezinos's possible crypto-Jewish background might have also been a contributing factor to his "discovery" of the Reubenites. In his analysis of Inquisitorial testimonies, David Gitlitz noticed that crypto-Jews incorporated notions about the Lost Tribes into their messianic speculations and hopes. In 1572 one Portuguese *cristãa nova*, Filipa Marques, reportedly said that "the Messiah still had to come, and he was going to bring with him the Twelve Tribes of Israel."[25] The famous crypto-Jewish martyr of Chile, Francisco Maldonado da Silva, was recorded almost a century later in 1627 as saying that he "was of the two tribes of Israel that were preserved in the earthly paradise awaiting the end of the world, which was imminent, for God to assemble them." An equally cryptic statement was heard from Ana Cortés, a Mallorcan conversa, who stated in 1678 "that there was a tribe and a half that were wandering, spread out and lost around the world, and that Moses and Aaron were going to come to take them out of their captivity."[26] Jonathan Schorsch sees the mention of the "tribe and a half" as referring to the tribe of Reuben and the half tribe of Menasseh, its neighbor on the east bank of the Jordan.[27] These images of a militarily powerful, yet geographically remote tribe waiting for God's orders to come and redeem the Jews share a strong resemblance to the Reubenites described in the *Relación* and clearly partake of the wider narrative context, both Jewish and Christian, describing secret armies living in far off kingdoms waiting to come to the rescue.

This network of circulating texts, ideas, and dreams deeply informed Montezinos's encounter with the Indians and the way that his experience was recorded and received by his audience. These cultural and religious currents also impact our analysis of the idea of brotherhood and its limits in the *Relación*.

As the narrative unfolds and the individual identities come into focus, we are better equipped to investigate the bond between these disparate individuals. Within the narrative space of the *Relación*, especially in its scenes of face-to-face encounter and self-disclosure, we can trace ideas of fraternity based on both blood and faith. His understanding of the origin and identity of the Indians is intimately tied to his evolving relationship with Francisco and his fellow Indians. The text points to the ethical complexities, possibilities, and limits of brotherhood as a spiritual concept and a social construct.

On the Mountain

The *Relación* begins on a windswept mountain ridge, where the merchant Antonio de Montezinos is traveling with his Indian porters, who are carrying his merchandise on their backs until a strong wind knocks the packs to the ground.

> Worn down by their day's toil, the Indians began to curse their fate, saying that this and much more did they deserve because of their sins. At that moment the aforementioned Francisco tried to cheer them up, telling them to have patience, because briefly they will have a day of rest. To this they responded that it was not right that they should have it because they treated such a saintly nation—indeed the "best of the world"—so cruelly. Furthermore, all of the affliction and atrocities [*inhumanidades*] that the Spaniards have inflicted upon them were well deserved because of their guilt.[28]

Montezinos hears the Indians bemoan their fate; they describe their downcast state as a punishment for their own past iniquities. They make a cryptic reference to an act of oppression and persecution they committed against a "holy people."

The next night when they set up camp and are finally resting, Montezinos takes out some crackers and brings them to Francisco, and says, "'take this, even if you speak ill of the Spaniards.'" The Indian responds that "he did not complain about them enough. They (the Spaniards) are a cruel, tyrannical and completely inhumane people. However, soon enough he will see their evil punished by means of a hidden people."[29] Montezinos does not grasp the meaning behind the porter's litany but he sees himself implicated in their suffering. As a Portuguese merchant in the Spanish colonial sphere, Montezinos would have worked hard to present himself as a Spaniard. In this scene it seems clear that he can easily pass as one. To the Indians in his employ he is clearly part of the colonial system responsible for their oppression. The fact that he is a Portuguese converso is of little consequence to them. His gesture of friendship, the gift of food, is given with the condescension of the powerful toward the weak. Francisco rebukes him and makes clear that his random act of kindness aside, Montezinos is no different from the Spaniards who have conquered and colonized their land. There is a stark division outlined in this exchange, which is blurred in the ensuing narrative. At this point, however, there is no common ground between these two social spheres.

In this scene Montezinos's Judaism is completely out of the picture. He appears as a Spaniard seeking his fortune in the Americas. He lives and acts exactly as any other Spanish colonizer would. He reaches out to the Indian with a gift, but he does so as a Spaniard toward a "downtrodden" Indian. He encourages Francisco to take the gift by saying "take some, even if you speak badly of the Spaniards." He seems to imply that he is being kind to the Indians despite Francisco's antagonism toward the Spaniards, himself included. Francisco throws his bitter indictment of the Spanish colonial project directly at Montezinos.

At this point in the story Francisco and Montezinos occupy clearly delimited spheres: Spaniard and Indian, conquistador and vanquished. As the story
unfolds, however, these lines begin to blur. Underneath Montezinos's performed
conquistador identity lies another narrative persona—the crypto-Jew—and it is
this persona that begins to emerge in the next scene as Montezinos makes sense
of Francisco's eschatology of oppression and deliverance brought about by the
"hidden people."

Prison Revelations

After this initial journey Montezinos is arrested by the Inquisition while passing
through Cartagena de Indias. He is accused of being an active Judaizer and remains under investigation for over a year and half. In jail he experiences an uncanny epiphany while reciting his morning blessings: "Blessed be the name of
Adonay who has not made me an idolater, a barbarian, a Negro nor an Indian.
Upon saying Indian he became overtaken by the thought that, these Indians
are Hebrews. He began to say the prayer again, and once more he was caught by
the same thought. He said, 'Am I crazy or out of my head [*juicio*]? How could it
be that these Indians are Hebrews?'"[30] This blessing is an idiosyncratic version of
a common Jewish prayer. Because access to Jewish books was prohibited by the
Inquisition, conversos who desired to recite Jewish prayers often relied on oral
traditions. Inevitably, their fragile memories of stories and prayers involved considerable distortions of the Judaic originals.[31] Whereas the original Hebrew liturgy includes blessings of thanksgiving for being "not made a heathen nor a
slave," Montezinos speaks of a racial hierarchy of people and gives thanks that he
is not one of any of them.

Montezinos returns to the same realization every morning during his
prayers. At the exact moment where he is affirming his difference from other racial groups, Montezinos finds himself convinced that there must be some truth
to his identification with the Indians. Montezinos swears that upon his release
from jail, with the help of the Almighty he will find the Indian Francisco and resolve the mystery.[32]

Montezinos tells us that "me retraté": "I made a portrait of myself." Confused
about the identity of Francisco and his fellow Indians, he has a new and bewil-
dered sense of himself. In saying a prayer that delineates who he is not, he begins
to question the rigidity of those distinctions. What began as his ethnic and religious opposite in a flash becomes his mirror image: "These Indians are Jews!" He
reads beyond the obvious markers of the Indians' difference and sees his own
hidden identity reflected in the Indians' secret.

When Montezinos was traveling across the mountains and first heard the
Indians' story he was unable to comprehend it; his sense of power and superiority

complicated his approach toward the Indians. He did not stand before them, but rather above them. Even his initial overture of kindness and humanity—his offering of crackers—reflects Montezinos's elevated status, not their shared humanity. Both he and the Indians were locked in the roles of master and servant. When he heard their cryptic history Montezinos could understand only the aspect of their narrative in which these roles are maintained—that is, in which he is master, who may feel guilty about his power and thus responds with a gift, and they are the servants, oppressed and helpless. He was unable to see the Indians as anything other than what they appeared to be: a generic group of "indios" complaining about their poor lot in history—certainly nothing extraordinary in the Americas of the seventeenth century.

It appears that while in prison in Cartagena, with his own sense of personal security, honor, and pride shaken, he began to intuit, however hazily and subconsciously, the basic shape of the Indian's story of persecution. Arrested on suspicion of Judaizing, Montezinos might have begun a reassessment and a new embrace of his Judaism which enabled him to begin to see his reflection in the Indian porters' tightly veiled narrative of redemption. The Indians became a mirror to his own desperate situation: both are oppressed by the Spanish, both hide an alternative identity, and both are awaiting redemption.

Arguably, Montezinos's identification with the Indians is little more than an instance of the appropriation of the subaltern into the intelligible categories of the imperial imaginary. The Indian cannot simply be an Indian; he must be me, in order for me to "grasp" his identity. Is not Montezinos, despite his apparent transformation, simply participating in what Emmanuel Levinas would call the "economy of same"? He seems to be able to accept the Indian only in terms of his own self.

This totalizing move of appropriation of the other into the self is at the center of early modern attempts to locate the Amerindians within the anthropological schema of the Old World, of which Montezinos's narrative is an obvious participant. But the details of Montezinos's experience with the Reubenites allows for a (perhaps only partial) rupture of the closed circle of appropriation. As reflected in the ensuing narrative, Montezinos seeks out the Indian, not to dominate him or to "enlighten" him, but rather to learn from him. His humility and curiosity, along with his apparently sincere transformation of identity, point to the possibility of a relationship of dialogue, vulnerability, and openness with the other on his own terms. The analysis that follows charts the possibilities and limitations of this intersubjective relationship as reflected within the text.

There is a dark side to this encounter. It could be argued that Montezinos's identification of the Indians as Jews paradoxically points to the ethical trap of universal brotherhood. Identifying the Indians as "brothers" calls into question his ability to care about the pain of the Indians who are *not* his brothers. Marc Shell identifies this paradox implicit in the concept of brotherhood when he writes that from the proposition that "'All men are my brothers' it comes to follow easily that 'only my brothers are men, all others are animals.' When only my siblings are human, all others are not human."[33]

Embracing the Amerindian other as part of the Christian fraternal order carries related but distinct ethical dangers. Bernal Díaz del Castillo describes an eloquent conversionary speech Cortés delivered to Moctezuma during an early encounter with the Aztec emperor. Cortés gave an account of creation and the basic elements of Christ's birth, death, and resurrection as a prelude to a plea that Moctezuma abandon his diabolical idols and the practice of human sacrifice. As part of his argument he invoked the bond of brotherhood between all people, including Spaniards and Indians: "And as all of us are brothers, sons of the same father and one mother who were called Adam and Eve, and as our brother the great Emperor was greatly pained by the perdition of so many souls, brought by those idols down into hell where they burn, subjected to live flames, he sent us, when he heard of it [the idolatry], so that we fix this situation, so that the idols will no longer be worshiped, nor will any more Indians, male and female, be sacrificed to them, for we are all brothers."[34] Cortés places Montezuma within the family of Adam and Eve and expects him to live by the implicit truth of universal brotherhood: Human sacrifice is wrong because we are all brothers. He includes the emperor within this family. His shared brotherhood with the Mexicans is what inspired this mission to save their souls. Darkly shadowing these expressions of shared humanity and brotherly concern, of course, is the fact that in just a few chapters of Bernal Díaz's *Verdadera historia* we will see Christian swords viciously cut down Moctezuma's people and destroy their metropolis. Brotherhood can be deadly, especially when it is imposed upon the other. Cortés's vision of shared brotherhood leaves no room for otherness, for difference. While at the outset the extension of universal brotherhood upon Montezuma and his people would appear to accord them dignity and love, in actuality it imposes the colonist's cultural system upon them, not allowing any room for difference. The difficulty of seeing others as brothers even when they do not fit into your cultural narrative or do not reflect back a part of your own self-image energizes much of the violence of the new world encounter. An awareness of the dark side of universal brotherhood can serve as both a counterpoint and cautionary note to our reading of the *Relación*.

Montezinos projects his own narrative of oppression, secrecy, and desire for redemption onto his Andean porters. In this move toward seeing the Indians as brothers, is he not erasing their identity? Can there be empathy for their story of oppression without it being connected to Montezinos's own narrative? Can there be concern for the other when he is not a brother, when he is clearly of a foreign ethnic, racial, or family group? The ethical encounter between Montezinos and the Indians at the heart of the *Relación* highlights these questions and points out the dangers implicit in embracing the other as a brother.

The Journey

At the beginning of the narrative, any sort of common bond between Montezinos and the Indians in his employ is inconceivable. His first encounter with Francisco in the mountains and his time in prison rattle Montezinos's solid sense of himself and allow him to move beyond clear racial and ethnic barriers. He begins to see the hazy outline of a common story and common origins. He is driven to unravel the details of this story, and upon his release from the Inquisitorial prison in Cartagena, Montezinos sets off to find Francisco. He locates him in the river port of Honda, reminds him of their laconic conversation in the mountains, and asks Francisco to accompany him on a journey. It is on this journey away from suspecting eyes and ears that Montezinos reveals his hidden Judaism to his would-be Indian brother: "He revealed himself to the Indian, telling him these words: I am a Hebrew of the tribe of Levi, my god is Adonay, and everything else is a lie."[35] In revealing himself to Francisco, Montezinos highlights both his faith, "my God is Adonay," and his sense of peoplehood, origins, and tribal lineages, "I am a Hebrew of the tribe of Levi." Francisco takes up the question of lineage when he responds to Montezinos with a seemingly simple question: "What are your fathers' names?" Montezinos replies, "Abraham, Isaac and Jacob." Francisco continues to question him: "Don't you have another Father?" "Yes, Luis de Montezinos." After some angry back and forth, the Indian asks, exasperated, "Are you not a child of Israel?" After his initial disclosure, Montezinos must provide proof of his Jewish authenticity. Faith in the God of Israel is not enough; Francisco wants to know about Montezinos's origins: Who is your father? Montezinos's uncanny prison revelation about the Jewishness of the Indians he met on his last Andean journey dissolves the markers of race and culture that separate Montezinos and the Indians. He has a sense that these individuals who on the surface appear to be far from the Jewish fold are actually connected to the Jewish story and can be trusted with his own admission of Jewishness. In Montezinos's assertion of his Jewish identity and in Francisco's verification of its authenticity, paternity and national origin are essential. Montezinos identifies himself not only as a believer, but as the descendant of a particular tribe of Israel. To be a Jew is not just a question of theology; it is also tied to sociology and genealogy. In this exchange Judaism is about both belonging to a group of believers and partaking of a common blood origin. In his desire to verify the authenticity of Montezinos's disclosure, Francisco demands more details, and he wants the details relayed in a particular form, almost like a password: "Some of the things that you have said have made me happy, but others make me want to not believe you because you do not know how to tell me who your fathers were."[36] When Montezinos offers Luis as the missing name of his actual father, Francisco rejects this detail and almost gives up on Montezinos. The interest in origins in this instance is an interest in mythic origins— Abraham, Isaac, and Jacob as opposed to consanguineous family connections.

As we will see later, Francisco is not a "Child of Israel," but he is the guardian of their secret; he and his family are not of the same tribe as the Reubenites, although they are attached to them. There is an affinity between the two groups that is so strong that Francisco feels obliged to scrutinize Montezinos's claims of belonging. Francisco is the guardian of this secret because of his own family's loyalty to the Reubenites, not because of any shared blood.

There is a conflation of the meanings of "child" here. "Hijo de Israel" reflects the genealogical link between a contemporary Jew and the biblical patriarch Jacob, also known by the name Israel. However, "Hijo de Israel" also carries the connotation of member of Israel, in the sense of being someone who is part of the covenant-, someone who subscribes to the group or the values of the group. This interrogation into Montezinos's origins highlights the interwoven nature of faith and blood.

Francisco's interrogation, while appearing to border on the absurdly pedantic, is his way of verifying Montezinos's Hebraic credentials: "Who are you? Are you really Jewish?" It is striking that the Indian who a few scenes earlier was Montezinos's servant is now in a position of power over Montezinos. Because Montezinos desires to unravel the riddle of the "story of the mountain," the secret history of the Indians and the "Holy People," he submits to Francisco's interrogations. He appears before him vulnerable and humble. In the ensuing scenes of the *Relación*, Montezinos defers to Francisco as his teacher and guide who deserves full disclosure and honesty. Instead of trying desperately to bury his Jewish ancestry, as would be expected for an upwardly mobile New Christian, Montezinos uncovers this heritage in hopes of finding common ground with Francisco, his former servant. It is interesting that while Montezinos reveals himself to Francisco and opens himself up to his questions, Montezinos does not ask the Indian anything about his own Jewish origins or associations. It is not clear why this would be the case. It is as though at this point the one who needs unmasking and whose Judaism must be revealed is Montezinos, the converso merchant, not the Andean native.

The detailed testimonies of accused crypto-Jews in Inquisitorial records point to the journey as a common locus for marrano unmasking. There are many instances where a converso child is initiated into the secret of his or her family's Judaism while taking a walk in the countryside with an older sibling or parent. In other cases, as in the *Relación*, one marrano would reveal himself to another while on a journey, far away from the prying eyes and ears of inquisitorial informers.[37] What is different about this unmasking, however, is that the marrano reveals himself, not to another marrano running from the Inquisition but to a hitherto unknown member of the Jewish people.[38] Montezinos reveals himself to Francisco believing that there is some sort of kinship between them. He tells him his Hebrew name, his tribal lineage, and his belief, despite his outward trappings of Catholicism, in the "Dios de Israel," hoping that these statements will resonate with the Indian. He does not understand why, but his experience in prison has made it clear to him that there exists a mysterious link between himself and Francisco. Somehow Francisco is also a secret Jew but instead of hiding beneath a cloak of Spanish Catholicism, his Jewishness is hidden beneath his "Indianness."

After this initial encounter, Francisco invites Montezinos to join him on another journey. Before moving forward, Francisco wants to be sure that Montezinos is ready for the trek: "The Indian said to him, if you are a man of initiative, courage and endurance who would dare come with me you will come to know that which you desire to know. However, I warn you, that you will go on foot, and you will eat toasted corn, and you will do everything as I tell you."[39] In order to learn the secret of their shared identity, Montezinos must become like his Indian brother. He must go by foot—no mules or Indian servants. He must eat corn like a poor Indian. He must obey the directives of the Indian who was previously his servant, but who in actuality is a *cacique*, a tribal leader.

Before the journey, Francisco tells Montezinos to "empty the contents of your saddle bags, put on these *alpargatas* [rope sandals], take this stick and follow me. And thus he did, leaving behind his cloak [*capa*] and sword [*espada*] and everything else that he brought with him."[40] The unraveling of his "Spanish-ness" continues. He must literally strip himself of the markers that signify him as a powerful member of the elite: He must empty out his bags of all their goods; he must remove the quintessential signs of Iberian privilege—the *capa y espada*—and follow Francisco into the jungle.

"Here You Will Meet Your Brothers": A Mediated Embrace on the Banks of the River

They travel together that entire week until the Sabbath and then again until Tuesday morning, climbing mountains and fording rivers until they encounter a river "as big as the Duero." At this point Francisco tells Montezinos that "here you will see your brothers." The journey helped to strip away his Iberianness and prepared him for his encounter with his Indian brothers, and it is in this unencumbered state that he can begin to understand the laconic conversation he had with Francisco in the mountains two years earlier.

From the other side of the river a group of Indians arrives on canoes and embrace their visitor, and together they recite the ancient Hebrew prayer of the

Shema.[41] In doing so, the Indians are at once testing and welcoming their guest into their inner circle. They are testing his Jewish credentials—waiting to see if he indeed knows and recognizes this Jewish prayer—and at the same time revealing their shared Hebraic origins.

After this initial welcome, the Indians relay a tightly worded nine-part messages to Montezinos. With Francisco as translator, they explain that they are the children of Abraham, Isaac, Jacob, Israel, and Reuben, that they believe in one God, and that they have a prophetic tradition stating that a "messenger" is due to arrive.[42] The Reubenites repeat their message multiple times throughout Montezinos's visit.

The nine-part message is translated by Francisco into Spanish but relayed by the Reubenites directly to Montezinos using a set text along with a particular choreography meant to clarify the meaning of each part. There are three stages of mediation between the original message and its presentation to Montezinos. The constant repetition can explain Montezinos's ability to record it with great detail in the *Relación*, where it becomes a fixed text. However, the constant repetition without any room for dialogue frustrates Montezinos greatly. After three days he is still unable to engage in a dialogue with his brothers: "It was impossible to extract anything else from them. . . . Montezinos was annoyed that they would not answer his questions, nor would they allow him to pass to the other side."[43] Montezinos grows frustrated with the constant repetition of these cryptic messages. Before arriving at the Reubenites' camp, Francisco warns Montezinos to be patient with the Reubenites' method of transmission: "Do not be shocked or upset, nor should you imagine that these men will tell you the second idea until you have fully grasped the first."[44] To a certain extent this is a continuation of the "molting" of the external features of his *hispanidad*, which began with his prison revelation.[45] Acknowledging his Jewishness is wrapped up with loosening his claim to power and privilege. To encounter his brothers and to hear their story, Montezinos must render himself humble and patient, without demands or expectations.

Montezinos, however, grew frustrated at the constant repetitions and the Reubenites imperviousness. By the third day he attempted to cross the river by himself. He was spotted and the Reubenites quickly flipped over his canoe before he could make it to the other side. Instead of uncovering the secret and entering the kingdom of his lost brothers, he was left looking like a fool, flailing in the water.

It is unclear why the Reubenites keep Montezinos at arm's length. Why so much mediation? Why do they not address his concerns and questions and why do they keep him out of their kingdom? Within the *Relación* these actions seem to function as part of Montezinos's humbling and shedding of his Iberian pretensions. From another perspective they reflect the uneasiness that the Reubenites have toward Montezinos, their Levite brother, despite any tribal/blood affiliation.

The inscrutability of the Reubenites' message and the impenetrability of their kingdom point to the distance between Montezinos and his fellow Israelites. Their shared ancestry—the tribal connection—is not enough for him to be fully embraced and let in. He must become more like them—stripped of his Old World pretensions and assumptions—before he can even begin to hear their message. However, after a certain point he still cannot enter directly into their secret or their society; for that he needs Francisco's mediation and guidance.

Full Disclosure

Montezinos cannot directly access the world of the Reubenites. He is unable to enter into dialogue with them or directly "extract" the meaning of their message. Montezinos is dependent on Francisco's mediation and guidance, and it is only after leaving the Reubenites that Francisco begins to explain the implications of the Reubenites' "nueve cosas" to him. In this instance as well, Francisco warns Montezinos not to press him to explain the secrets: "The Indian Francisco responded, I will tell you what you will come to know, but do not rush me. I will show you the truth as I learnt it from the tradition of my ancestors. However, if you press me, which I am afraid you will, . . . then I will be forced to tell you lies."[46] Montezinos must learn how to read the messages of the Reubenites on their terms, not his. If he approaches Francisco with force, instead of respect, he will be treated with guile and lies. Montezinos's frustrated attempts to comprehend the Reubenites' message is integral to his story of spiritual transformation; it is a test of his humility, of how far he has gone in renouncing his power over the Amerindians, and it is a test he initially fails. Only through patience and respect for his interlocutor does Montezinos come to understand that which he desires to know.

Despite being referred to as a brother of the Reubenites, Montezinos is not fully accepted by them. Despite their physical embrace of Montezinos at their first meeting, there is a sense that his filial or tribal connection is only a starting point. His time in prison and his week-long trek with Francisco play important roles in Montezinos's transformation: As these experiences strip him of his elite status he becomes a suitable vessel for receiving the message of the Reubenites and for encountering them as "his brothers." Francisco is authorized by the Reubenites to explain their secret history to Montezinos. However, his ability to disclose the full meaning of the Reubenites' message and the wider history that informs that message is based on his own family legacy. He reminds Montezinos that he will tell him the "truth as I learnt it from the tradition of my ancestors."

On their return journey, Francisco explains the pre-Columbine history of the lost tribe and its relationship to other Indian tribes: "Your brothers, the Children of Israel, were brought to this land by God. He made great miracles for them—wondrous mysteries—things that if I tell you, you will not believe. This is what my parents told me. We, the Indians, came to this land, we waged war on them [the Israelites], we treated them worse than the Spaniards treat us."[47] Francisco explains that his forefathers followed the deceptive leadership of their *mohanes* (translated within the text as magicians or *hechizeros*) and persecuted the Children of Israel, chasing them into the depths of the jungle.[48] None of those who pursued the Israelites into the jungle, however, would return alive. After a succession of military failures the *mohanes* admitted their error. They told their people that "the God of these Children of Israel is the true God, all which is written on their stones is true; at the end of days, they will become masters of the nations of the world, people will come to these lands who will bring many things with them and once all of the land is well stocked, these children of Israel will come out from where they are and become the rulers of the entire land, as it once was theirs. Those of you who desire to be fortunate, attach yourself to them."[49] Francisco's family heeded this advice and became trusted servants to the "Children (Hijos) of Israel," forming a special alliance between the Israelites and this select group of Indians. While these Indians are not "Hijos de Israel" in a genealogical sense, in the secret Hebreo-Indian alliance the eschatological fortunes of the Jewish diaspora come to be intimately linked up to the oppression and redemption of the Indians.

Francisco and his family, along with a network of other Indian families, become allied with the Children of Israel despite not sharing any blood relationships with the Reubenites. Francisco's family's historic error and act of repentance along with their long history of devotion to the Reubenites solidifies their bond. However, there are also signs of the fragility of that bond. When the Reubenites cross the river and come to greet Francisco and Montezinos, Francisco bows down to them, expressing subservience and remorse.[50] The Reubenites try to dispel his unease and shame by lifting him up and embracing him. This scene reflects an unresolved element in the relationship between the Reubenites and their allies. Are the Hebreo-Indians converts who become part of the nation of Israel despite not sharing in the blood and lineage of Abraham, Isaac, and Jacob? Or are they in a quasi-fraternal alliance? Their relationship to the Reubenites, and by extension to the wider Jewish diaspora, is left unresolved. However, their role in the millennial battle for redemption is made clear in the *Relación's* final scene.

The cycle of oppression and redemption—of violence and divine justice—is about to turn again: Those who were once the oppressors became the oppressed, and now the new oppressors—the Spaniards—are about to receive their due. Montezinos's *Relación* offers a counternarrative of European colonialism; instead of conceiving of the Indian as the passive recipient of European mastery and control, the Reubenites and their Indian allies share an epic prehistory that is linked to a prophetic future wherein they, the downtrodden, will bring about a global redemption.

This point is made clear to Montezinos upon his return from meeting with the Reubenites. Back in the river port of Honda where they began their journey, Francisco introduces him to three other Indian *hermanos*. Montezinos reveals himself to them as "a Hebrew from the tribe of Levi whose God is Adonay." Hearing this they embrace him and say: "One day you will see us and you will not recognize us. We are all brothers; with Compassion did God make us all. Do not be worried for this land. All of us Indians have our orders. Once we finish off these Spaniards we will go and take you all out of your captivity, if God wills it, which He does will it because his word can never falter."[51] Montezinos has come full circle. He begins as a colonizer, part of the engine of oppression exploiting the Indians. Standing before the other and (literally) discovering him—seeing beyond his mask—he is able to reveal an identity that he himself has been hiding and suppressing. He sheds the cloak of his "Spanish-ness" and is able to hear a message of redemption for both the Indians and his own people. Seeing himself in their face and in their story, Montezinos realizes his brotherhood with the oppressed—"We are all brothers"—and is able to embrace his secret Judaism and become a messianic emissary to the Jews of the diaspora. Despite his outward appearance the Hebreo-Indians accept him as one of their own.[52] They remind him that on that great day they too will cast off their masks: "One day you will see us and you will not recognize us."

The Reubenites are unable to fully express their message of hope to Montezinos. He depends instead on the insight and trust of Francisco and his fellow Hebreo-Indians in order to decode the secret history. He has gained their trust, and they see him as part of their fraternity: "We are all brothers; with Mercy did God make us all." Who is included in this declaration of brotherhood? All of God's creatures? Is this a declaration of the Hebreo-Indian's solidarity with the Jews of the diaspora, or is there a larger claim to some sort of universal brotherhood that goes beyond bloodlines or tight alliances?

The *Relación* does not directly address these questions. I contend, however, that while claiming the *Relación* as his proof text, in several important ways Menasseh's ideas about race and brotherhood and specifically the relationship of the lost tribes to their Amerindian allies is at odds with aspects of Montezinos's narrative. Reading the *Relación* against the grain of the *Esperanza* can illuminate some of the underlying ideas animating both works.

Menasseh ben Israel makes a strong case throughout his *Esperanza* against the notion that the Indians of the New World are of Jewish origin.[53] In Menasseh's view, Montezinos's text sets up the following historical narrative: the Reubenites were the first inhabitants of the Americas and had almost no contact with the overwhelming majority of nations that followed them to the New World. Menasseh argues that while the Reubenites might be the original inhabitants of the

Americas, this does not explain the origin of the rest of the Amerindian groups. As he writes early on in his analysis:

> The Spaniards who dwell in those Indies, are of the opinion generally that the Indians descend from the Ten Tribes, but they clearly err: because even though in my opinion these [the Ten Tribes] were the first people to populate [the Americas], afterward, . . . new peoples came from the East Indies. . . . These being of greater military power waged war upon them [the Ten Tribes], as a result it was necessary for them (as our Montezinos tells us) to retreat into the most remote and hidden areas of those regions, by divine approval.[54]

On this point Menasseh relies firmly on Montezinos's account. However, the two texts differ significantly in the emphasis on racial and cultural markers to prove this distinction.

To further elaborate his ideas about the origins of the Amerindians and the distinction between the Reubenites and the rest of the Amerindian population, Menasseh cites a wide variety of classical and contemporary sources in addition to the *Relación*, which point to the differences between the hidden tribes of Israel scattered throughout Asia and Africa and their gentile neighbors.[55]

These include tribes such as the Danites and Naphtalites, which were dispersed in remote regions of Asia.[56] The Naphtalites, for example, are described as clearly distinct physically and culturally from the "barbarous" people surrounding them: "for in their face one can see . . . that these are not ugly nor black like the Huns, among whom they dwell."[57] In Menasseh's view, it is obvious to anyone who just looks at them that they are different and actually superior to their neighbors. He goes on to highlight their cultural distinction: in contrast to the nomadic and barbarous Huns, these Naphtalites "live with laws and civilization, in the way of the Romans, being well governed by their prince."[58] Menasseh sets up a dichotomy between the uncivilized and nomadic Huns and the Naphtalites who conduct themselves like the Romans, with law and order under the good governance of their ruler. It is interesting how Menasseh sets up this dichotomy between the civilized Israelites who comport themselves like the Romans and the actual Huns who live like savages. Another proof of the Naphtalites' distinct cultural identity can be found in their care for the dead: "They do not just toss them anywhere like the barbarians and the neighboring peoples among whom they dwell."[59] As opposed to their neighbors who leave the corpses of their loved ones to rot, the Naphtalites, following Jewish custom and basic civilized practice, bury their dead.

Menasseh brings examples that follow these basic patterns from Africa and the Far East and reveal that the lost tribes are racially and culturally distinct from their neighbors and that they maintain their commitment to the Torah after all of these centuries. These examples are used to show that indeed the tribes still exist as viable and identifiable parts of the Jewish people awaiting the messiah. But they also serve to foreground his understanding of the racial and cultural divide between the Reubenites and their neighbors.

As a prelude to his discussion of the Reubenites, Menasseh brings an array of testimony from European travelers who have brief encounters with mysterious groups of Americans who are bearded, sometimes blond, and clothed in elaborate robes. In describing one group from the Salomon Islands, Menasseh writes that they are "white people, blond, of large body and sumptuously dressed, with tunics and long beards."[60] These groups generally live in secluded cities with impressive architecture and are marked by their development of "comercio y política." That is to say they are civilized, sophisticated both technically and socially, just like the Israelite tribes of Asia and Africa.[61] Another feature of these secluded and mysterious Americans is that they are revered (even feared) by their indigenous neighbors for their bravery. Menasseh reports that after a run-in with one of these groups in South America, the intrepid conquistador and cousin of the emperor, Phelipe de Utre, reported that he called off the pursuit because he was "so impressed with their bravery and daring."[62] This echoes earlier accounts of the lost tribes such as Eldad HaDani's and David Reubeni's, which emphasize their martial prowess and dominion over their neighbors.[63] For Menasseh these racial and cultural features all point to a fundamental distinction between the Israelites dwelling in the Americas and the rest of the Amerindian population.

Montezinos's account, while important to Menasseh's wider argument, is at odds with this emphasis on racial and cultural difference. In the *Relación* there is a brief description of the Reubenites' physical attributes: "These people are somewhat tanned by the sun, some of them wear their hair down to their knees, others wear it shorter, others wear it in the usual style, cut evenly, they are well proportioned with good faces, good feet and legs: around their heads they wear a cloth [paño]."[64] This description echoes many others. Columbus, for example, writes that the natives of Guanahaní (today the Bahamas) "all go about naked as their mother bore them, and even the women, . . . well formed, with handsome bodies and very good faces, their hair is thick, almost like the silk of a horse's tail and cut short. . . . There are those of them that are dark [skinned], and others are of the color of the Canary Islanders, neither black nor white. . . . They are all of good stature and of good gestures, well formed."[65] Montezinos's physical description of the Reubenites clearly echoes Columbus's early impressions; as opposed to the sharp racial distinction between the scattered Israelite tribes and their neighbors that Menasseh stresses in the *Esperanza*, in the *Relación* there is no clear physical distinction between the Reubenites and their neighbors.[66]

Montezinos makes only one reference to their clothing: it is to their turban-like headgear. What this may signify about their civilization and their primitive, exotic, or noble "nature" is not clear. Early explorers such as Columbus, Pané, Bernal Díaz, and Cabeza de Vaca and others paid close attention to clothing as an indication of the native's level of culture and access to resources.[67] The Reubenites are not described as naked, but there is no indication of any elaborate clothing. This scant reference to their headgear tells us little. That Montezinos had to dress in the simple tunic and rope sandals common among Amerindians may indicate that this was the way the Reubenites also dressed. The Reubenites cross the river on a canoe, a common Amerindian mode of transportation. Nothing in this description would differentiate them in any particular racial or cultural way from other Amerindian people; no mention is made of beards or blond hair, and depiction we get no sense of the elaborate robes or technological advantages that Menasseh emphasizes finding in the previous accounts. Montezinos does point out in the next paragraph that the Reubenites "enjoyed all of the products that the Spaniards have, for instance in food, clothing, livestock, seeds and everything else."[68] Does this mean they have access to these products or that they are able to produce them on their own, thus signifying a fundamental sociological and technological superiority over their neighbors?[69] Because Montezinos never crosses over to where the Reubenites actually live, we are not privy to descriptions of their architecture or the structures of their society—what Menasseh would refer to as their "policía." Their ability either to have access to or to produce European products, however, points to a technical advantage that the Reubenites have over the vast majority of indigenous groups. Schorsch reads their act of giving Montezinos and Francisco gifts of these products for their journey home as an indication of their magnanimity toward their vassals. While the *Relación* clearly distinguishes between the Reubenites and their Indian allies, this difference is not framed in any stark racial or sociocultural terms; rather, the distinction is based on history and a particular power dynamic between the two groups.

Menasseh seems to be commenting on this relationship without directly saying so, toward the end of the *Esperanza*. After cataloguing the punishments meted out to the princes who persecuted the Jews throughout the ages, Menasseh describes the culmination of Jewish suffering as foretold by the Hebrew Prophets. He reminds his readers that "the Lord will not forgive the spilt blood of Israel; thus those that will reject being their enemies and will pledge their goodwill and benefit [to the Jews] will be saved with them."[70] Those gentiles who abjure their former hatred and instead open their hands to the Jews, helping them, will share in the blessing that God gave to Abraham: "And I will bless those who bless you and I will curse those that curse you."[71] Menasseh wrote the *Esperanza* with Jewish and gentile readers in mind, and this passage can be easily read as an invitation and encouragement to gentiles to aid the Jews of the world in their time of need. However this passage also serves as a gloss on the *Relación*. Francisco and his family, along with the other Hebreo-Indians, are clearly implicated in this vision of Jewish-gentile cooperation and the promise of future reward. While Menasseh works hard throughout the chapters of the *Esperanza* to maintain a stark distinction between the Israelites and their neighbors, in this passage we can see a vision for cooperation and alliance that echoes, but falls short of, the sort of bond described by Montezinos between Francisco's people and the Reubenites and the wider Jewish diaspora. For Menasseh these gentiles are included in the blessings of the messianic era, and they are on the "side" of the Jews, but there is no indication that they become part of the Israelite community.

The *Relación,* however, goes further. As noted previously, Francisco and his comrades embrace Montezinos as a brother. Their brotherhood is based not on claims of tribe or family, but on the fact that they are all created by God. Through the course of the narrative Montezinos becomes initiated into a brotherhood based on a shared past, strong bonds of loyalty, and mutual commitment but without any claim to a shared genealogical origin. The Reubenites, Montezinos's actual blood/tribal connections, remain a distant presence in the narrative. They are referred to as Montezinos's "brothers" but as discussed previously, his interaction with them is limited and heavily mediated. However, with Francisco and his fellow Hebreo-Indians, he forms an intimate connection based on shared dreams and sacrifice. As Aharon, a "Hebreo del tribu de Levi," he is welcomed into this intimate circle and is given insight into an alternative narrative of the redemption of his farflung people and the turning wheels of world history.

Afterword

Sources are neither open windows, as the positivists believe, nor fences obstructing vision, as the skeptics hold: if anything we can compare them to distorting mirrors.

Carlo Ginzburg, *History, Rhetoric, and Proof* (25)

One of my goals in writing the book was to show that the narratives of Carvajal, Cardoso, and Montezinos belong to both Iberian and Jewish culture. In fact, my reading of these works points to the ways that post-expulsion Sephardic society and culture and the wider Atlantic world were intimately related. Commercial activity, socioeconomic bonds, and religious commitments linked people in the Old World and New and forged connections across religious, ethnic, and political lines. Family in both its socioeconomic and spiritual forms—families of blood and families of faith—were essential to the structure of converso and Sephardic life in these contexts. By reading the autobiographical texts, we have come to see the complexities of these structures, the emotional and material limitations of brothers and sisters and parents, and the disappointment and betrayal of family, as well as the vital importance of teachers and comrades who come to be like family, who become part of a fraternity of faith. I do not make claims about the larger trends within the early modern Atlantic world or even within the Western Sephardic diaspora. However, these three texts afford the careful reader an opportunity to see how three individuals made sense of the complexities and vicissitudes of those worlds and transformed their experiences into personal narratives of religious enlightenment.

I have investigated the autobiographical texts at the center of this book not as "windows" transparently exposing the realities of their historical moment. Neither have I seen them as another sort of window, a "window into the soul" of their authors. They are narrative constructions written for particular reasons under particular conditions. They reflect the wider historical reality wherein they were produced; however, this reflection is fractured and multidirectional. Another challenge these texts pose is that to some extent they are, as Carlo Ginzburg writes, mirrors reflecting back to the reader an image, distorted and distorting, of his or her own time. We are always reading from the present, and I believe that it is important to account for my own stake in the story I have been telling.

This is a project inspired by books—books sitting on shelves for years, often neglected, misunderstood, misplaced. I think of a particular fat volume that sat on a bookshelf in my childhood home. Its spine was grayish white with a sketch of a menorah on the bottom, and written above that obviously Jewish symbol was the title, *LA FAMILIA CARVAJAL*. I remember the title catching my eye for years. I was curious why a book title with no obvious Jewish content would be adorned with a menorah. It was not until I was a graduate student that I took this book off the shelf and began to explore its pages. The same volume of Toro's classic history of the Carvajal family is now quite ragged with use and sits on my own bookshelf.

The book was a gift from one of my parents' clients. My parents sold South Florida condominiums to wealthy Mexicans in the late 1970s, and they became quite close with several of their clients. These Mexicans were eager to have a small piece of America, and my parents were not only their real estate brokers but served as cultural intermediaries as well. Their clients were Syrian Christians and Jews— in those days they all did business and socialized together: a Catholic family, children of Spanish Civil War exiles who made it big by manufacturing the eyes and hands and hair for dolls, and Ashkenazi Jews, people whose grandparents arrived in Mexico with nothing and remade themselves in the bustling metropolis of Mexico City and in the outlying dusty towns throughout Mexico. Toro's *La Familia Carvajal* was a gift from one of those Ashkenazi Jews; he was a physician, well read and worldly. (He even wrote a novel at some point that also sat unread on that book shelf.) I am not sure why he chose that volume as a gift for my parents. Did he know how much my father loved history? Was he trying to give my parents a concrete marker of Jewish *Mexicanidad*? How curious that a history of a sixteenth-century Mexican crypto-Jew and his family could express a sense of rootedness and pride in being both Mexican and Jewish for my father's client and friend, Dr. Zajdenweber.

Another book at the right place and time: In the summer of 1999 I was lucky enough to get a job at the rare book room at the Jewish Theological Seminary. Ostensibly I was hired to catalogue the Spanish and Portuguese books in their collection. I was fortunate because my supervisors were not at all vested in the completion of this project, and so I was able to spend as much time as I would like with each of these volumes. Most came in as part of the personal collection of Elkan Nathan Adler, the great bibliophile and cosmopolitan traveler. There were prayer books and Bibles from Amsterdam, collections of sermons and the classic philosophical and polemical texts from the great early modern intellectuals of the Western Sephardic diaspora, Menasseh ben Israel, Usque, Aboab, and so on. But there were also titles that did not seem to belong in a Jewish library: books of secular verse, drama, and history. One title in particular stood out: Pedro Teixeira's travel account, *Relaciones de Pedro Teixeira del origen, descendencia y svccesion de los Reyes de Persia, y de Harmuz, y de un viaje hecho por el mismo autor dende la India Oriental hasta Italia por tierra.* According to several bibliographic sources, Teixeira was a converso who, after years of global travels, openly embraced Judaism later in life. Did his possible Jewishness inform his account of his journey in the Middle and Far East? There is no indication of any such thing, and so this book's presence among the more openly Jewish titles was a puzzle to me.

His account of his travels in the Far East reminded me of the colonial Latin American travel accounts I read avidly in some of my graduate seminars. In his own way, he echoed the experience of Columbus, Cabeza de Vaca, and other travelers who were able to convey the sense of wonder, strangeness, and uncertainty throughout their American wanderings. Teixera's volume got me thinking about the large numbers of conversos who found their way to the Americas, and I wanted to find their narratives of travel, dislocation, discovery, and wonder. Would their Jewish background color their encounters? And thus began my search for converso autobiographical texts that unfolded across the Atlantic. I wanted to see the Americas through their eyes and through their words; I wanted to see them negotiate their religious identities with the otherness of the New World and within the structures of the Iberian colonial systems.

My interest in books is ultimately an interest in people, their stories, and the details, complexities, and mysteries of their lives. I was drawn to that thick volume on my father's bookshelf because of my own family history. My grandparents left their *shtetlach* in Poland and Transylvania and arrived in Cuba in the 1920s and 1930s. Havana was warm and welcoming and full of promise. They fell in love with Cuba and felt deeply grateful for the refuge it offered them from the stifling economic and political troubles of the Old World, not to mention the looming horrors of World War II. As deeply connected as they were to their families, and no matter how marked they were by their Eastern European childhoods, all of my grandparents embraced their new life in Cuba. They mastered Spanish— my grandmother Sara was proud of the fact that the locals assumed that her slight accent was a sign that she was a Gallega, someone from Spain; they fell in with the rhythm of island life, working hard selling ready-made dresses or hand-tailored men's suits or shoes, but also enjoying their siestas and summers at the beach at Varadero.

With the Communist takeover of the island, almost the entire Jewish population, mostly small store owners whose businesses were nationalized, did not want to wait and see if Fidel would be "good for the Jews" or not. Most left the island by 1961. My family also left, mostly for Miami, but some relatives went to Panama and Israel. New languages, new rhythms, opportunities, and challenges. I grew up as part of this reconfigured Cuban-Jewish community—a community with feet in multiple worlds: American, Jewish, Cuban. It all made perfect sense, and it was all so ephemeral, contingent, and in flux. The notion of periphery and center, of an elite and marginal culture, were constantly renegotiated and reconfigured. Was being Cuban an asset or a stigma? Was being Jewish a social bridge to make connections or another marker of foreignness? Hybridity, along with a fierce attachment to the "tribe," was the norm.

I have spent the last decade and a half searching after three spiritual seekers, individuals who were deeply attached to their families and yet restless in their pursuit of enlightenment. All three were shape-shifters, skilled in masking and revealing themselves and in connecting across lines of race and culture. Did I see traces of my own story in their heroic self-fashioning(s)? I see in these three individuals striking examples of the fluidity and dynamism of identity, of the multiple ways that our social networks anchor us and give us the ability to make meaning out of our experiences. However, in all three cases we have individuals who were not limited by their bonds of blood and whose attachment to their tribe did not prevent them from being true to their dreams and visions, whatever the costs.

At this point the reader should notice the obviously autobiographical echoes between my own life and the individual lives we have just explored in such detail in this book. I know that my own narrative inspired and informed my interest in Carvajal, Montezinos, and Cardoso. I am attracted to their chameleonic adventures, identity games, and transatlantic and transcultural transformations because I see these men as kindred spirits. I also know that while this affinity has led me to this subject and has fed my passion for understanding and discovering the nature of the Sephardic Atlantic and in particular these powerful tales of personal religious enlightenment, it is also a possible liability in my quest to engage this subject analytically and critically. This is a danger that I am willing to hazard.

When I first began to analyze these texts, I saw them as writings of spiritually vibrant individuals crafting their narratives of religious enlightenment and heroism. Only later was I able to begin to see that these texts are not discreet self-portraits; rather they reflect the myriad ways that identity is deeply tied to our most intimate human connections. It is clear to me now that these narratives are driven to a great extent by a charged Freudian-style family romance often transposed or projected onto a religious drama. The texts point to the dialectical relationships of parents, children, and siblings, along with all of the displacements of these relationships, the search for surrogate parents and siblings to fill in the void left by our family's failures and disappointments. This sociopsychic dynamic is refracted through the experience of travel, dislocation, and the need for cultural morphing and reinvention. The encounter with the otherness of new terrain, new cultures, and new people serves as a catalyst for the authors' transformations and reconsiderations of their own lives and their place within their families and communities.

Notes

Introduction

1. See Jonathan I. Israel, *European Jewry in the Age of Mercantilism* and *Diasporas within a Diaspora*. For one excellent study of the interconnected nature of converso and Sephardic business and social networks, see Yosef Kaplan, "The Travels of Portuguese Jews from Amsterdam to the 'Lands of Idolatry,'" as well as his "Amsterdam, the Forbidden Lands and the Dynamics of the Sephardi Diaspora."

2. *Limpieza de sangre* is fundamental to understanding converso life and will be discussed in greater detail later in this introduction.

3. The bibliography of works related to the events surrounding 1391 and the powerful aftershocks within Iberian society is too long to review here. However Yitzhak Baer's *History of the Jews in Christian Spain*, 2:95–169, will provide the reader with ample context and analysis.

4. In the first chapter of his groundbreaking study of seventeenth-century marranism, *From Spanish Court to Italian Ghetto*, Y. H. Yerushalmi presents a comprehensive analysis of the inherent confusion of New Christian identity. Echoing Cecil Roth, he writes: "Names had been altered, religious allegiances had shifted, but even discounting the question of religious sincerity, today's Christian was still recognizable as yesterday's Jew" (13).

5. Before moving any further, I would like to define and clarify some terms particular to my project. In the present study, "Sephardic," in its broadest sense, refers to those Jews of Iberian descent who settled throughout the Ottoman Empire, Italy, North Africa, and eventually northern Europe after the expulsion of 1492. These communities maintained close linguistic, cultural, and religious ties among themselves throughout most of their history.

"New Christian," or "converso," refers to those individuals of Jewish descent who converted, or whose ancestors converted to Christianity. These interchangeable terms refer to a very wide range of individuals regardless of their actual religious beliefs and practices; i.e., fervent Catholics could share this appellation with Judaizing heretics, as long as at some point in the past they or their ancestors converted to Christianity. Converso identity, while having its roots in religious experience, actually developed into an ethnic and socio-economic phenomenon and was maintained to a great extent through the stigma and prejudice inspired by *limpieza de sangre*.

"Marranos," or "crypto-Jews," in the present context, refer to those Iberian New Christians who, while externally observing Catholic practice, secretly maintained varying degrees of Jewish belief, identity, and ritual. Thus crypto-Jews are a subgroup of the wider conversos. Searching for relief from inquisitorial persecution as well as new mercantile opportunities, many of these individuals found their way out of the Iberian Peninsula throughout the sixteenth, seventeenth, and eighteenth centuries. As opposed to the first generation of Sephardic exiles, who settled primarily in the Ottoman Empire, most of these individuals relocated to the Jewish communities of Amsterdam, Hamburg, and London and followed the global trade circuits leading into and out of these ports. These communities retained Spanish and Portuguese as their internal language of business and culture well into the eighteenth century. They also kept a distinct ethnic identity within the global Jewish community, while maintaining family, business, and wider ethnic ties with Iberian conversos who lived as Catholics throughout the Iberian world. See Kaplan, "The Travels of Portuguese Jews to the 'Lands of Idolatry'" and Miriam Bodian, *Hebrews of the Portuguese Nation*, 132–51. "Marrano," a pejorative term used colloquially to refer to New Christians, was appropriated by many twentieth-century Jewish historians as a sort of romantic "badge of honor" to describe those Jews who resisted inquisitorial persecution. However, in comparison with "converso" or "New Christian," it is rarely used in the early modern period, especially in inquisitorial documents. The Inquisitors labeled those individuals accused of maintaining Judaism in some form as "Judaizers" (*Judaizantes*), which points to the nature of their heresy. For a sociolinguistic history of the term see Yakov Malkiel, "Hispano-Arabic Marrano and Its Hispano-Latin Homophone." See also Julio Caro Baroja's treatment of the term's history in his *Los Judíos en la España Moderna y Contemporánea*, 1:405–6. As will be seen in great detail within the individual case studies included here, the Judaism that crypto-Jews participated in rarely was a direct iteration of the religion that Jews in the early modern period practiced. This was certainly the case after the expulsion of 1492. Crypto-Jewish belief and practice were idiosyncratic and often inspired by individual readings of the Old Testament; they would be somewhat unrecognizable to contemporary Jews.

6. Antonio Domínguez Ortiz, *Los Judeoconversos en España y América*, 77. For an in-depth analysis of these issues, see David Nirenberg's "Mass Conversion and Genealogical Mentalities: Jews and Christians in Fifteenth-Century Spain." María Elena Martínez offers an insightful and nuanced analysis of the development, implementation, and theoretical currents informing the laws of *limpieza* in Spain and colonial Latin America in her *Genealogical Fictions*, where she incorporates the classic scholarship on this topic, such as Albert Sicroff's *Los estatutos de limpieza de sangre*, as well as more recent analysis, such as the work of David Nirenberg. Martinez's book traces the transplantation of Iberian concerns with converso blood onto the colonial American context, pointing to the surprising and complex ways that anxieties about Jews and heresy became transformed in the course of the conquest and conversion of New World societies into new forms of racial anxieties.

The essays included in *Race and Blood in the Iberian World*, ed. María Elena Martínez, David Nirenberg, and Max S. Hering Torres point to the variety and complexity of ideas about race, blood, and identity as they developed in late medieval Iberia and continued to unfold throughout the Atlantic world into the modern age. These essays are helpful because they broaden and complicate the converso phenomenon by placing it within a much more expansive sociocultural context.

7. This quotation from the text of the Edict of Expulsion comes from Jeffery M. Green's English translation of Haim Beinart's *The Expulsion of the Jews from Spain*, 50. Beinart's volume provides an extensive collection of primary documents regarding the expulsion, revealing the complexities surrounding the order of expulsion along with its implementation.

8. The carefully developed arguments of the edict point to Ferdinand and Isabella's need to justify their actions. The rhetoric of the edict seems to indicate that this was not a decision they took lightly. I believe that the antiquity and ubiquity of Iberian Jewry within Spanish society forced the monarchs to carefully justify their decision. For a discursive reassessment of the lachrymose vision of fifteenth-century Iberian history as an inevitable and unmitigated series of calamities so common in Jewish historiography see Eliezer Gutwirth's "Towards Expulsion."

9. The numbers of those who chose exile over conversion are notoriously uncertain. For a balanced consideration of the question, see Henry Kamen, "The Mediterranean and the Expulsion of the Spanish Jews in 1492."

10. See Domínguez Ortiz, *Los Judeoconversos en España y América*, 13–104, and Y. H. Yerushalmi's introduction to *From Spanish Court to Italian Ghetto*. David Gitlitz offers a concise overview of the topic in his *Secrecy and Deceit*, 3–96.

11. Benzion Netanyahu makes the case that within a very short time following the expulsion, most conversos were completely disconnected from Jewish practice and beliefs; see his "The Marranos According to the Hebrew Sources of the 15th and Early 16th Centuries." Even a scholar like Renée Levine Melammed, who finds evidence for crypto-Jewish practice among sixteenth-century Spanish conversos, makes the point that after the expulsion the conversos' commitment to Judaism waned and morphed into other forms of religious heterodoxy with less and less connection to Jewish practice; see her *Heretics or Daughters of Israel?*

12. How exactly the Portuguese authorities managed to baptize the entire Jewish community within a matter of weeks is difficult to fathom. Contemporary accounts make it difficult to tease out a timeline of events that would explain how thousands of men, women, and children scattered in the major Portuguese cities as well as many small towns came to be baptized. François Soyer provides a comprehensive analysis of these events and a compelling description of the conversions and their aftermath in his comprehensive new history, *The Persecution of the Jews and Muslims of Portugal*, 182–240.

13. Yerushalmi, *From Spanish Court to Italian Ghetto*, 5–6.

14. On the establishment of the Portuguese Inquisition, see Alexandre Herculano's *History of the Origin and Establishment of the Inquisition in Portugal*; the 1972 edition has a prologue by Y. H. Yerushalmi.

15. For a contrary view regarding the Jewish commitments of the Portuguese conversos, see António José Saraiva, *The Marrano Factory*, 19–42.

16. Stuczynski, "Harmonizing Identities."

17. This term was sometimes stretched to *Gente da Nação Hebrea, Men of the Hebrew Nation*. The centrality of commerce to this social group's identity is apparent from the interchangeability of the term with *gente* (or *homen*) *de negocios* (meaning "business men"). Miriam Bodian analyzes the nature and use of these terms in Iberia and in Amsterdam in the introduction to her *Hebrews of the Portuguese Nation*, 6–13.

18. Inquisitors referred to the belief in the Law of Moses as the defining feature of the Judaizer's heresy, and it became the way many crypto-Jews referred to their own belief system. The religious ideas and practices developed by Judaizing conversos in the Iberian world was quite distinct from the religion practiced by Jews living in open Jewish communities. The divergence between the two became even more pronounced in the generations following the expulsion of 1492 and the forced conversions of 1497.

19. Yerushalmi, *From Spanish Court to Italian Ghetto*, 3–20.

20. Domínguez Ortiz, *Los Judeo conversos en España y América*, 131.

21. Gitlitz, *Secrecy and Deceit*, 52–63.

22. For a comprehensive account of this global phenomenon see Israel, *Diasporas within a Diaspora*.

23. On the historiography and sociological context of these scholars, see Jonathan Schorsch's insightful, "American Jewish Historians, Colonial Jews and Blacks, and the Limits of *Wissenschaft*."

24. In the last fifteen years there have been several important essay collections dedicated to the Jewish Atlantic, which have helped establish the idea of a "Sephardic Atlantic" within academic discourse. These collections delineate geographic and thematic areas for further exploration and have begun an important interdisciplinary discussion about Jewish life in the first three centuries of European colonialism. Three prominent examples are: Bernardini and Fiering, *Jews and the Expansion of Europe to the West*; Kagan and Morgan, *Atlantic Diasporas*; and Gerber and Bodian, *Jews of the Caribbean*.

25. An excellent example, which "proves the rule," is Daniel López Laguna's *Espejo Fiel de Vidas* (London, 1720), in which the author gives very little expression to his crypto-Jewish past

or to his experience with the Inquisition. I explicitly deal with the question of the "absence" of autobiographical discourse among the Western Sephardim in my "Daniel Israel Lopez Laguna's *Espejo Fiel de Vidas* (London 1720)." This question is also addressed in the following chapter.

26. Carvajal's autobiography was transcribed and recorded in *Procesos de Luis de Carvajal, el mozo*, ed. Luis González Obregón. It will be referred to as the *Vida* and cited as LCMA (for Luis de Carvajal, *el mozo*, autobiography). Hereafter, his trial records will be cited as LCM I for the first trial and LCM II for the second trial.

27. Montezinos' *Relación* can be found in Menasseh ben Israel, *Esperança de Israel* (Amsterdam, 1650).

28. Manuel Cardozo de Macedo, *La vida del buenaventurado Abraham Pelengrino*. Hereafter, I will refer to the proceedings from Cardoso's two inquisitorial trials, which come from the *Processo de Manuel Cardoso*, as CM-PT-TT for the first trial and CM-PT-TT II for the second trial.

1. Audience and Archive

1. My use of the term "archive" is informed by Roberto González-Echevarría's *Myth and Archive*.

2. The ensuing archeology of early modern Iberian self-writing begins with a consideration of Roberto González-Echevarría's analysis of the *relación* and its generic offspring. See his "Humanismo, retórica y las crónicas de la conquista," as well as "The Law of the Letter," which is an important supplement to the earlier essay.

3. "Is there anything more 'novelesque' than the autobiography?" Miguel de Unamuno.

4. "Lo cual yo escribí con tanta certidumbre, que aunque en ella se lean algunas cosas muy nuevas, y para algunos muy difíciles de creer, pueden sin duda creerlas." Alvar Nuñez Cabeza de Vaca, *Naufragios*, 76.

5. "En 18. de Ilul del año 5404. vulgo, 644. llegó a esta ciudad de Amsterdam Aron levi, y en otro tiempo en España, Antonio de Montezinos, y declaró delante de diversas personas de la nacion Portugueza la Relacion siguiente." *Relación de Aharon Levi*, 1.

6. González-Echevarría, "The Law of the Letter," 111.

7. Nuñez Cabeza de Vaca, *Naufragios*, 77.

8. Yosef Kaplan uses this term to describe the former conversos who embraced Judaism upon their arrival in open Jewish communities of Western Europe such as Amsterdam, Hamburg, and London. See his "Wayward New Christians and Stubborn New Jews."

9. It is impossible to know what Montezinos thought about the veracity of his narrative. It is also hard to ascertain what his motives were beyond what he claims—namely, the desire to spread the "good news." It seems that he did not have material motives in mind when he approached the Portuguese Jews of Amsterdam. This can be ascertained from his refusal to accept community money and support during his six months living in Amsterdam, as attested to by Menasseh in the *Esperanza*: "He ate up all of his wealth with his trip to (Amsterdam), afterward living in extreme need and poverty because he did not want to sit in any anybody else's house nor did he try to gain any material benefit from his efforts" (42). It should be noted that this claim serves Menasseh's own purposes in bolstering the validity of the source of his main proof text for the *Esperanza*.

10. Reflecting on the intense mediation of "Columbian" writing, Margarita Zamora asserts that "the very signature 'Columbus' must be seen as an aggregate, a corporate author as it were" (*Reading Columbus*, 7).

11. I am indebted to Richard Kagan for pointing out the possible connections between my texts and the *discurso de la vida*. The introduction, bibliography, and collection of extraordinary "brief lives" contained in Richard Kagan and Abigail Dyer's recent book, *Inquisitorial Inquiries*, have been important resources for the following analysis.

12. Ibid., 17.

13. I have tried to describe the function of confession from the perspective of the Holy Office. In no way is it meant to be an apology for the coercion and violence of inquisitorial procedures. However, it is important to be able to look beyond the smokescreen of *leyendas negras y blancas* and put the Inquisition's methods within the wider context of secular juridical procedures throughout Western Europe. What went on within the secret cells of the Inquisition was on the whole no more extreme than the torture, harsh interrogations, and cruel punishments of the secular courts. The infamy of the Inquisition lies less in its actual acts of cruelty than in its ability to terrorize, like a sword of Damocles, certain segments of the Spanish and Portuguese population. Kagan and Dyer, *Inquisitorial Inquiries*, 18–19.

14. Ibid., 6.

15. Ibid., 16.

16. Ibid., 14. The passage is Kagan and Dyer's translation, from Miguel Jiménez Montserín, *Introducción a la inquisición española*, 198–240.

17. Ibid., 15.

18. In a recent essay James S. Amelang describes the peculiar power dynamics of the *discurso de la vida* and its relationship to autobiographical discourse:

> One might describe the situation as one in which the Inquisitors
> themselves open an autobiographical space, and then order the suspect
> to fill it as he or she sees fit, in a free format that lacks specifications as
> to length, detail, and thematic breadth. (Amelang, "Tracing Lives," 39)

19. One example of this tactic can be found in the fascinating case of Luis de la Ysla, a converso who left Spain in 1506 and lived as a Jew while in Italy and in Turkey. Upon his return to Spain in 1514, he went to confess his errant ways to the Inquisition in Toledo. Ysla confesses to living as a Jew during his time in Italy and Turkey but begs the tribunal's mercy and understanding that he Judaized out of necessity and coercion. Ysla asserts that he abandoned Judaism as soon as he could, as evidenced by his re-conversion to Christianity upon his arrival in Alexandria and his subsequent return to Spain. Kagan and Dyer, *Inquisitorial Inquiries*, 21–35.

20. "La figura del confesor o del superior estaba siempre presente bien fuera un defensor benigno o bien un duro capataz, ya que a la monja le estaba prohibido llevar a cabo un acto tan individualista como la escritura de su propia historia a no ser que fuera autorizada u obligada a hacerlo por alguna autoridad religiosa masculina. . . . De tal modo, que en las vidas se hace constante referencia al acto de la escritura como una pesada tarea, emprendida por el amor de Dios y en obediencia a su representante terrenal, el confesor" (Ross, "Cuestiones de género en *Infortunios de Alonso Ramírez*," 596).

21. Ross uses the example of the *escritura de monjas* to contextualize Alonso Ramírez's mediated autobiography. This poor Puerto Rican's story of shipwrecks, tortuous captivity among infidel pirates in the Far East, and his eventual arrival in New Spain was recorded and revised by the erudite pen of Carlos de Sigüenza y Góngora (1645–1700).

22. Gitlitz, "Inquisition Confessions and *Lazarillo de Tormes*."

23. Antonio Gómez-Moriana makes a similar claim in his tightly analytic and insightful essay "Autobiografía y discurso ritual." Gómez-Moriana focuses on the generic connections between inquisitorial discourse and the *Lazarillo* and the *Libro de la Vida* of Santa Teresa. However, unlike Gitlitz, he does not take the next step (a lá Américo Castro) of considering

how these practices might affect the wider sociocultural situation. Gitlitz's assertion that the fear of inquisitorial interrogation distributed itself throughout the converso and intellectual classes and produced scores of potential autobiographers points to the possible subterranean pathways of culture and mimesis. While intriguing and very suggestive, this theory is difficult to prove in any conclusive fashion.

24. Gitlitz, "Inquisition Confessions and *Lazarillo de Tormes*," 60.

25. Ibid., 59–60.

26. Ibid., 60.

27. Ibid.

28. Molloy, *At Face Value*, 4.

29. "Vuestra merced escribe se le escriba y relate el caso muy por extenso . . . porque se tenga entera noticia de mi persona" (*La vida de Lazarillo de Tormes*, 26).

30. Gitlitz, "Inquisition Confessions and *Lazarillo de Tormes*," 61.

31. Ibid., 55.

32. Ibid.

33. González-Echevarría, "The Law of the Letter," 111.

34. Within this dynamic hybridity there are certain generic elements that these texts share: (1) They are written with a particular end in mind, i.e., they are "interested texts," regardless of whether their interest is spiritual or material; (2) the texts are intended for an audience (or multiple audiences) and this intended audience affects their composition; (3) the texts engage in different generic practices to achieve multiple ends.

35. Zemon Davis, "Fame and Secrecy."

36. Ibid., 57.

37. Ibid., 53.

38. James Amelang's *The Flight of Icarus* analyzes a variety of early modern autobiographical texts written by artisans in multiple genres. Amelang explores the way these texts interact with a wide range of cultural modes and social expectations to create a textual space for the authors (especially those of the lower classes) to craft personal narratives. For a suggestive example from the German-Jewish context, see Debra Kaplan's "The Self in Social Context." Kaplan's reading points out the possibilities and limitations of treating autobiographical texts as sources for social history. J. H. Chajes engages many of the theoretical issues relating to the genre of autobiography in the early modern Jewish context in his "Accounting for the Self."

39. "Vendo os meyos tão estraordinários que el D[eus] B[endi]to teve para me trazer a seu conhesimento, . . . quis poor memória ás calamidades y rodeos com que me troxe a seu serviso, para que continuamente lhe desse grasas pella mercê que me fez" Cardoso, *La Vida del buenaventurado Abraham Pelengrino*, 6.

40. There is an extensive bibliography on the issue of the transition from converso life in the Peninsula to the open practice of Judaism in Amsterdam. The following citations are in no way meant to be comprehensive. Yosef Kaplan's classic study, *From Christianity to Judaism*, provides an in-depth analysis of the social and intellectual environment of converso assimilation into normative Jewish practice in Amsterdam. Miram Bodian's *Hebrews of the Portuguese Nation* and Daniel M. Swetschinski's *Reluctant Cosmopolitans* also deal with the issue of converso assimilation and dissent from a social historical perspective. David Graizbord's *Souls in Dispute*, analyzes the phenomenon of "renegade" Jews—conversos who embraced normative Judaism in southwest France, only to later renounce it upon their voluntary return to the Peninsula. These fascinating cases reveal the complexities and unresolved allegiances at the center of the return of these conversos to their ancestral faith. Before their formal encounter with a normative Jewish community, most conversos had only a vague notion of Jewish practice and

belief, and many were surprised by the religion that they found. This shock caused some "New Jews" to reject Judaism, or at least to challenge the way it was practiced by the community. Baruj Espinoza, excommunicated in 1556, is the most famous heretic of the Amsterdam community, but he was joined by several other notables—Uriel da Costa and Dr. Juan del Prado in particular—who were forced out of the community because of their heterodox beliefs and refusal to conform. These individuals are extreme examples, but they are indicative of the anxieties and concerns of a wider group of ex-conversos. Resolving their doubts and guiding them in the ways of normative Judaism became a primary goal of the Western Sephardic intelligentsia in the seventeenth century.

41. Some examples include Miguel de Barrios's poem lamenting the death of his first wife, "Exclamación de Mirtilio" in his *Coro de las Musas* (1660). Barrios uses his young bride's death as an opportunity to reflect on his own life. In "The 'DePinto' Manuscript," the author describes his escape from Portugal and arrival in Holland; For another example see also H. P. Salomon *Portrait of a New Christian.* Daniel López Laguna's "Espejo Fiel de Vidas" (London, 1721) includes some references to his imprisonment in Lisbon veiled in his poetic paraphrase of the Psalms. For a discussion of the place of the autobiographical in this work and the wider Western Sephardic context, see my "Daniel Israel Lopez Laguna's *Espejo Fiel de Vidas* (London 1720)." Laura Leibman deals with some aspects of Laguna's life in her "Poetics of the Apocalypse." Mayer Kayserling was the first to identify many of the autobiographical motifs in Laguna's paraphrase in his "The Jews in Jamaica and Daniel Israel Lopez Laguna."

42. The essential work on Sephardic literary production in Amsterdam is Harm den Boer's *La literatura sefardí de Amsterdam*, which provides a thorough history of Northern Sephardic literary culture and its religious and secular orientations, and includes a comprehensive bibliography. Because of a mixture of economic and inquisitorial restrictions, many of the great Spanish authors were published in Belgium instead of the Peninsula, giving the Dutch Jews easy access to the latest literary developments in their *patria*. Bodian shows how the Amsterdam Sephardim at once embraced and rejected aspects of Iberian culture in chapter 4 of her *Hebrews of the Portuguese Nation*, "Iberian Memory and Its Perpetuation," 76–95.

43. Delaney, *British Autobiography*, 36.

44. In a paper on "The Reformed Spaniards," James Amelang recently presented new research into three cases of Iberian Catholics who embraced Protestantism in England in the 1620s, just two decades after Cardoso's time there. His analysis points to many similarities with Cardoso's experience, in particular their youth at the time of their conversions and their emphasis on scripture and an ill-defined "reason" as the basis of their conversion.

45. In addition to Montezinos's text, two other works of travel literature come to mind: one, written by a Portuguese converso with unclear Jewish affiliations about his travels in the Middle East, is Pedro Teixeira's *Relaciónes del origen, descendencia y sucesión de los reyes de Persia, y de Harmuz, y de un viaje hecho por el autor dende la India hasta Italia por tierra* (Relation of the origin, geneology, and succession of the Kings of Persia and Harmuz and a journey undertaken by the author from India until Italy by land) (Antwerp, 1610); the other, by the Amsterdam Jewish merchant Moseh Pereyra de Paiva, is *Notisias dos Judios de Cochim* (Report on the Jews of Cochim) (Amsterdam, 1687); both point to the dearth of first-person travel writing among this very mobile group. See also Jonathan Schorsch's insightful analysis in "Mosseh Pereyra de Paiva." Teixeira's *Relaciónes* was edited and translated into English by William F. Sinclair and Donald Ferguson as *The Travels of Pedro Teixeira.* See also Scholberg, "Teixeira, Pedro"; Fuente del Pilar, "Pedro Teixeira y su viaje por Mesopotamia."

46. García-Arenal and Wiegers, *A Man of Three Worlds*, 3.

47. Bodian contextualizes the experiences of several "dogmatizing martyrs" in her *Dying in the Law of Moses*. Her nuanced and piercing treatment of the phenomenon of those seeking martyrdom for their beliefs when faced by inquisitorial persecution points toward larger intellectual and cultural trends in the Iberian world.

48. I have referred to this absence of converso and Sephardic autobiographical texts as the "ghost of marrano autobiography" in my "Daniel Israel Lopez Laguna's *Espejo Fiel de Vidas* (London 1720)."

49. "Dando prinsípio a minha ventura, eu sou filho em sanguinidade de hum homem chamado António Cardozo de Macedo, natural de Guimar[ãe]s, morador e asistente na sidade da Ponta Delgada na Ylha de São Miguel, escudeiro e mercador" (Macedo, *La Vida del buenaventurado Abraham Pelengrino*, 7).

50. "Recibidas mercedes y dones de la mano del muy alto" (LCMA, 685).

51. "Que en el santo de los santos creen y esperan sus grandes misericordias" (LCMA, 685).

52. See Toro, *Los judíos en la Nueva España*, 498. As seen elsewhere in the text, Italy represented the ideal "tierra de libertad" for Luis and his family (LCMA, 686). Italy also played an important role in the religious life of the Mexican crypto-Jewish community in the late sixteenth century. Undercover teachers came to Mexico from Italy; it was to Italy that the marranos of New Spain hoped to escape. Jonathan Israel discusses the arrival in Mexico of Jews from open Jewish communities in Italy in *Diasporas within a Diaspora*, 97–124. The most audacious case he records is the Diaz Nieto father and son who came to Mexico with official licenses from the Vatican to collect alms but who managed to teach the Carvajals and their fellow crypto-Jews aspects of the liturgy in Spanish translation as well as important rabbinic texts.

53. "Las puso con su vida hasta los beinte y cinco años de su peregrinación en orden de brebe historia" (LCMA, 686).

54. God also assures the veracity of Joseph's account. In the *Vida*'s introductory paragraph Carvajal tells the reader that "con las rodillas por el suelo . . . promete trayendo por to.[do] Al sr. de las verdades, de tratar lo punctual en todo lo que aqui escribiere." [I purposefully keep the Spanish in its original, condensed form.] God, "el Señor de las Verdades," knows the truth and cannot be fooled.

55. "Saliendo de la inmundancia gentílica, venía a gozar del deleite de la congregación de sus deseados compañeros" (as quoted in Carsten Wilke, "Políticos franceses, criptojudíos portugueses"). Wilke offers a nuanced analysis of the double and even triple meanings inscribed into Enríquez Gómez's poetry.

56. LCMA, 686.

57. I use Dámaso Chicharro's edition of Santa Teresa de Avila's *Libro de la vida*. Sonja Herpoel's study of nuns' autobiographic writing "on demand" in early modern Spain, *A la zaga de Santa Teresa*, is a helpful introduction to this generic practice.

2. "Hermanos en el Señor"

1. LCMA, 686. LCMA refers to Luis de Carvajal, *el mozo*, as author of his *Vida*. Carvajal did not give his autobiography a title. Toro refers to it as the *Autobiografía*, and Gonzalez Obregón uses the term *Memorias*. I use *Vida* because it is the term most often used for autobiographical texts in the early modern Iberian world. The pagination follows the edition included in *Procesos de Luis de Carvajal, el mozo*, ed. Luis González Obregón. The actual text is identical to that included as an appendix to Alfonso de Toro's *La familia Carvajal*.

2. The territory stretched from Tampico to San Antonio, Texas, and reached six hundred miles inland from the Gulf of Mexico. See Liebman, *The Enlightened*, 27. For a full treatment of the older Carvajal, see Cohen, *The Martyr*, 37–66, and Samuel Temkin's biography, *Luis de Carvajal*.

3. Throughout the autobiography and the trial records, mention is made of the dire financial straits of the Carvajal family, despite their being relatives of the governor. Wealth did not come automatically with the title, and the fact that they settled in a rather inhospitable part of Mexico pushed the men of the family to earn extra money through petty commercial activities in Mexico City and the countryside. The Carvajals' more modest economic activity serves as an interesting counterpoint to the stereotype of the wealthy Portuguese merchant.

4. Cohen, *The Martyr*, 142–48, 174–81.

5. Toro, *La familia Carvajal*, 377–400, and Cohen, *The Martyr*, 198–212. For an in depth analysis of the activities at this unique New World institution, see Tzvetan Todorov's *The Conquest of America*, 219–41.

6. These letters are included in *Procesos de Luis de Carvjal el Mozo*, 497–522. See also Seymour Liebman's English translations in *The Enlightened*.

7. "De los peregrinos de la occidental India y de los captivos" (LCMA, 463).

8. "Para que sean notorias a todos los que en los santos de los santos creen y esperan sus grandes misericordias que usa con los pecadores" (ibid.).

9. All subsequent scholars of the Carvajal family must be grateful to Toro. In preparing his study of the Carvajals, he carefully transcribed Luis's *Vida* and other documents. Soon after, the original text of the autobiography, along with other precious artifacts related to the Carvajals, were stolen by a mysterious foreigner in 1932. While some of the artifacts were anonymously returned, the *Vida* has never resurfaced and would have been lost for all time if not for Toro's copy. Toro gives a detailed account of this heist and the ensuing scandal relating to the use of his own transcriptions in the publication of the trial documents under the authorship of Luis Gónzalez Obregón, the chief historian of the Archivo General de la Nación (AGN). See Toro, *La familia Carvajal*, 15–23. See also Rafael López's introduction to *Procesos de Luis de Carvajal (el Mozo)* (1935). Toro's ambivalent feelings toward Jews and Judaism are seen quite clearly in his treatment of the theft of the documents. The suspected thief, a certain Professor Jac Nachbin, is the target of Toro's latent anti-Semitism. Nachbin, Toro informs us, was a Brazilian citizen of German origin, who was a professor at the University of New Mexico. But most importantly, it seems that Nachbin was Jewish. Toro constantly refers to him as "el professor judío" or "el doctor judío." Throughout the work there are many bouts of atavistic anti-Semitism. Referring to the Jews as cheap, money-hungry, and fanatical is commonplace in his description of the Carvajal family. What is most perplexing and fascinating about these comments is that they appear in a work dedicated to the heroic suffering and brutal persecution of Judeo-conversos. A study of the historiographic orientation of the early Latin American scholars of the Inquisition such as Toro and the eminent Toribio-Medina remains a desideratum.

10. Cohen, *The Martyr*. For Liebman, see his translation of primary sources relating to Carvajal in *The Enlightened*, as well as his collected essays on conversos in colonial Mexico, *The Jews of New Spain*.

11. Bodian, *Dying in the Law of Moses*. It is worth mentioning three contemporary scholars who look at the wider reverberations of the Carvajal family story. Lucía H. Costigan places Luis de Carvajal's writings within their New World literary context and the wider culture of the Iberian Counter-Reformation world in *Through Cracks in the Walls*. Erin Graff-Zivin's *Figurative Inquisitions* explores ways that twentieth-century Latin American authors and artists utilize the Carvajal family story for their contemporary concerns. In her very

promising dissertation, "The Other Sephardic Diaspora: Feminine Representations of Sephardic Identity in the Early Modern Atlantic World," Emily Colbert Cairns turns her attention to the trial records of Isabel, Carvajal's sister, as part of a wider study of converso women in the early modern Iberian world.

12. I have carefully studied the complete trial record of Luis de Carvajal, *el mozo*, as well as that of his uncle the governor and the testimonies of other witnesses pertaining to these two trials. However, I did not examine the entire inquisitorial archive related to the Carvajal family. I have relied on Toro and Cohen's impressive synthetic work to establish larger contextual questions.

While this study focuses on the autobiography, the interplay between Carvajal's autobiography and letters and the extant documentation from the trial records will also be considered. I want to stress that I am not attempting a positivistic "reconstruction" of the events; rather I am interested in using the varied textual currents in order to see how Luis and his family shape their respective self-images.

13. See chapter 3 of Daviken Studnicki-Gizbert's *A Nation upon the Ocean Sea*, 67–90. Studniki-Gizbert also deals with this issue in his essay "La Nación among the Nations," 86–87. For other treatments of the centrality of family within the early modern converso and Sephardic world, see Graizbord, "Converso Children under the Inquisitorial Microscope in the Seventeenth Century." See also the various contributions to *Familia, Religion y Negocio: el sefardismo en las relaciones entre el mundo ibérico y los Países Bajos en la Edad Moderna*, ed. Jaime Contreras, Bernardo José García, and Juan Ignacio Pulido Serrano. Most recently Francesca Trivellato has questioned the overriding centrality of family in economic activity in the early modern Sephardic diaspora in her *Familiarity of Strangers*. For a comprehensive look at family life in the Western Sephardic, converso, and Ottoman contexts, see the excellent essays collected in *Sephardi Family Life in the Early Modern Diaspora*, ed. Julia Lieberman.

14. Cohen, *The Martyr*, 55–57; see note 43 for the textual history of this official patent.

15. "Tío miserable y ciego" (LCMA, 465).

16. There is considerable speculation about how much the governor would have known about his family's Judaizing. His own background as the child of conversos is obviously not proof of his commitment or even exposure to crypto-Jewish practices in his youth. His own wife, Doña Guiomar, the daughter of his Portuguese New Christian business partner, refused to go to Mexico with him, apparently over religious differences. There is evidence that she asked Isabel, Luis's sister, to try to convert her husband, which she attempted to do with disastrous effects. The governor spent most of his adult life in the Americas and had limited contact with his family until he received his title to govern Nueva León. It would have been reasonable for Carvajal (the elder) to have assumed that they were committed to assimilating into the Catholic fabric of Iberian society, as he was, not in maintaining an atavistic faith in the dead law of Moses. Thus the degree to which he knew of his family's Judaizing proclivities is unclear. In the years leading up to the first arrest, however, the governor and his sister's children had theological confrontations, and thus their Judaizing had to be obvious to him. See Cohen's chapter dedicated to Carvajal, el viejo, "The Governor," in *The Martyr*, 37–66, as well as Bodian, *Dying in the Law of Moses*, 47–52.

17. "Dijo: que no lo sabe, aunque presume haber nacido este mal del dicho Gobernador Luis de Carvajal, su tío, que casi es enemigo capital, por controversias que con él han tenido sus padres y hermanos, y por haberles hecho tanto mal como traerlos engañados de España, de cuya causa están pobres y perdidos, o haberle algún enemigo levantado algún testimonio" (LCM I, 16).

18. This claim is not as preposterous as it may seem. Within the arguments that circulated relating to the nature of *limpieza* there were those who believed that after several generations

a converso could/should be considered as an Old Christian. María Elena Martínez analyzes these arguments and their reception and transformation in the Americas in her *Genealogical Fictions*, 52, 82–84. Martinez's important contribution to questions of race and identity in the Iberian world is made more poignant by her untimely passing; it is clear that there were many more dark corners she would have been able to illuminate.

19. We will look at these two instances in greater detail in chapter 4, in considering Isabel's Judaizing and her role within the Carvajal family dynamic.

20. "Los rudimentos o principios de la Trinidad," "la luz de su conocimiento santo" (LCMA, 463).

21. "Un dia señalado que es el que llamamos de las perdonanças día santo y solemne entre nosotros a diez días de la luna séptima y como la verdad de Dios es tan clara y agradable no fue menester mas que advertirle de ella su madre hermano y hermana mayores y un primo suyo" (ibid). In this section I invert the syntax at times for greater clarity, but I still try to maintain the idiosyncratic baroque style of Luis's writing, in particular the long and winding sentences.

There is an echo of the original biblical Hebrew in Luis's Spanish rendering of "Quipurim/ כפורים" as "perdonanças." This is similar to the calque-style translation that was common within medieval Spanish Jewish circles and that continued after the expulsion. For one of many examples of this usage, see the *Biblia en dos columnas*, a bilingual Bible (Hebrew and Spanish) from Amsterdam (1762), 70, 71, 105, and 138. The great Spanish bibliophile Joseph Rodríguez de Castro uses the term "día de perdonanças" in discussing the content of Leviticus in his *Biblioteca Española* (Madrid, 1781).

22. Julia R. Lieberman dates the ritualization of Bar Mitzva among the Western Sephardim to the mid- to late seventeenth century. Lieberman finds the use of a recurring term to mark this age of religious maturity in some of the sermons delivered by thirteen-year-olds, "gremio dos observantes dos preceytos divinos," or "the guild of [commandment] observers." We cannot know whether Carvajal was initiated into his family's crypto-Judaism close to his thirteenth birthday because his family understood that age to be the beginning of religious responsibility in rabbinic sources. At minimum, their decision to entrust him with this secret only at this age points to the reality that in the early modern period, this was an age at which an individual would begin taking on markedly more responsibilities and even begin supporting himself. Lieberman insightfully illustrates the connection between the practice of apprenticeship and religious maturity. See her *Sephardi Family Life in the Early Modern Diaspora*, 153–58.

23. In the trial records, this description of Luis's father as religiously in the background is contradicted. A cousin, Felipe Nuñez, quotes one of the sisters ("la viuda") as attributing their initiation and instruction in the Law of Moses to the father: "sabed que mi padre nos dijo" (know that my father told us) (LCM I, 8). A few lines later: "su padre les había dicho, porque era leído, que habia leído que un profeta decía" (her father had told her, because he was lettered, that he had read that one of the prophets said) (LCM I, 9). Blaming the father, who was already dead, might have been a convenient way to deflect guilt from other living members of the family.

24. "En donde el verdadero Dios pudiera ser mejor servido" (LCMA, 463).

25. "Soldados y capitanes gentiles" (ibid., 468).

26. "Con mucho temor del s[eño]r mientras vivio, avia resistido el defunto padre atendiendo a su smo. Mand[a]to en que lo prohibe" (ibid.).

27. "Le preguntó esto a solas, en una comunidad de indios, no se acuerda, que día, que por que se guardaba el domingo y no el sábado y éste le respondió" (LCG, 231).

Gapsar's testimony comes from the *proceso* of the governor, Luis de Cravajal, *el viejo/the Elder*, which was transcribed and edited by Alfonso Toro in *Los judíos en la Nueva España*; citations from this trial record will be given as LCG (Luis Carvajal Gobernador).

28. "Que andaba confuso de ver que los predicadores declaraban las figuras del Testamiento Viejo unos a un propósito y otros a otro" (LCG, 231).

29. "Por qué el Papa consiente en Roma juderías" (ibid., 232).

30. "Por qué se había metido fraile pues sabía que no lo podía ser" (ibid.).

31. "El temor de que no volvessen a algo de su ralea y casta; de que descendían, y que este no había de volver" (ibid.).

32. "Todos piensan eso de si" (ibid.).

33. Gaspar must explain his reasoning for not alerting the Holy Office to his family's Judaizing. He brings up these assorted questions, apparently to point to the fact that whatever doubts he might have had about his father's orthodoxy, they were always based on vague statements, and whatever was problematic was always dealt with clearly and conclusively. However, it is fair to wonder what meaning these questions had for Gaspar. Gaspar, like the other witnesses, might also have been pressed to place the blame for the family's Judaizing on the deceased father instead of other living family members.

34. LCG, 226–27.

35. He had a bad premonition about said Francisco Rodríguez: "teniendo mala espina del dicho Francisco Rodríguez" (ibid., 287).

36. "Ha oido decir que los de Portugal se van a Francia a vivir, o a Flandes, o a otras partes remotas, es huyendo de Inquisición y por vivir en la Ley de Moisés" (ibid., 228).

37. "Tan mala gente" (ibid.).

38. "Si por ventura han alcanzado algún resabio de su padre. . . . por si acaso, por ventura, hubiese sido enseñado de doctrina mala" (ibid., 288).

39. Catalina claims that Isabel blames her dead husband in order to protect her father, during his lifetime, from the governor's wrath.

40. "No se lo consintió; sino traerla consigo a la dicha provincia de Pánuco, con intento de enseñarla la ley de Moisés" (He did not consent; instead he brought her to this province of Pánuco with the intention to teach her the Law of Moses) (LCG, 274).

41. "Estaban en la dicha Ley porque el dicho su padre se lo había asimesmo dicho y enseñado" (LCM I, 42).

42. Ibid., 48–49.

43. "¿Sabéis cómo vuestro padre vivió en la Ley de Moisén?, y este respondió llorando: es muy gran maldad, y el dicho Luis de Carvjal le dijo entonces: mira que por eso os quiero más que a todos vuestros hermanos. Porque sabed que a mi quiso engañar vuestro padre, persuadiéndome que me volviese a la guarda de la Ley de Moisén" (ibid., 45).

44. "Un medico afamado. Y especialmente en el temor de Dios nuestro señor" (ibid.).

45. "Un tullido hebreo" (LCMA, 470). This old man is Luis's father's friend Machado. In the trial testimonies Luis credits his father with connecting Luis to this devout Jew. This is yet another example of Luis diminishing his father's role in his spiritual development.

46. "Un libro, o medicinal emplasto para sanidad del anima" (ibid.).

47. Miriam Bodian deals with this relationship in great detail, showing the clear intellectual affinities between these two New World religious visionaries in *Dying in the Law of Moses*, 57–58.

48. "Guarda la Ley de Moisén con mucha más perfección que él" (LCM II, 151).

49. "Ojalá fuera como su zapato" (ibid.).

50. Díaz is the antithesis of Ruiz de Luna. Carvajal was certainly lured into trusting him because of his powerful experience with the lapsed monk with whom he shared a cell during his first trial. Carvajal apparently overestimated his power of religious persuasion, believing that he was able to "flip" the priest toward Judaism so quickly. However, because Carvajal

seemed to have earnestly believed Díaz's sincerity, his exchanges with this informer reflect a sense of security and comfort—as if he can voice his true feelings. In this way Díaz's testimony functions most like the *Vida*—Luis does not think that the Inquisitors would ever hear his words, which were destined only to his cellmate.

51. "Le avisase con el camino que iba a morir, porque pensaba como éste vería, ir cantando y predicando la Ley de Moisén, y le diesse tambien cuenta de la alegría que tenía en la cárcel cantando y bailando con mucho regocijo, porque moría por su Dios y Señor" (LCM II, 151–52).

52. "Que en el Señor se amaban como el agua y la tierra" (LCMA, 470).

53. Cohen, *The Martyr*, 34–36, discusses the issue of whether or not Gaspar knew of the family's Judaizing.

54. "Parecioles lastimosa dejar a un hermano mayor suyo ciego y fraile dominico predicador y maestro ya en su orden, y ansi con animo fuerte y amoroso ambos dos hermanos se fueron a verle en su convento que estaba junto a la carcel de la inquisicion" (LCMA, 472).

55. Touring the colonial district of Mexico City, one can easily see the Palacio de la Inquisición where Luis was eventually imprisoned, right across the street from the Dominican monastery where his brother lived.

56. "El fraile ciego . . . desaventurado, . . . triste," "hermano mayor suyo" (LCMA, 472).

57. "Mas que bueno era leerla más no guardarla" (ibid.).

58. "Vuestros mismos predicadores," "vuestro crucificado" (ibid., 473).

59. "Dixoles viendose convencido no tratemos mas desto" (ibid.).

60. "Bendito sea Dios que me saco de entre vosotros" (ibid.).

61. "Me saco de entre vosotros" (ibid.).

62. "Ambos hermanos replicaban uno de un lado y otro de otro glorificado sea n[ues]tro. D[ios]. y S[eño]r que no nos dexaste en la ceguera y perdición que a este miserable" (ibid.).

63. For a sophisticated discussion of Luis's bibliocentric approach to religion, see Bodian, *Dying in the Law of Moses*, especially 57–58.

64. "El que fuese convenzido por la x[ver]dad quedase en ella" (LCMA, 473).

Although the context of this passage seems to indicate reading *xdad* as *verdad*, Claude Stuczynski suggests that the word may actually be "cristianidad," with the "x" indicating "Xpo"/Christo (email exchange, March 5, 2012).

65. "Se disculpo con dezir que las vedaba su ley el inquirirla, ni augmentarla" (LCMA, 473).

66. The absorption of inquisitorial concepts and terminology by crypto-Jews is seen in many surprising ways. See Yerushalmi, "Marranos Returning to Judaism in the 17th Century," 202.

67. Despite our focus on the *Vida*, it is important to point out that in Gaspar's version of this episode in his testimony before the Inquisitors, while both brothers engage in the debate, it is Baltasar who does most of the talking (LCG, 231). Gaspar's sidelining of Luis could point to his desire to place the blame on the brother who was far away from the Inquisitor's grasp, namely Baltasar who eluded arrest and fled to Italy. Alternatively, his testimony may highlight the depth of Luis's drive to craft a particular self-image in the *Vida* and the liberties he took with the events of his life. From Gaspar's point of view, the essence of the exchange was meant to show how he adequately dealt with the religious doubts of his brothers, and thus can justify not turning them in to the Inquisition.

68. "Por que razón hace estos grados de sospecha, entre unos mismos hermanos, nacidos y criados de unas puertas adentro de unos mismos padres?" (ibid., 230).

69. LCM II, 695–96.

70. My reading of the relationship between Fray Francisco and Luis is enriched by some ideas developed by Professor Thomas Cohen of York University in his recent keynote address

to the Early Modern Workshop in Jewish History (Brown University, February 26, 2012) entitled, "Entanglement: How the Whole World Worked and How Jews Joined In." In particular, his idea of the relationship between sacrifice and communion was very illuminating and provocative.

71. See Cohen, *The Martyr*, 166–167; Bodian, *Dying in the Law of Moses*, 63–64. Luis asserts that he was placed in the cell because of the Inquisitors' concern over his poor health and depressed spirits (LCMA, 475).

72. "Despues de los dos presos aberse comunicado un rato y alegrado de la junta y compañia" (LCMA, 476).

73. "Con sumo gozo y alegria de ver que el s[eño]r D[ios] suyo abia ymbiadole por aquella orden lo que deseaba tanto que era tener por donde rezar los ps[alm]os como solia" (ibid.).

74. "Alumbrado y convertido" (LCM II, 478).

75. "Se alegraba y consolaba y cantaba himnos y loores al s[eño]r" (ibid.).

76. Certeau, "Reading as Poaching."

77. Presumably these were stories from the Hebrew Bible, but quite possibly this general category might include a wider array of religiously edifying stories. It is important to notice that in this case in particular, Luis is the teacher: He is the one regaling Francisco with the stories.

78. "Quien me dierra sido alumbrado en la berdad de Dios fuera de esta carzel y caido en ella estando en los monasterios, que solyan donde tienen librerias abiertas con la sagrada escriptura y otros muchos buenos libros" (LCMA, 478).

79. Ibid., 479.

80. "A quien me diera en unas de ellas" (ibid.).

81. "Bamos a hacer el sacrificio" (Let's make the sacrifice) (ibid.).

82. "Confesor de D[ios] verdadero y de su ley s[antis]ma," "corona de martir"(ibid.).

83. "Imprimiosele tambien en el anima a este buen estrangero la berdad divina como si toda su vida ubiera sido criado en ella y enseñado por fieles p[adr]es" (ibid.).

84. Cohen, *The Martyr*, 253, based on Medina *La Inquisición en México*, 109.

85. LCMA, 479.

86. "El compañero de Joseph confeso aquella vez al D[ios] del cielo delante de los tyranos con tan valerosos animo q[uan]to no se a vista semejante cosa en ho[mbr]e de estraña nacion" (ibid.).

87. It is not clear if this exchange is the invention of Luis's fertile imagination or not. How Luis knew that Francisco used this creative piece of biblical exegesis before the Inquisitors is hard to know. However, the application of the Exodus story to the plight of the conversos before the Inquisitors could very well be an indication of the extent to which this monk had already begun to absorb Luis's bibliocentric hermeneutic.

Calling the Inquisitors "dogs" is a fascinating reversal or appropriation of the classic anti-Jewish epithet "perro judío." This is just one of many examples whereby Luis's Judaism is actually a Judaizing of Christianity, a reorientation of Catholic ideas and terminology toward an idealized vision of the Law of Moses.

88. Manuel Cardoso de Macedo, another Old Christian convert to Judaism whom I will discuss in chapter 4, was deeply troubled by his Old Christian blood and felt that it was a hindrance to his full conversion.

89. LCMA, 480.

90. "Sacristan de los idolos" (ibid.).

91. "Regando primero el suelo con muchas lágrimas" (ibid.).

92. The Colegio was founded in 1537 and in 1590 lost its most famous teacher, Fray Bernadino de Sahagún. Sahagún oversaw the monumental project of recording indigenous religious practices, history, and science, which was collected in various massive codices over several decades. These histories were generally recorded in order to understand indigenous idolatrous

practice as a means of policing the neophyte Indians' atavistic paganism. Along the way, many of those who worked on these projects came to find points of contact between the indigenous and the Christian. Tzvetan Todorov, *The Conquest of America*, 219–41, sees Fray Bernardino de Sahagún's monumental translation project as a model of a form of cultural inquiry that is not solely interested in the possession and control of the other. By the time that Luis arrived at the monastery, most of the focus on indigenous culture had shifted to more classical humanist pursuits of which Luis benefited greatly.

93. "Un anciano fraile hombre de mucha virtud . . . le amaba [a Joseph] y queria estrañamente no solo a el sino toda su g[en]te Y como les habian quitado los lobos carnizeros sus haciendas y ellos quedaban en pobreza, este de su mismo plato y mesa, todos los dias desta vida los regalaba" (LCMA, 481). For further discussion of the texts Luis gained access to, see Toro, *La familia Carvajal*, 459–80; Cohen, *The Martyr*, 198–212; and Bodian, *Dying in the Law of Moses*, 64, n. 101 and 102.

94. Fray Pedro's piety and intellectual intensity are attested to in book 20, chapter 78 of Juan de Torquemada's monumental, multivolume history of the Franciscans in the New World: *Monarquía Indiana onarquía indiana de los veinte y un libros rituales y Monarquía indiana*, originally published in Seville in 1615 and available online at: http://www.historicas.unam.mx /publicaciones/publicadigital/monarquia/

95. This would be the meaning from the context. However, *gente* also refers to "people," and it may mean something more expansive, such as the larger group of conversos. Oroz was deeply interested in the culture and languages of the indigenous group his monastery serviced, but we do not have any indication that this interest extended to New Christians.

96. "Esta m[e]r[ce]d. Del sr. fuese mas colmada de la mano de su liberalisima magnificiencia" (This mercy from the Lord was most desired from his generous and magnificent hand) (LCMA, 481).

97. We can hear a clear echo of the biblical Joseph's experience here. Despite his trials and hard times, Joseph always "finds favor" with people in power—Potiphar, the jailer, and later Pharaoh. For more on this trope see Ronnie Perelis, "Marrano Autobiography in Its Transatlantic Context," 162–65.

98. "Y quando se los truxeron le vino el mismo como a pedir las albricias y Joseph diziendole o que ricas cosas trahemos a nuestro colegio" (LCMA, 481).

99. "En este libro le descubrio el Sr. los santos treze articulos y fundamentos de nuestra fee y religión cosa no sabida y oida en las tierras de captiverio" (ibid., 482).

100. "Matalotage para el anima" (ibid.). *Matalotage* refers to the provisions taken on a journey. In this sense these texts provided nourishment for Luis on his spiritual journey of discovery and deepening of his commitment to crypto-Judaism. For more on Luis's poaching of the texts see Perelis, "Marrano Autobiography in Its Transatlantic Context," 140–70.

101. "Bolbio a faborezer a Joseph como de antes" (LCMA, 491).

102. Miriam Bodian's treatment of Carvajal's religious ideas points to the Christian nature of his "Judaism." One prominent analysis of the Jewish and Christian symbiosis in the Medieval period is Israel J. Yuval's *Two Nations in Your Womb*.

3. A Prophetic Matrix

1. Renée Levine Melammed's work on conversa Judaizers is an eloquent illustration of this approach. See her *Heretics or Daughters of Israel?*

2. I want to thank both Claude Dov Stuczynski and Stan Mirvis for helping me consider this historiographic angle, each at a different decisive moment in the evolution of this project.

It was in discussions with Silvia Arrom at Brandeis University that I was able to first perceive the centrality of family dynamics to Carvajal's writings. I am grateful for her critical eye and open mind.

3. "Un dia señalado que es el que llamamos de las perdonanças día santo y solemne entre nosotros a diez días de la luna séptima y como la verdad de Dios es tan clara y agradable no fue menester mas que advertirle de ella su madre hermano y hermana mayores y un primo suyo" (LCMA, 463).

4. "Estraños y gentilicas mugeres" (ibid., 468).

5. "Dando el parabien a la dichosa madre muchas de las gentilicas mugeres le dezian. Señora, y que buena oracion rezasteis: mas cmo dixo la santa Sara 'no está a toda a los meritos del hombre, que siempre son pocos, o ningunos, la divina my[sericordi]a'" (ibid.).

6. "La dichosa madre, la cual aunque herida con el fiero golpe de tan cruel enemigo cubrio su manto con mansedumbre y llorando sus trabajos y alabando al Señor Dios por ellos, fue llebada por aquellos ministros de maldición, verdugos de nuestras vidas, a la prision escuricísima" (ibid., 474).

7. "Lobos carnizeros" (ibid., 481). While Luis often presents himself as fearless and brave, we can find plenty of instances in the trial records where he expresses real trepidation and fear; see ibid., 477 and 487 for just two small examples.

8. "Tu madre estando entera antes de ser encarzelada y partida con tormentos bien olia fructa era de buen olor de paciencia ante el sr. mas agora que está partida con tormentos da mejor olor de paciencia antes el Señor" (ibid., 477).

9. Ibid., 486.

10. This is one of the many patterns and mentalities that the Spanish imported from their centuries of military struggle against the Moors. In the wars of the *reconquista*, soldiers were often rewarded with land in the newly conquered territories, thus opening the door for them to become *hijos de algo*, literally sons of "something" or "substance." Américo Castro identifies this connection when he writes: "El español cristiano bajaba a las regiones de la Plata en el siglo XVI, lo mismo que en los siglos X y XI se había extendido hacia el sur de la Peninsula, a fin de ganar honra y mantener señorío" (*La realidad histórica de España*, 216). Another stunning example of this transference of *reconquista* motifs to the New World can be seen in the use of the iconography of Santiago Matamoros, with Indians replacing Muslims as the dead soldiers are trampled underneath Saint Jaime's horse. Besides appearing in churches throughout Latin America, this image was included in a variety of historical works. Filipe Guamán Poma de Ayala's Nueva *Corónica y buen gobierno* (Caracas: Biblioteca Ayacucho, 1980) records how St. James sealed the "conquista milagrosa" of Cusco. P. Alonso de Ovalle's *Histórica relación del reino de Chile* (Santiago: Instituto de Literatura Chilena, 1969 [1646]) has the patron saint defending Santiago from Indian hordes in an engraving entitled, "El Apóstol Santiago en la defensa de Santiago de la Nueva Extremadura."

11. The genealogy he provides to the Inquisitors as part of his "discurso de la vida" points to a classic Portuguese converso merchant family. His family moves from Mogodorio in Portugal to the nearby Spanish town of Benavente. Of his maternal uncles, three out of the five were involved in Atlantic trade: "Francisco Jorge de Andrade, que fué en la Guinea factor de esclavos por el Rey de Portugal, que después fue fraile augustino en San Agustín de México Antonio de León, mozo soltero que murió en manos de Franceses yendo de Indias a españa Duarte de León-Contratador de los pueblos de Guinea por el Rey de Portugal" (LCG, 279). Carvajal himself was involved in Atlantic trade from a very young age. His father died around the time of his eighth birthday, after which his uncle Duarte de León took him to work with him in Cape Verde, where he lived for thirteen years, eventually holding the position of "treasurer

and accountant of the King of Portugal." He comes to the New World seeking to recuperate his loses from a lost shipment of wheat. His wife was born in Lisbon and moved to Seville with her family. This was an extremely common move for Portuguese conversos seeking to have easier access to the Atlantic trade coming in and out of Seville's port (ibid., 280).

12. Cohen, *The Martyr*, 111–13.

13. "Oyeron derrepente chirimias, y tormpetas a sus puertas y era la causa aver llegado a su casa dos maridos que el S[eño]r ymbiaba a las huerfanas temerosos suyos y de su pueblo" (LCMA, 468).

14. "Temeorsos suyos y de su pueblo" (ibid.).

15. "Vio a las hermanas huerfanas, por el Señor amaparadas y en lugar de las sayas rotas, las vio cubiertas de terciopelos, joyas de oro y otras sedas en las casas de sus maridos, y en ellas repartidas y amparadas las demas viudas y huerfanas, amparadas sean del Señor" (ibid., 469).

16. Psalms 118, 22.

17. Cohen, *The Martyr*, 146.

18. Ibid., 190–94, 197–98.

19. Almeida's escape from the Inquisitors is dramatized by Luis into another instance of divine intervention. The official who was sent to Tasco to arrest Almeida was gored by a bull, right outside Almeida's door: "Embio el sr. D[ios] un toro el qual le embistio con este tan fieramente que le mato a cornadas antes que lo dexase en la misma puerta de su casa" (LCMA, 484). As has been seen throughout the narrative, this is not a freak accident; rather, it is God who sends the bull. That the official is gored right in front of his door seems to prove this assertion.

20. In his testimony Luis describes how he brought a copy of Fray Luis de Granada's *Símbolo de la fe* to Almeida while he was hiding. Together they read "autoridades y cosas de la Ley que dio Dios a Moisén." The "poaching" of relevant Jewish material from Christian books is a phenomenon already discussed in this chapter. However, here we have a scene of this poaching in practice, and its related social dynamic: "Se rio mucho con éste de dicho Fray Luis, diciendo, que escribía éste borracho estas cosas de la Ley de Dios, y que no lo entienda, y allí se declaró con éste cómo guardaba la Ley de Moisén y era judío." The text is brought by Luis and they read it together. We are not told if Almeida requested this or any other book. Are we meant to see this as Luis's initiative? Or did Almeida request uplifting reading material? The *Símbolo* brings the primary sources they crave and Fray Luis's Christological commentary/frame serves as the strawman for their zealous ridicule. Fray Luis has Jewish sources right before his eyes, and yet he "drunkenly" twists them in a Christological key. Does Luis want the Inquisitors to think that he is converting Almeida over to Judaism during these sessions? Does Luis want the Inquisitors to believe that this is the first time he and Almeida revealed their Judaism to each other? Many of the witnesses against Luis, as well as his own testimony, mention aspiring crypto-Jews coming to visit Luis at Tlaltelolco and their spending time reading texts together. Clearly he was seen as a resource and a guide in the thicket of religious texts.

According to Cohen, Almeida seems to have hidden in the same safe house that Baltasar used (*The Martyr*, 193).

21. See the letter Almeida wrote to Leonor from Havana on his way to Spain, quoted in ibid., 193–94.

22. The letter was intercepted on May 13, 1596. The Carvajals were re-arrested in early 1595. Luis was the first one arrested on February 1, 1595.

23. Baltasar, writing from Spain on the eve of his trip to Italy, refers to the vast distance between them and how it only makes him love his family more. For evocative examples of the impact of distance on family connections, see the marvelous collection of personal letters from

both sides of the Atlantic in Sánchez Rubio, Testón Núñez, and Domínguez Ortiz, *El hilo que une.*

24. "Que ningún género de concierto haga con él, sino con todo rigor cobre mi hacienda de él y le destruya, y cuando no pudiera pagar lo que me ha hurtado, le pierda y le deje comer piojos en la cárcel" (LCM II, 170).

25. Almeida's change of heart regarding his uncle reflects what Francesca Trivellato charts so lucidly in her *Familiarity of Strangers.* Trivellato's careful analysis of cross-cultural interactions of Livorno-based Sephardic merchants challenges the cliché of ethnic cohesion as the essential feature of premodern merchant diasporas. She notes the tensions and difficulties involved in relying on family members and argues that often enough, merchants looked for business connections that crossed familiar and ethnic lines for the sake of efficiency and profit.

26. "y vive el Señor que si deseo volver a esa tierra es para vengarme de ese ladrón, mas aunque no vaya, yo haré de acá que no se pose en rama verde él ni los hijos que tiene de puta, ni tenga lugar con mi hacienda casar las hijas de su manceba" (LCM II, 170).

The expression "Posar en ramo verde" is borrowed from the popular ballad "Fontefrida," in which the "widowed" dove, mourning her dead husband, tells the nightingale who tries to woo her that she is not interested—that since she lost her true love she no longer "dwells on green branches, nor on prairies adorned with flowers." For an analysis of the development of this popular ballad see Francisco Rico, "Los orígenes de 'Fontefrida,'" esp. 18–23, where Rico considers this phrase. I thank Professor David Wacks for his help in contextualizing this phrase and pointing out the way that literary texts were so seamlessly integrated into everyday discourse.

27. "Las enfermedades de mis hermanas me pesa como es razón" (LCM II, 170).

28. "Cuyas manos beso mil veces" (ibid.).

29. It is not clear if the brothers first went to Rome, or if Almeida refers to Rome as a general term for places of open Jewish life. See Baltasar's letter upon his departure from Spain for Italy (ibid., 251).

30. "Aunque en cuatro años no se ha acordado de escribirme" (ibid., 170).

31. Marrying two sisters was already forbidden within the Bible (Leviticus 18:18). Almeida's romantic plan either points to the piecemeal nature of crypto-Jewish knowledge of the Bible or is simply a reflection of his own personal sexual predilections.

32. Cohen, *The Martyr,* 122–23 presents a vivid description of this affair, based on varied inquisitorial confessions from Mariana and Díaz de Cáceres and others.

33. Cohen, "Antonio Díaz de Cáceres"; Cohen, *The Martyr,* 169–84, 186–90; Toro, *La familia Carvajal,* 413–59.

34. "El otro cuñado de Joseph ya entiendo que el d[ic]ho como estando el y su m[adr]e y her[man]as presos se partio pa[ra] la china de donde para remedio de su mujer y de una niña que dexaba lo truxo el sr. no con falta de milagros" (LCMA, 484).

35. Cohen, *The Martyr,* 213.

36. "Si no hacía las ceremonias de la dicha ley era por temor de no ser preso por la inquisición" (quoted in Cohen, *The Martyr,* 327, n. 2); taken from Díaz de Cáceres's trial of September 26, 1596. Díaz de Cáceres consistently, even under torture, pleads "negative," which may reflect more on his iron will and commitment to this risky strategy than to his "innocence." Despite the evidence against him, he is able to go free.

37. "Nunca jamás nos comunicamos antes delante de todos nosotros se mostraba el mejor cristiano de la tierra" (LCM II, 362). Cohen brings additional testimonial evidence regarding Díaz de Cáceres's Judaizing in *The Martyr,* 316, n. 65.

38. "Tuvieron pesadumbre con los dichos sus cuñados, que llamaban a éste y a su madre de confesos y que por ellos pierdan honra a causa de la dicha prisión" (LCM I, 66).

39. The stakes were much higher after their first reconciliation to the Church because a lapsed Judaizer was punished with death at the stake. Almeida's long absence from Mexico during this period was certainly another element that created greater pressure on Díaz de Cáceres.

40. Cohen, *The Martyr*, 209, 220.

41. Ibid., 221.

42. "Mi yntento no es sino escribir los inmensos benef[ici]os y my[sericordi]as que el señor D[ios] de israel hizo a Josep y toda su g[en]te" (LCMA, 485).

43. "Por que el cuñado viniese para amparo de su mujer y hija le libro" (ibid.).

44. Isabel testified about herself to the Inquisitors after her first arrest. The sessions began on April 14, 1589. Her testimony was preserved as part of the case against her uncle and was printed as part of the trial proceedings against her uncle in Toro, *Los judíos en la Nueva España*, 210–23; henceforth, all references to the governor's trial record will be given as LCG (Luis de Carvajal Gobernador).

Seemingly in an attempt to shield her family from the charge of indoctrinating her, she first points to her deceased husband, Gabriel Herrera, as her teacher. Eventually she identifies her father as the source of her indoctrination into crypto-Judaism. This would still shield her mother from the charge and place the blame on her dead father. Her claim that Doña Guiomar, the wife of the governor, was the first to initiate her into Judaism is hard to believe, and not only because she recants it later. It is also hard to imagine that she could be won over to a completely new religious idea, with all of its danger and consequences, so quickly and by someone whom she just met. However, while some aspects of this encounter between Guiomar and Isabel may be questionable, the description of their time together is very evocative and points perhaps to a formative experience for Isabel. Guiomar would have been a model of piety and tenacity—she retained her crypto-Judaism despite her marriage to the governor. Guiomar also gave Isabel a mission: to convert the governor as well as his friend and trusted assistant Felipe Nuñez. It is possible that this mission built up Isabel's confidence and zeal.

She later states that her parents were the ones who encouraged her to speak to her uncle (LCG, 213). This is a bizarre claim: Why would she implicate her mother who was still alive? And why would her parents want to put her in that situation to begin with?

45. He tried to forget about their encounter but eventually he went to clear his conscience and denounced her to the Inquisitors (Cohen, *The Martyr*, 142–43).

46. "Sin aguardar otra palabra le di un bofetón que dí con ella en el suelo" (LCG, 323).

Isabel's sisters Catalina and Mariana both echo the violence and fury of this encounter in their testimony (ibid., 274–75, 277).

47. Ibid., 217.

48. According to Isabel, Guiomar is too afraid of her husband's rage to raise the issue of Judaism with him. Why Isabel would be more suited for this confrontation is not discussed.

Using Isabel and the governor's confessions to reconstruct the scene is problematic because both are committed to a particular juridical end: to get the lightest sentence possible. Within the context of this trial, the governor is interested in showing his zealous reaction to Isabel's heresy. He may not have reported her to the Inquisition, but he took care of the issue on his own by laying down a firm line. Isabel actually also bolsters this line of defense, describing his deep Catholicism and staunch rejection of Judaism. In this she has no real ulterior motive. Isabel wants to give as complete a confession as necessary in order to be deemed "contrite and repentant." At the same time she would prefer not to incriminate any living relatives.

Originally, Isabel claims that the idea to try to convert Nuñez and the governor came from Doña Guiomar. Later she recants and points to her parents as the initiators of this plan (LCG,

223). It is unclear why she would switch her story and incriminate her mother, unless she sensed that her mother had already confessed to that crime.

49. "En casa de la dicha Doña Ysabel guardaron y celebraron la pascua del cordero el viernes en guarda y observancia de la ley de Moysén y por ceremonia comieron pan cenceño sin levadura y gallinas cojidas y asadas y la guardaron en memoria que Dios libro el pueblo de Israel del cautiverio de Egipto" (*Segundo proceso de Isabel de Carvajal*, mss. 95/96, 4: 358v). This description comes from the record of Isabel's second trial transcribed from the original manuscript by Emily Sarah Colbert. I thank her for sharing this material here and for her advice, especially in connection with Isabel's case. For a full treatment of this trial see Colbert, *The Other Sephardic Diaspora*, 24.

50. While the biblical Sarah is a powerful figure in the Genesis story, she is rarely held up as a figure associated with the redemption of the Jewish people. The conflating and compounding of biblical personae and their possible symbolic significance is quite common among post-expulsion crypto-Jews.

51. "Dixo que porque entiende que es para la dicha doña Isabel, es porque sabe leer, porque las demás no saben leer letra tirada, y que aunque dize en el papel, que se embía a las demás, no save con que fin lo hiziesse porque como dicho tiene no saben leer" (*Segundo proceso de Isabel de Carvajal*, mss. 95/96, 3:187v).

52. As quoted in Colbert, *The Other Sephardic Diaspora*, 42.

53. "Su hermana viuda, la cual fue acusada de un herege aunque de nra. Nación a quien ella un año antes abia intentado enseñar la verdad diuina" (LCMA 473–74). The reference to Nuñez as "a heretic but of our Nation" reveals the complexity of converso identity: Nuñez is a member of the nation, but he is outside the community of believers. Nonetheless, his ethnic connection to the community of believers places him within the circle of intimates who are concerned for his soul, and thus Isabel feels compelled to "enlighten" him, in a way that she would not feel toward an Old Christian.

54. Baltasar is the only one who could be considered a peer throughout the *Vida*, and yet it is clear that Luis is "first among equals" in that relationship: He is the first to circumcise himself; he leads the theological debate with Gaspar; after Isabel's arrest he returns to Mexico City to check on his mother while Baltasar stays behind at the safe house in the countryside.

55. Cohen, "Antonio Díaz De Cáceres," 190.

56. "Particularmente enemiga de los ydolos e ydolatrias," "otra hermana del pueblo ysraelitico y del sr. temerosa." "otra hermana del pueblo ysraelitico y del sr. temerosa" (LCMA, 487). This is a reference to Justa Mendez, one of the more active Mexican crypto-Jews, whose family was very close with the Carvajal. She is another figure who barely registers in the *Vida* but who was a regular presence within the Carvajal family's orbit. It appears that Luis and Justa even had a possible romantic connection (Cohen, *The Martyr*, 209–11). It is unclear why Luis would leave out Justa and Isabel from the *Vida* considering their piety and commitment as reflected in the trial records. As already stated regarding the elision of Isabel from the autobiography, there is an unease with strong females like Isabel and Justa. Luis could hold up his mother as a saintly matriarch, endowed with the spirit of prophecy, but to share the stage with two spiritually dynamic women might have been too destabilizing for his self-image as the family's spiritual leader. This, however, is not only an issue of gender. As noted earlier in the chapter, he also diminishes his father's role in the *Vida* as compared with the inquisitorial record. That narrative choice reflects a related but distinct psychological dynamic.

57. LCMA, 487.

58. Ibid., 488. Regardless of Luis's deep rejection of Catholicism, the classic New Testament story of the miracle of the loaves would have been subliminally in the literary air he breathed.

59. "Mas ni entonces falto a la paciente enferma el divino consuelo y reparo por que fue el sr. seguido de abrir el entendimiento a su hermana la que caso con jorge de ameyda para que le entendiese todo quanto hablaba y ansi el medico y el cirujano y todos los demás se servian della como de interprete para entender a la enferma a quien sano la infinita mya. De sr. D." (ibid., 493).

60. "De dia y de noche habla sin sesar y a buelta de pocos disparates de locura dize muchas verdades descubiertas" (ibid., 494).

61. Cohen, "Antonio Díaz De Cáceres," 222–23.

62. For in-depth studies of the connection between madness, religious enlightenment, and heresy, see Richard Kagan's *Lucrecia's Dreams*, as well as Sarah Nalle's *Mad for God*.

63. Cohen, "Antonio Díaz De Cáceres," 180, 197.

64. "Venido a la compañia de su madre y hermanas hallo que por los grandes miedos que los enemigos les ponian y por consejo malo de algunos amigos, compraban y comian de los manjares que las gres. por la ley de D. vedados, lo qual estorbo Joseph" (LCMA, 480).

65. "Con el favor divino poniendoles por delante el exemplo de los s[an]tos que antes consintieron ser hechos pedazos que en los crueles tormentos que comer cosas vedadas por el sr. ni aun fingir que la comian y como los corazones estaban con su D. y sr.aunque por el temor hazian estas cosas, fue poco menester para estobarles, porque con muchas lagrimas y temor se convirtieron a su D. y sr. y deshecharon todas estas inmundincias y comidas lo que fue pa[ra] su bien" (ibid.).

66. For one notable example of this trope, see Santa Teresa de Avila's protestations of ignorance, simplicity, and unworthiness in her introduction to the *Libro de la Vida*. For a wider discussion of this phenomenon, see Electa Arenal, Stacey Schlau, and Amanda Powell's collection of testimonials written by Mexican nuns from the colonial period, *Untold Sisters*. Also of interest is Josefina Ludmer's "Tricks of the Weak"/Tretas del debil, which analyzes the seventeenth-century Mexican poet and philospher Sor Juana Inés de la Cruz's rhetorical declarations of her indignity and foolishness as she defends her right to pursue her scientific and philosophical inquiries.

67. Just to point to a few examples from outside his family: In his testimony against Luis and his family, Manuel de Lucena offers an intimate portrait of the Carvajal's prayer rituals. He describes hearing them sing psalms late into the night, between the hours of ten and eleven, with Luis leading the prayers and his sisters responding. Many of the witnesses against Luis describe meeting him at Tlaltelolco, where he would show them textual discoveries vindicating another aspect of Judaism. Luis himself seemingly regales the Inquisitors with his accounts of celebrating and often leading Passover and Yom Kippur celebrations with fellow Judaizers throughout Mexico.

68. "y la verdad es: que habrá de un año poco más o menos que su hermano de ésta, Luis de Carvajal, le dijo a ésta y le preguntó si se había apartado de la Ley de Moisén, y respondiéndole ésta que sí, le dijo el dicho Luis de Cravajal, su hermano: no hagas tal ni creas en la Ley de Jesucristo, porque es cosa de burla, sino solamente cree en la Ley de Moisén" (LCM II, 193).

69. It should be noted that to a great extent the practices and beliefs she recounts echo the phrasing and content of the inquisitorial edicts of grace. Leonor's testimony conforms to the ways that the Inquisitors themselves imagined conversos Judaized and not the actual practices of normative Judaism of the early modern period. This might reflect her desire to tell the Inquisitors what they expected to hear in order to be treated by the Holy Office as a true penitent who is able to give a full account of her sins. This might also indicate to what extent crypto-Jewish practices were a sort of inverted mirror of their oppressors' own projections. Without access to normative Jewish models, many conversos would latch onto the version of Judaism

that the Inquisitors themselves crafted. What is of most interest in the following analysis is how she describes the interactions between the different members of her family and the leadership roles they take on within their family unit.

70. LCM II, 293–94.

71. "Como ésta los guardaba antes que fuera reconciliada" (ibid., 194).

72. "y ésta por la persuación del dicho su hermano Luis de Carvajal, de un año a ésta parte que pasó con él lo que tiene dicho, se determinó ésta de dejar la Ley de Jesucristo y pasarse a la dicha Ley de Moisén" (ibid.).

73. "El verdadero mesías que había de venir era el Anticristo que dicen los cristianos, el cual había de congregar el pueblo de Israel, que andaba desparcido y sacarlo del cuativerio y cárceles, y llevarlo al Monte de Sinaí donde les había de dar palmas y coronas por haber guardado la Ley de Moisén" (ibid.).

74. This eschatology is reminiscent of the converso messianism analyzed by Renée Melammed in her *Heretics or Daughters of Israel*, 45–72.

75. LCM II, 195–204.

76. "Salmos de David en romance que él había sacado de la Biblia que estaba en el colegio de Santiago de Tlaltilulco" (ibid., 195).

77. "Cantaba el dicho Luis de Carvajal a ésta y las dichas su madre . . . sus hermanas" (ibid., 199).

78. "Iban respondiendo porque también la saben de memoria" (ibid.).

79. "A sus hermanos, que están Judaizando fuera de los reinos de Su Majestad" (ibid., 204). It is not clear to which book Leonor is referring in this instance. The *Vida* does mention Leonor, referring to her as the wife of Jorge de Almeida, and notes her piety, but by no means would one consider the entire book about Leonor. The "book" that she is referring to might be a different text that Luis produced and that was passed around as an inspirational text for other crypto-Jews.

80. "y ésta tomaba el dicho libro algunas veces para leer en él, y lo mismo hacía la dicha doña Isabel, su hermana" (ibid., 205).

81. "Mediante sus méritos, usaba Dios de milagros con ellos" (ibid., 204).

82. "Llamaba de santa y de bendita martir y a quien reconocia por una grande sierva del Señor y asi el dicho Luis de Carvajal la animaba por billetes que le enviaba desde su cárcel, metidos en plátanos" (ibid.).

83. "Estuviese fuerte para padecer el martirio por Dios, y pidiéndole albricias de que con brevedad había de gozar de la gloria teniéndola por santa y celebrándola como tal" (ibid.).

84. Regarding this aspect of inquisitorial protocol, see Boleslao Lewin and others in *Confidencias de dos Criptojudíos*, 11–12. Lewin points out that the Mexican tribunal's use of spies was often criticized by the Suprema in Madrid because it was too invasive. Also see Solange Alberro's *Inquisicion y sociedad en México*, 229–35. Diaz, like Ruíz de Luna, was imprisoned on light charges. However, these would have been enough for the Inquisitors to use as pressure to force him into spying.

85. "Para conocerlos y amarlos como a hermanos" (LCM II, 164).

86. "Me diréis quién son tus hermanos . . . [?]" (ibid., 165).

87. "Donde tenía yo mi juicio cuando os descubrí mi pecho" (ibid., 157).

88. "y diciendole éste que él era su hermano" (ibid.).

89. At a certain, point his interrogations took place within the torture chamber itself.

90. Zemon Davis, "Fame and Secrecy," 50–72.

4. Writing His Way into the Jewish People

1. Cardoso's autobiography has certain key points of dissonance with the version of his life and experiences that Cardoso presented to the Inquisitors during his two trials before the Lisbon tribunal in 1608–9 and 1610–11. H. P. Salomon identified the trial records and connected Cardoso to several important individuals in the Dias Milão family as part of his study, *A Portrait of a New Christian*. I would like to thank Professor Salomon for first alerting me to the existence of this trial record. I would like to also thank Dr. José Alberto Rodrigues da Silva Tavim for helping me gain digital access to this precious document. Throughout this chapter's analysis I will make reference to those points of dissonance between the *Vida* and the trial testimony with an eye toward understanding what might be at play between these different versions of his life story. I would also like to thank Miriam Bodian for her early suggestion that I look at Cardoso's *Vida* in light of his trial record.

The trial proceedings will be referred to here as CM-PT-TT for the first trial and CM-PT-TT II for the second trial.

2. In her *Dying in the Law of Moses*, Miriam Bodian includes two fascinating cases of Old Christians who embrace the "Law of Moses" while still in Iberian territory: the Portuguese Capuchin monk, Diogo da Asumpção (79–116), and a student of Hebrew at Salamanca, Lope de Vera y Alarcón (153–177). Neither of these individuals was able to join an open Jewish community and neither was ever able to formally convert.

3. Toward the end of Miguel de Barrios's "Relacion de los poetas y escritores Espanoles de la Nacion Judaica Amstelodama," one encounters the name of "Lorenzo Escudero/por otro nombre Abraham Israel/famoso "Peregrino" de Israel." In his critical edition of this short yet invaluable treatise, Mayer Kayserling directs the reader to Lucien Wolf's *The Jews of the Canary Islands*, where Wolf documents an inquisitorial deposition regarding the whereabouts of certain lapsed Catholics living in London. The witness refers to one of these lapsed Catholics by the name of "Escudero." Wolf identifies this Escudero with the "famoso Peregrino" of Barrios's poem, Abraham Israel Peregrino, and refers to an autobiography he reportedly wrote. The identity of the famous *Peregrino*, Lorenzo Escudero, however is more complicated than Wolf had imagined. In fact there were two (not one as most sources believed) Lorenzo Escuderos. One, an entertainer from Andalucía, who despite his known conversion to Judaism, was a beloved comedian at the Spanish governor's court at Antwerp. While the other also converted to Judaism in Amsterdam, this Escudero was not a clown, but a former Cappuchin friar who wrote a polemical tract defending the Mosaic faith, *Fortaleza del Judaismo*. These two men took the Jewish name adopted by yet a third Old Christian convert to Judaism, Manuel Cardoso de Macedo, the author of the *Vida del buenaventurado Abraham Pelengrino*. This Abraham Pelengrino (also spelled "Pelegrino" or "Peregrino" or in its Hebrew equivalent, "Guer") was a Portuguese, not an Andalusian, Old Christian who lived from 1585 to 1652 and spent most of his life wandering the north Atlantic in search of religious truth. This identity game was unraveled by Yosef Kaplan in his "Jewish Proselytes from Portugal in 17th Century Amsterdam."

4. I follow B. Teensma's transcription of the eighteenth-century copy found in the Ets Hayyim collection and published in "La vida del buenaventurado Abraham Pelengrino."

5. "Seu conhesimento" (*Vida*, 6).

6. "Sendo de gente tão apartada delle y de sangue gentílico y aboresido en seus olhos, como diz Malahy cap[ítulo] 1, v[ers]os 2, 3: Y amey a Jahacob, y a Esaf aborrecí" (ibid.).

7. For a history of this evolving typology, see Cohen, "Esau as Symbol in Early Medieval Thought." Also see Louis Ginzburg's monumental *Legends of the Jews*, 254, n. 19.

8. "Sao de huma sepa tão enemiga de seu povo, em tanto extremo como ante elle hé manifesto que era pouco o fogo se fose em sua mão para os acabar" (*Vida*, 6).

9. "Dar grassas a D[eu]s de Israel pellas mizericórdias q[ue] me fez de me trazer a seu conheseminto por meyos tão tresordináarios como estes, pello q[ue] tenho obrigasão contìnuamente de alabá-lo por me tirar de entre meos irmãos e me dar lugar entre seu Povo" (ibid., 15).

10. Friedman, "Jewish Conversion, the Spanish Pure Blood Laws and Reformation." See also Y. H. Yerushalmi's *Assimilation and Racial Anti-Semitism* for a thorough treatment of the racial elements of *limpieza* and the academic disputes surrounding their origins and the nature of their application.

11. Friedman, "Jewish Conversion, the Spanish Pure Blood Laws and Reformation," 16. See also Nirenberg, "Mass Conversion and Genealogical Mentalities."

12. Yerushalmi, *Assimilation and Racial Anti-Semitism*, 17.

13. Kaplan, *An Alternative Path to Modernity*, 56.

14. Clearly the concern with blood and lineage does not have only one source within the early modern Iberian context. David Nirenberg rejects the idea of a "'genetic' transmission" of the concern with blood, lineage, and nobility and its effect on an individual's religious character. He writes that these notions "were the outcome of a specific historical process of conflict in which lineage became a newly meaningful way of thinking about religious identity amongst Christians and Jews alike" ("Mass Conversion and Genealogical Mentalities," 6). To a great extent, by subscribing to the kabbalistic notion of reincarnation, Cardoso figures out a way to free himself from the claim that his Old Christian lineage had on his own religious identity.

15. "Creo ser esta minha alma de algu[m] Israelita mao e profanador da Ley Divina, e o S[enho]r B[endi]to por suas piedades uzou com ella benignamente, metendo-a neste vazo imundo apartado de seus caminhos, para nelle tornar de suas maldades" (*Vida*, 56).

16. On the development of reincarnation in Jewish mystical sources see Gershom G. Scholem, "*Gilgul*," where he charts the widespread acceptance of the idea of transmigration of souls within kabbalistic circles in pre-expulsion Spain and the refinement of the idea among the students of Isaac Luria in Safed in the second half of the sixteenth century. For Scholem, the fact that these mystics were almost entirely the children of Sephardic exiles (Luria being the main exception) was not coincidental to the prominence of transmigration within their theosophy. Scholem writes that "Lurianic Kabbalah placed the Jew in an ineluctable entanglement of transmigrations. These ideas linked an ancient teaching to the conviction of these generations that all things are in exile, that all things must wander and transmigrate in order to prepare, through a combined effort, for redemption" (*Gilgul*, 241).

The Safed school of kabbalah became the dominant influence on kabbalistic activity throughout the early modern period, radiating its ideas throughout the diaspora. While it had its critics within the Spanish and Portuguese community of Amsterdam, Lurianic kabbalah attracted a wide following there. The idea of reincarnation featured quite prominently within the theological discussions surrounding the immortality of the soul,both popular and erudite, which erupted after the public apostasy, excommunication, and eventual suicide of Uriel da Costa in the 1630s. Around 1635 R. Isaac Aboab de Fonseca wrote an unpublished but widely circulated tract entitled *Nishmat Hayim*, in which the transmigration of souls was central to his argument against "eternal damnation." In 1651 Menasseh ben Israel wrote a work by the same name that also made ample use of transmigration in his defense of the divinity of the soul. On the ex-converso context of Aboab's work see Alexander Altman, "Eternality of Punishment." The end of Aboab's tract, cited by Altman, reflects the intellectual landscape informing Cardoso's assertion of his soul's transmigratory past: "This is what our Rabbis, of blessed memory, meant when coining the phrase, 'Though he sinned, he is still an Israelite.' They intended to convey the idea that though he sinned, he was not cut off thereby forever from the tree but remained a Jew; and even if he apostatized from the Lord and chose new gods, he will again be called a Jew as a result of transmigrations and punishments" (19).

Regarding Menasseh's eclectic use of kabbalistic material, see Chajes, *Between Worlds*, chap. 5. Chajes brings out the complexity of Menasseh's intellectual project, which is at once modern—universalistic, ecumenical and empirical—and retrograde—insisting on the reality of demonic possession, witchcraft and sorcery. Chajes's suggestive description of Menasseh's complicated intellectual project as a "'fundamentalist', or perhaps 'Protestant' Jewish response to modernity" (132) is deserving of further inquiry. I am grateful to Professor Chajes for his advice and guidance in these areas of early modern esoterica.

17. "E assy queira Elle conservar-me em a observasão de sua Ley para que assy venha a alcansar a Luz Divina" (*Vida*, 17).

18. This assessment comes from one of the first witnesses who accuse Cardoso of heresy. He recalls a conversation they had previously when Cardoso scandalized him with his newfound protestant radicalism. "Athe agora tive a nossa merce por portugues, Mas ia agora os tem por Ingres" (CM-PT-TT 14).

19. From a note on the outside file of the processo of Cardoso's first trial (ibid.): "Que este mozo se ficao perto de algua porto de mar pella comunicasao que té có os ingreses Seha de ir ao que delle me parece e pella affeicao que lhe Sinto a esta gente."

20. "Me não pareseu bem a secta de meus pais, e vendo a variedade de algumas religoims que ouvia, me não quis resolver a tomar nenhuma athé mais comonicasão e veer qual milhor me contentava" (*Vida*, 7).

21. "Considerey na Escritura, que foy a primeira couza que me meterão na mão depois de ABC" (ibid.).

22. The scribe refers to the location as Tapçon. I want to thank my friend and colleague Will Stenhouse for helping me figure out the actual toponym this referred to.

23. In the *Vida* we hear about a certain Mestre Gordon, "an Englishman who did business on behalf of the Scots" (7). This Gordon is described as having business with Cardoso's father in the dye business. In the trial record we do not see the name "Gordon"; rather, he is referred to as Mestre Escot. Escot is a Hispanicized version of "Scot" or "Scott," which refers either to his origin or to his first name. These appear to be the same person. Cardoso describes him as having some "trato nestas ilhas" ("dealing in these Islands"), referring to the Azores, which explains how Cardoso's father is acquainted with him (CM-PT-TT, 24).

24. CM-PT-TT, 27.

25. "Os naturais das terra forão gostando de me ver continuar na sua cercha e mostrar-me tão zelozo de sua religão, e assy erra estimado delles" (*Vida*, 7).

26. "Com seus filhos e filhas como irmãos, sem haver outra differensa" (ibid.).

27. "Para com isso me ligar mays à constânsia de sua religâo" (ibid.).

28. Cardoso never mentions the fact that Catholicism was officially banned in Elizabethan England. Under the Act of Uniformity of 1559 the Church of England was the only official church and all subjects of the crown were required to attend its services and no others. Elizabeth did not conduct inquisitorial-style investigations into possible heresy; rather she demanded "conformity to the national church." Failure to conform was met with a range of fines and certain disabilities (Zagorin, *Ways of Lying*, 132–33). Catholic foreigners were able to practice in private, as attested by the comment of the Spanish ambassador regarding Cardoso's absence from Mass at his residence. While Cardoso would not have faced outright persecution for keeping faith with his Catholicism, he certainly would have been ostracized or marginalized

by his "popish" allegiances. Omitting this fact from his *Vida* helps bolster Cardoso's self-portrait as a courageous searcher after the truth.

29. "Sua Exelência tivese conta com seus criados e não commigo" (*Vida*, 8).

30. "Athe agora tive a nossa merce por portugues, Mas ia agora os tem por Ingres" (CM-PT-TT, 18). This witness's exact family name is hard to make out from the manuscript; "Castro" seems to be the most probable rendition.

31. Ibid., 20–21.

32. "Manuel Cardoso respndeu que per elle morreira y que ainda qua tornasse as ilhas quando obrigare air a igreia iva por comprimento" (ibid., 20).

33. It is hard to verify the veracity of this testimony. The heretical statements find a clear echo in Cardoso's own self-portrait. In addition he readily confesses to expressing heretical statements and asks forgiveness and help from the Mother Church to come back to the source of his salvation. However, he is not asked about his long-term plans or any sort of deception toward his father. While these issues fall outside of the interest of the Holy Office, they might be relevant to this last encounter between father and son.

34. "Mais nunca tornara" (ibid., 21).

35. See Ephraim Shoham's careful analysis of two examples of adolescent converts in medieval England who end their lives in suicide in his "'Vidam finivit infelicem."

36. This information was compiled by Don Jerónimo Teixeira Cabral, the archbishop of Angra in Sao Miguel in January 1608. Cardoso was first imprisoned in Angra before being transferred to the Lisbon Holy Office (CM-PT-TT, 41–43).

37. "Filho natuaral de Antonio Cardoso y Breatiz Ruiz mulher soltera" (ibid., 41).

38. This document's assurance that Breatiz's family has not a single drop of "Moorish, Jewish or English blood" only solidifies the classic "salt of the earth" image of the poorer Iberian classes who would have had little occasion to have mixed with such foreign elements. Sancho Panza's boasting of his pure blood is a classic literary example of this phenomenon.

39. Sebastián de Covarubias's *Tesoro de la Lengua Castellana o Española* (Barcelona: S. A. Horta, 1943) defines *hijo natural* as "one who is not legitimate but is also not a bastard" ("hijo natural, el que no es legítimo ni tampoco bastardo") (824). This is a child who, while not born in wedlock, was not the result of a forbidden union. Isabel Dos Guimarães Sá, in "Up and Out" (23–24, n. 12), points out the high rates of illegitimate births in Portugal (from 10 to 20 percent in the north), which would indicate that Cardoso's status would not have been seen as problematic.

40. "Filho, as tu ditto alguma couza contra a nossa Santa Fé? Porque aqui está hum precatorio para te prender pella Ynquiz[is]ão, que se for a por ladrão, matador, salteador, te livrara e dera-te meo cavalo e dinhiero, e quando o não tivera, tomara-te às costas, porque assy fazem pais por filhos, e os filhos por pais; mas por couza tocante a Fee yrey 7 légoas a pé para buscar lenha para te queimar" (*Vida*, 8).

41. In the *Vida* Cardoso echoes his father's words as he calls out to God from the boat that would bring him to Lisbon's inquisitorial prison: "S[enho]r, não hé por ladrão nem por maofeitor, hé por buscar o caminho de miña Salvasão" (9). His plea is an inversion of his father's distinction between criminal and theological crimes. Cardoso calls out to his heavenly Father and pleads his case by saying that he did not sin criminally; all he did was search after His path. Even as he writes these lines after several years of living as a practicing Jew in Amsterdam, it is easy to hear in it an allusion to the tragic irony of Jesus being crucified alongside two lowly criminals. It is Cardoso who suffers, like Jesus, for the crime of searching for the true path of salvation.

42. "D[eu]s lhe pague a V[ossa] M[ercê] essa boa vo[n]tade" (ibid., 8).

43. The trial record gives very little information about Cardoso's discussions with the bishop. It consistently recounts the date of his arrest and that he was sent from Sao Miguel to Lisbon for this crime. There is no explicit mention of his family background or a desire to give him a light sentence—or for that matter, Cardoso's bold proclamations of Calvinist faith. That he is consistently given light sentences reflects the Inquisition's more lenient approach to heresies perpetrated by Old Christians.

44. "Lhe respondy como mosso temerário: 'Eu sou Calvino, e Calvino ei-de morer, salvo ouver quem me comvensa com rasoms que me cayão no entendimento'" (*Vida*, 8–9).

45. "Se me apartey da religião de meos pais hé por ver as abominasoins da religião pap[is]ta" (ibid., 9). He goes on to list the basic repertoire of Protestant criticisms of Catholic dogma and practice. In his telling, the Inquisitors are unable to convincingly respond to any of these points.

46. "Eu sou Calvino, e Calvino ei-de morer" (ibid., 8).

47. "Ahy vos tocará o Espírito S[an]to, para que vos convertais ao leyte da Ygreja que mamasteis." (ibid., 12).

48. As is often the case in trials of Portuguese conversos, it is very hard to ascertain the veracity of the accusations of Judaizing. That his children work hard to leave Lisbon in the years following their father's execution at the auto-da-fé of 1609 only proves that they feared being caught in the Inquisition's web a second time. On the other hand, that many of the Dias Milão children move to Northern Europe and become members of open Jewish communities does indicate some awareness of and commitment to Jewish belief and practice. This consciousness, however, might have been inspired by their brush with the Inquisition. Regardless of the veracity of the Inquisitor's accusations, what is of interest to our present discussion is how Cardoso describes this encounter with the booklet listing Dias Milão's "Judaizing crimes."

49. "Libelo de suas culpas," "se havia gente que guardasse aquela religião, porque tudo o que aly estava concordava com a Escritura" (*Vida*, 12). Regarding the attraction of some radical Protestants to Judaism see the collection of essays edited by Muslow and Popkin, *Secret Conversions to Judaism in Early Modern Europe*; and Popkin and Weiner's *Jewish Christians and Christian Jews*. In *The Dutch Revolt*, Geoffrey Parker mentions that many marranos of Antwerp served as an important resource for the Protestant cause in the Low Countries. In addition to providing monetary support, some marranos converted to Calvinism and shared strategies of dissimulation with their fellow "brethren." Parker cautions, however, against seeing too much religious sincerity in these moves, "for many of them [the Marranos] it was no more than a façade for crypto-Judaism. It is significant that few *marranos* became Protestants in 1577–1584 when it was easy but there was no persecution" (60, n. 36). See chapter 2 of the present study for an analysis of Cardoso's conversion within the wider context of Christian religious experimentation in the early modern period.

50. "He deitando-me amanhesi sem hum modo de religião, borando todas as Escrituras e não creher nada dellas, e ter tudo por fábula. Finalmente fiquey libertino formado" (*Vida*, 13).

51. "Disbarates" (ibid.).

52. "Ao seguinte determiney a hir à Meza e desdezir-me por não morer" (ibid., 13).

53. "Desdezir-me" (ibid.).

54. In his second trial two officials from the *escola* testified that they knew Cardoso from his time at the school and were aware that he moved into the Santa Marinha neighborhood. They do not explicitly vouch for his piety, but they do not say anything to contradict it. Their main focus is on Cardoso's close relationship with Fernão Lopes and his mother. They describe Cardoso as a servant of this family and their acquaintants, setting their table and preparing

their meals. See the testimonies of Jorge DaCosta, the director (*alcalde*) of the school and Antonio de Ruiz, a former guard, in CM-PT-TT II, 50–54.

55. We have seen the "edifying" nature of inquisitorial prisons already in the case of Montezinos and Luis de Carvajal. I am currently working on a project analyzing Inquisitorial prisons as sites of cross-cultural encounter and enlightenment.

56. "E nunca aqueitando com o juizo me chegava a algumas pessoas que me paresião, y lhes preguntava: 'Porquê vos prenderão?' e dizendo-me por Judeu lhe tornava a preguntar se o avia sido. Se me dezia que sy. Tirá-lla delle couza era, y dizendo-mo tomava dahy o que me paresia" (*Vida*, 14).

57. "Fuy com presuposto de guardar o Sabat e yr pouco a pouco tomando nottísia da Ley de Mosseh, porque me pareseu ser a verdadeira, da qual de antes não havia tido nottísia, por cuidar que os Judeos adoravão huma toura, como em caza de meo pay se dezia" (ibid., 13).

58. In his edition of *La vida del buenaventurado Abraham Pelengrino*, Teensma defines the word "Toura" to mean wooden disc or chopping block (30, n. 13). My reading is supported by the straightforward definition found in the *Dicionário du Língua Portuguesa Contemporânea: Academia das Ciências de Lisboa*, 2.2 (Lisbon: Verbo, 2001) and other Portuguese dictionaries. This definition also supports an allusion to the "Golden Calf" implied by word play.

59. "Fuy tomando afeisão à gente da Nasão, e pasar-me a seus trabalhos como própios" (*Vida*, 13).

60. This seems to be a clear allusion to Ruth, the righteous convert, who told her mother-in-law, Naomi, "Wherever you go, there shall I go, and wherever you will sleep, I will sleep, your people are my people and your God my God" (Ruth 1:16). Ruth left the comfort of her homeland to return with her impoverished and widowed mother-in-law to a strange land. Her commitment to Naomi on a personal level was intimately tied to her relationship with Naomi's God.

61. Cardoso writes at the beginning of his narrative that his goal in writing his *Vida* was to record the "meyos tâo estraordinários que el D[eus] B[endi]to teve para me trazer a seu conhesimento, . . . [e] poor memória às calamidades y rodeos com que me troxe a seu serviso" (*Vida*, 6).

62. The proceedings for the second trial began March 5, 1610. The title of the dossier was: "A fugida que fazia Isabel Henriques Milão, Victoria Dias y Manuel Cardoso/The Escape Made by Isabel Henriques Milão / Victoria Dias y Manuel Cardoso," and it was stored, like the first proceedings, at the Archivo Nacional Torre de Tombo, Lisbon. I refer to these records as CM-PT-TT II and all page references are to the pdf page number because the manuscript file is not paginated.

63. CM-PT-TT II, 7–9.

64. Dias's racial identity is somewhat unstable in the trial records. At times she is referred to as *mora* (black) and other times as *india*, which could either refer to East India, meaning the Asian subcontinent or even the spice islands farther east, or to Native Americans. Eventually it is established that this maidservant was born in China and raised in Goa (Salomon, "The 'DePinto' Manuscript," 60, n. 28). This global trajectory is another indicator of the peripatetic and multinational career of this Iberian converso family. There is evidence that this maid eventually embraces Judaism, another indicator of the complex dynamics informing identity in this unstable and fluid context.

65. Thanks to "Google Maps" (https://www.google.com/maps) I was able to verify the location of the church, its proximity to the water, and the approximate distance of about fourteen miles from the church to Belem.

66. CM-PT-TT II, 22–23.

67. "Criado" (ibid., 45).

68. Ibid.

69. He tells the Inquisitors that he was indebted to them and would do whatever they asked of him: "por obrigacao que lhe tinha" (ibid.).

70. Ibid., 39.

71. Ibid., 37–38.

72. Ibid., 38.

73. "Lioins arebatadores" (*Vida*, 14).

74. "Se vingarem em não poder condenar a ninguém, que elles não dexaivão de entender a verdade, mas não podião mal fazer, porque em minha boca estava tudo, tiverão-me preso thé outro Auto, sem poderem nunca tirar de mim huma só palavra, no qual sahi solto i livre" (ibid.).

75. "Huma só palavra" (ibid.).

76. The Hebrew *Guer*, or "convert," is also used instead of "Pelegrino" in other documents.

77. Drawing on Hermann Kellenbenz's *Sephardim an der unteren Elbe*, Teensma documents the background to this murder (*Vida*, 31–32, n. 15) and he states that Abensur, alias Paulo de Milão, alias Paul Dirichesen, was the brother-in-law of the Hamburg-based sugar importer Álvaro Dinis. Abensur set up a sugar operation in Danzig in 1613 and remained there until this incident in 1617, the same year he hired Cardoso, his father's former cellmate. Abensur's hot temper and abusive treatment of his servants was well known. The death of this unfortunate and unnamed mulatto servant is further evidence of his infamous cruelty. It should be noted, however, that the townspeople's violent reaction was not a result of their moral outrage over the death of the servant at the hands of his master. Their fury was brought on because the murder was conveniently cast into the classic template of the blood libel. Cardoso writes that because the murder occurred a few days before the holiday of "Quipur," the people ("o povo") believed that the servant was killed for ritual purposes: "p[ar]a lhe bebermos o sangue em sacrefísio na Páscoa que vinha" (ibid., 14). This mulatto servant and the Abensur's involvement in the Brazilian sugar trade connect Danzig's cold Baltic port with the harsh realties and lucrative economics of the colonized tropics.

78. "Eu lhe dixe que se fosse elle, e que eu ficaria" (ibid., 15).

79. "E assy tomara hum mez antes de Inqizisão q[ue] hum dia de tal prisão. Cada dia cu[i]dava q[ue] sahia a padeser, e já não sentia a morte por estar muy enfadado da vida e cansado de trabalhos" (ibid.).

80. "Consider[a]ndo m[os] dava para provar se estava fixo na Sua Ley, ou não" (ibid.).

81. "E hijos de los estranhos, los ajuntados a A[donay], para servirlo y para amar a nombre de A[donay], para ser a Elle por siervos todo guardando Sabat de abiltarlo tratantes en mi firmamento, traer los he en mi monte de mi santidad, y alegrar-los hé en caza de mi oración, . . . que my caza caza de oración será llamada; dicho de A[donay] Dios a todos los pueblos apanhan empujados de Israel, aun apanharé a él a sus empujados" (ibid.).

Cardoso's translation of this section of Isaiah is based on the Spanish translation "palabra por palabra" of the Ferrara Bible with some minor Lusophonic peculiarities such as "estranhos" instead of "estraños" and "Elle" instead of "Él." Versions of the Ferrara Bible were published both in Italy and in Amsterdam and were widely circulated among the Western Sephardim. Cardoso's translation follows the Hebrew structure of many phrases such as "Hijos de los Estranhos" for בני הנכר, and other "calque" forms that were common in Jewish translations into Spanish. There is a chance that this is Cardoso's own translation from either a Hebrew or an English Bible. Cardoso's command of Hebrew, however, is unknown and thus it is unlikely his own translation. A version of the Ferrara Bible would be the most likely source.

This passage has a special resonance for Cardoso and his fellow Jews living in Amsterdam because it is the designated reading from the Prophets (the *Haftara*) for the "Sabat de contrision que es antes de Quipur," the Sabbath dedicated to repentance between the Jewish New Year and Yom Quipur in the Western Sephardic tradition. As such, this passage would have been familiar to his potential readers and would have made a natural connection to the rhythm of their liturgical life. See the table listing these special readings, "Ordem de las Aphthoras," on the second page of the *Biblia en lengua espanola*. This version is similar to Menasseh ben Israel's revised version of the Ferrara Bible of 1611. I wish to thank Theodor Dunkelgrün and Jesús de Prado Plumed for their illuminating guidance through the thicket of early modern vernacular Bible culture, which led me to consult this version of the Ferrara Bible.

82. "Sangue e sepa" (*Vida*, 6).

83. "My caza caza de oración será llamada; dicho de A[donay] Dios a todos los pueblos" (ibid., 15).

5. "All of Us Are Brothers"

1. See Menasseh's comments in the *Esperanza de Israel*, 41–44. Jonathan Schorsch meticulously traces possible family connections that Montezinos might share with other known conversos from the small town of Villaflor to across the Atlantic world but finds no definitive relationships. Villaflor had a large converso population, and many prominent Amsterdam Jews hailed from this small Portuguese village close to the border with Spain. See *Swimming the Christian Atlantic*, 379–477.

2. All translations are mine unless otherwise noted. For a thorough introduction to the text, along with a seventeenth-century English translation of Montezinos's narrative and Menasseh's treatise, *The Hope of Israel* (referred to as M&N hereafter).

Schorsch adds a new dimension to the question of Montezinos's authorship of the *Relación* in an appendix to his *Swimming the Christian Atlantic*, 505–12. Schorsch tracked down a letter, said to be a direct copy of one penned by Montezinos to a certain Elia Perera in Venice, in which Montezinos elaborates on the details of his experience for this curious Italian Jew. This fascinating document seems to corroborate the basic elements of Montezinos's *Relación* while disclosing some interesting differences. I concur with Schorsch that it cannot definitively prove anything about the text of the *Relación* except the fact that its fixed nature would not preclude Montezinos himself from slightly altering his narrative in a different context. This letter also indicates that Montezinos stood by the basic details of his story and was willing to clarify it to curious and interested readers. Schorsch's extensive archival work and intrepid sleuthing did not, however, locate the original recording of Montezinos's account or the French translation that Dury claims to have received from Menasseh.

3. *Relación*, 1–2.

4. Ibid., 7–9.

5. Thomas Thorowgood, *Iewes in America*; M&N, 64–65.

6. M&N, iv, 46–51, 64.

7. Ibid., 64.

8. "En otro tiempo en España, Antonio de Montezinos" (*Relación*, 1).

9. Ibid., 2–3.

10. Ibid., 42.

11. *Esperanza*, 41.

12. Ibid.

13. Menasseh describes his impoverished state: "He ate up all his wealth with his trip [to Amsterdam], afterwards living in extreme need and poverty because he did not want to eat at anybody else's house, nor did he try to gain any material benefit from his efforts" (ibid., 42).

14. Ibid.; M&-N, 69. Schorsch notes that in the Yiddish version, the names of two witnesses are included at this deathbed confession, the famous Rabbi Isaac Aboab de Fonseca,

who was rabbi of Recife in those years, and the unknown Ya'acob Asher ben Alexander (*Swimming the Christian Atlantic*, 388, n. 37, based on Shlomo Berger, "Ashkenazim Read Sephardim in Seventeenth- and Eighteenth-Century Amsterdam," *Studia Rosenthaliana* 35, 2 [2001]: 261).

15. There is an inquisitorial document which refers to a certain "Antonio de Montessinos, born at Villaflor in the Kingdom of Portugal who concealed himself and fled, was caught in this city with sequestration of goods and locked up in the secret prisons on 3 September 1639, after a testimony of complicity made against a certain Montessinos accused of Judaism: he is suspected of being the same as the man who has been apprehended" (*Archivo Histórico Nacional, Cartagena de las Indias, Inquisición*, folio 49; quoted and translated by Montezinos, "The Narrative of Aharon Levi," 75). Also see M&N, 73–74, and Proodian, *Los Judios en America*.

16. Ortiz, *Los Judeo-conversos en España y América*, 134–42. Also see Silverblatt, "New Christians and New World Fears in Seventeenth-Century Peru."

17. Roth, *A History of the Marranos*, 176.

18. Two exceptions to this pattern are Schmidt, "The Hope of The Netherlands," and Schorsch's *Swimming the Christian Atlantic*, chap. 9. Schorsch appreciates the text's literary nature but also grounds it within its colonial and native context. His linking the text to multiple indigenous discursive practices helps clarify many of the more obscure passages.

19. Zamora, *Reading Columbus*, 7.

20. These issues of genre and authorship are dealt with more extensively in chapter 2 of this study. On the subject of early modern self-writing, see Kagan and Dyer, *Inquisitorial Inquiries*; Amelang, *The Flight of Icarus*; González-Echevarría, "Humanismo" and "The Law of the Letter"; Molloy, *At Face Value*, 3.

21. Natalie Zemon Davis rejects the idea that the "interestedness" of premodern autobiographic texts precluded any development of consciousness. She writes, "Certain forms of embeddedness and most especially in the family could assist in consciousness of self. Not only were kinsfolk imagined as the audience for which the life was recorded, but also playing oneself off against different relatives was a major part of self-revelation" ("Fame and Secrecy," 53).

22. He was, however, unique in reporting that he personally met a group of people who themselves claimed to be a lost Israelite tribe. For the wider context of Jewish conceptualization of the Americas and the Americans, see Limor Mintz-Manor's ambitious dissertation, "The Discourse on the New World in Early Modern Jewish Culture," where she develops an extensive analysis of a wide range of Jewish thinkers, from both Europe and the Middle East who deal with the Americas. Her bibliography is exhaustive and very useful.

23. See Grafton, *New Worlds*; Elliott, *The Old World and New*; Greenblatt, *Marvelous Possessions*; Popkin, "The Rise and Fall of the Jewish Indian Theory;" Glaser, *Indians or Jews*; Neher, *Jewish Thought and the Scientific Revolution of the Sixteenth Century*; Neubauer, "Where Are the Ten Tribes?"; Huddleston *The Origins of the American Indians*.

24. M&N, 45–65.

25. "O Messias ainda havia de vir e havia de trazer as doze tribus de Israel" as quoted in Gitlitz, *Secrecy and Deceit*, 106.

26. Ibid.

27. Schorsch finds many suggestive associations between Iberian and Jewish messianic discourses that focus on Reuben as one of the first tribes to begin the ingathering. See Schorsch, *Swimming the Christian Atlantic*, 420–27.

28. "Los Indios enfadados del trabajo del dia, empeçaron a dezir mal de su fortuna, diziendo que esso y mucho mas merecian por sus pecados: a lo que el dicho Indio Francisco,

animandolos dixo, que tuviessen paciencia, que en breve tendrian algun dia de descanço: a esto respondieron, q'[ue] no era justo le tubiessen, pues que trataron tan mal a una gente santa y al mejor del mundo, y que todos los trabajos y inhumanidades que los españoles uzavan con ellos, tenian bien merecidas por esta culpa" (*Relación*, 1–2).

29. "No se avia quexado dellos con mucha parte de lo que devia, por ser gente cruel, Tirana, y de todo inhumana: pero que en breve se veria bien vengado dellos, por via de una gente oculta" (ibid.).

30. "Bendito sea el nombre de Adonay que no me hizo idolatra, barbaro, negro, ni indio, y al decir Indio, se retrató luego diziendo, estos Indios son Hebreos: Mas tornando en si, de Nuevo bolvio a retratarse, diciendo estoy loco, o fuera de juicio? Como puede ser que estos Indios sean hebreos" (ibid., 3).

31. Schorsch traces the history of these prayers and the possible sources for Montezinos's particular version (*Swimming the Christian Atlantic*, 404–7). For a discussion of crypto-Jewish prayer practices among Judeo-conversos in general see Gitlitz, *Secrecy and Deceit*, 443–50. See also Yerushalmi, "Marranos Returning to Judaism in the 17th Century," 202.

32. *Relación*, 3.

33. Shell, *Children of the Earth*, 22. Shell's book is filled with fascinating and provocative explorations of race, nation, and family in a variety of historical and cultural contexts. I believe he sets up a suggestive but overly facile dichotomy between Christian universalism versus Jewish particularism: Christians' seeing "all men as brothers" leads to seeing non-brothers as non-human, whereas Jews are able to see "others" as humans because they acknowledge the special relationship to those of the tribe and the less intimate, yet fully human "stranger."

34. "E como todos somos hermanos, hijos de un padre, E de una madre que se dezian adan y Eva, E como tal hermano n[uest]ro gran Emperador, doliendose de la perdiçion de las animas que son muchas, las que aquellos sus ydolos llevan al ynfierno donde arden a bivas llamas nos Enbio para questo que aya oydo lo rremedia y no adorar aquellos ydolos, ni les sacrifiquen mas yndios ni yndias, pues todos somos hermanos" (Díaz del Castillo, *Historia verdadera de la conquista de la Nueva España*, 275).

35. "Se descubrió con el Indio, diziendole estas palabra. Yo soy Hebreo del tribo de Levi, mi Dio es Adonay, y todo lo demas es engaño" (*Relación*, 4).

36. "Por algunas cosas que me has dicho, me as causado content, y por otra parte, estoy para no darte credito, por cuanto no me sabes dezir, quien fueron tus padres" (ibid.).

37. For some examples see Salomon, "The 'De Pinto' Manuscript," 13.

38. It is an act of extreme audacity that reflects Montezinos's sincere belief in his identification with the Indians. The details of this narrative are as much the product of the assumptions of what was "possible" in the eyes of Montezinos's readers and his transcribers/publishers, as well as himself.

39. "Le dixo el indio, si eres hombre de animo, valor y esfruerço, que te atrevas a yr conmigo, sabras lo que dezeas saber; pero adviertote, que as de yr a pie, as de comer mais tostado, y as de hazer en todo y por todo lo que yo te dixere" (*Relación*, 5).

40. "El dia siguiente, un Lunes, vino a su aposento el Indio diziendole, quita todo quanto tienes en las faltiqueras, calçate estos alpargates, tomas este palo y sigueme. Assi lo hizo, y dexado la capa y espada y todo lo demas que consigo llevava" (ibid., 5–6).

41. This verse from Deuteronomy is the closest approximation to a Jewish credo or catechism; it expresses connection to the nation of Israel and to the belief in one God. Observant Jews traditionally recite it twice daily.

42. Schorsch explores the possible resonances of these nine cryptic messages in *Swimming the Christian Atlantic*, 417–32.

43. *Relación*, 9.

44. Ibid., 7.

45. I borrow this exquisite term from Schorsch's analysis of the *Relación* in his *Swimming the Christian Atlantic*, 414.

46. *Relación*, 11.

47. "Tus hermanos los hijos de Israel, los truxo Dios a esta tierra, haziendo con ellos grandes marravillas, muchos asombros, cosas que si te las digo, no las as de creer y esto me lo dijeron assi mis padres. Venimos los indios a esta tierra, hezimos les Guerra, tratamoslos peor de lo que los Españoles nos tratan" (ibid., 11–12).

48. Schorsch discusses the term *hechizeros* and its regional meaning in *Swimming the Christian Atlantic*, 438–44.

49. "El Dios destos hijos de Israel, es el verdadero dios, todo lo que está escrito en sus piedras, es verdad; al cabo de los tiempos, ellos seran señores de todas las gentes del mundo, vendrá a esta tierra gente que os trayga muchas cosas, y después de estar toda la tierra abastecida, estos hijos de Israel saldran de donde estan, y se enseñorearan de toda la tierra, como era suya antes. Algunos de vosotros que quizierdes ser venturosos, pegaos a ellos" (*Relación*, 12–13).

50. The *Relación* describes how a group of Reubenites crossed the river by canoe, greeted Montezinos by embracing him, and then approached "el Indio Francisco" who "kneeled to his feet, but they [the Reubenites] lifted him up with signs of humanity and affection[se arrojo a s sus pies, pero ellos le levantaron con muestras de humanidad y afficion]" (ibid., 7). There is a clear hierarchy and a real sense of shame or guilt that still hangs over Francisco.

51. "Algun dia nos veras, y no nos conoceras: todos somos hermanos, merced es que Dios nos hizo. Desta tierra no te dé cuydado, que todos los Indios tenemos a nuestro mandado, en acabando con estos Españoles iremos a sacarvos a vos otros del captiverio en que estays, si quisiere Dios que si quererá, que su palabra, no puede faltar" (ibid., 15–16).

52. "Todos somos hermanos" (ibid., 15).

53. In the *Esperanza*, Menasseh argues forcefully against such blurring of the racial distinctions between the Reubenites and their Indian allies (118). For the wider intellectual context of Menasseh's racial views, see Kaplan, *An Alternative Path to Modernity*, 51–77.

54. "Los españoles que habitan en dichas indias, siendo generalmente que los indios proceden de los 10 tribos, pero erran manifiestamente: por q[ue] aun que estos a mi ver, fueron los primeros pobladores, despues, . . . , vinieron nuevas gentes de la India oriental. . . . Estos pues prevaleciendo en fuerças, les hizieron Guerra, con que les fue necessario (como dize nuestro Montezinos) retirarse a lo mas interior y oculto de aquellas regions, por permission divina" (*Esperanza*, 23).

55. He makes a similar argument based on travelers who encountered the lost tribes throughout Africa and Asia. In every case the members of the lost tribe were seen as clearly distinct from their neighbors, both in terms of racial/physiogenetic and cultural characteristics. This was part of Menasseh's larger argument that the lost tribes, even in their dispersion, have maintained their connection to the Torah.

56. This particular description comes from the sixth-century Byzantine historian Procopius, *De Bello Persico*, which was published in Rome in 1509. Menasseh uses a wide and eclectic range of sources to make his arguments—from contemporary travelers such as Pedro Teixeira to biblical and classical texts. See M&N, 130, for the exact citation.

57. "Que en la cara se les echa de ver . . . que estos no son feos y negros, como los *Hunos*, entre los cuales habitan" (*Esperanza*, 56).

58. "Viven con leyes, y policia, a modo de los Romanos, siendo bien governados de su principe" (ibid., 56–57).

59. "No los echan por ahi como hazen los barbaros, y las vezinas gentes, entre las quales biven" (ibid., 57).

158 | Notes to Pages 118–119

60. "Gente blanca, rubia, agigantada, y ricamente vestida, con tunicas y barbas largas" (ibid., 31).

61. Yosef Kaplan has shown how "gente política" carried a distinct sociocultural meaning for the Portuguese Jews of Amsterdam in his "Gente Política." One striking example of how the distinction between barbarous and civilized behavior crept into the details of everyday life can be found in the language of the communal regulation forbidding the use of hammers to drown out the name of Haman. The men of the Mahamad said of this noisy synagogue custom, "It appears more as a practice of barbarians and not of civilized (*política*) people. [Que mais parece acsão de bárbaros que de gente política] (*Livro de Ascamoth* of the Sephardi community of Amsterdam, in the Amsterdam Municipal Archives [GAA], PA 334, no. 19, fol. 143, cited by Kaplan, "Gente Política," 28).

62. "Por lo qual admirados del valor y atrevimiento destos hombres, dejaron la empresa" (*Esperanza*, 31).

63. The image of the lost tribes as fierce, self-sufficient warriors who live off pillaging and warfare is a standard trope found in Eldad Hadani, Benjamin of Tudela, and David Reubeni.

64. "Es esta gente algo tostado del sol, el cabello en algunos les llegava hasta las rodillas, otros le trahian mas corto, otros como se trahe cumunmente en general cortado por parejo, Buenos talles, buenas caras, buen pie, y pierna: en las cabeças un paño al derredor" (*Relación*, 10).

65. "Ellos andan todos desnudos como su madre los parió, y también las mugeres, . . . Muy bien hechos, de muy fermosos cuerpos y muy buenas caras, los cabellos gruesos cuasi como sedas de cola de cavallos e cortos . . . De'ellos se pintan de prieto, y [d']ellos son de color de los canarios, ni negros ni blancos. . . . Ellos todos a una mano son de buena estatura de grandeza y Buenos gestos, bien hechos" (Colón, *Los cuatro viajes*, 62–63). Columbus gives a similar description throughout the diaries. Columbus explains the similarity to the natives of the Caribbean to the Canary Islanders in terms of their shared latitude.

66. Columbus's description of the natives in sociocultural and technological terms resonates less with Montezinos's description. Columbus notes that they have no iron tools or weapons; however, he is impressed with the swiftness of their canoes—"y anda a maravilla" (ibid., 64). He surmises that they would be good servants because they are "de buen ingenio, que veo que presto dizen todo lo que les dezía"—that is, they are intelligent but in a passive and imitative way; they can follow the orders or words of the Spaniard. In the *Relación*, however, the Reubenites are nobody's servants!

67. To some extent, the often semi-naked state of the Amerindians inspired visions of prelapsarian noble savages, guileless childlike beings, impoverished brutes, or demonic monsters. For an overview of these varied and interrelated phenomena, see Jara and Spadaccini, "The Construction of a Colonial Imaginary."

68. *Relación*, 10–11.

69. This detail seems to refer to one of the messages that they give Montezinos regarding their readiness to take on the Spanish. Schorsch posits that this group might have been founded by runaways/renegades who would be good at stealing from the Spanish or at reproducing Spanish agricultural and industrial practices. For a full analysis of how these products fit into a wider matrix of indigenous practices see *Swimming the Christian Atlantic*, 434–35.

70. "No perdonará el Señor la sangre de Israel vertida; assi sera[n] salvos con ellos, aquellos que se negaren de enemigos, y les obligaren con su beningnidad y beneficios" (*Esperanza*, 113–14).

71. "Y bendiziré tus bendizientes, y tus maldizientes, maldizire" (ibid., 114).

Bibliography

Abbreviations of Frequently Cited Sources

CM-PT-TT   Cardoso Macedo's first trial before the Lisbon Inquisition
CM-PT-TT II   Cardoso Macedo's second trial before the Lisbon Inquisition
LCG   Luis de Carvajal, the Governor's trial
LCMA   Luis de Carvajal, *el mozo*/the Younger *Vida*/autobiography
LCM I   Luis de Carvajal the Younger's first trial
LCM II   Luis de Carvajal the Younger's second trial

Primary Sources

Barrios, Miguel de. "Relación de los Poetas y Escritores Espanoles de la Nación Judaica Amstelodama." *Revue d'études Juives* 32 (1896): 281–89.
Ben Israel, Menasseh. *Esperança de Israel*. Amsterdam, 1650. Biblioteca Nacional, Madrid. R 3768—5410 1650.
———. *The Hope of Israel*. Edited by Moses Henry Méchoulan Wall and Gérard Nahon. Translated by George Richenda. Oxford: Oxford University Press, 1987.
———. *Orígen de los Americanos . . . esto es, Esperanza de Israel*. Edited by Santiago Perez Junquera. Madrid: S. Perez Junquera, 1881.
Biblia en dos columnas, Hebrayco y Español. Amsterdam : En casa y a costa de Joseph, Iacob y Abraham de Salomon Proops, A. 5522 [i.e. 1762]
Biblia en lengua Española traduzida palabra por palabra de la verdad Hebrayca por muy excelentes letrados . . . : Con privilegio del . . . duque de Ferrara. Amsterdam, 1630. New York Public Library DM 8479.
Cardozo de Macedo, Manuel. *La Vida del buenaventurado Abraham Pelengrino*. Edited by B. Teensma. *Studia Rosenthaliana* 10 (1976):1–36.
Colón, Cristóbal. *Los cuatro viajes. Testamento*. Edited by Consuelo Varela. Madrid: Alianza, 1986.
Covarrubias Orozco, Sebastián de. *Tesoro de la lengua castellana o española según la impresión de 1611, con las adiciones de Benito Remigio Noydens publicadas en la de 1674*. Barcelona: S. A. Horta, 1943.
Díaz del Castillo, Bernal. *Historia verdadera de la conquista de la Nueva España*. Mexico: Oficina Tipográfica de la Secretaría de Fomento, 1904.
Guamán Poma de Ayala, Felipe. *Nueva coronica y buen gobierno*. Caracas: Biblioteca Ayacucho, 1980.
La vida de Lazarillo de Tormes y de sus fortunas y adversidades. Edited by Germán Bleiberg. Madrid: Alianza, 1980.
Núñez Cabeza de Vaca, Alvar. *Naufragios*. Edited by Juan Francisco Muara. Madrid: Catedra, 1989.

Obregón, Luis González, ed. *Procesos de Luis de Carvajal, el mozo*. México: Talleres gráficos de la nación, 1935. LCMA and LCM I & II.

Ovalle, Alonso de. *Histórica relación del reino de Chile y de la misiones y ministerios que ejercita en él la Compañía De Jesús*. Santiago: Instituto de Literatura Chilena, 1969.

Pereyra de Paiva, Moses. *Relacion delas noticias delos Judios de Cochin*. Amsterdam, 1687.

Processo de Manuel Cardoso. Tribunal do Santo Ofício, Inquisição de Lisboa, Instituto dos Arquivos Nacionais / Arquivo Nacional Torre do Tombo. PT-TT-TSO-IL-28-319 and PT-TT-TSO-IL-28-319-1.

Procopius. *De bello Persico*. Rome: Eucharium Silber, 1509.

Relación de Aharon Levi, alias Antonio de Montezinos. In Menasseh ben Israel, *Esperança de Israel*. Amsterdam, 1650. Biblioteca Nacional, Madrid.

Segundo proceso de Isabel de Carvajal. Bancroft Special Collections, University of California, Berkeley.

Teixeira, Pedro. *Relaciones de Pedro Teixeira d'el origen descendencia y succession de los reyes de Persia, y de Harmuz y de un Viage Hecho Por El Mismo Autor Dende La India Oriental Hasta Italia Por Tierra*. Antwerp: H. Verdussen, 1610.

———. *The Travels of Pedro Teixeira with His "Kings of Harmuz" and Extracts from His "Kings of Persia."* Translated and annotated by William F. Sinclair, with further notes and an introduction by Donald William Ferguson. London: Hakluyt Society, 1902.

Teresa de Avila, Santa. *Libro de la vida*. Edited by Dámaso Chicharro. Madrid: Cátedra, 1997.

Thorowgood, Thomas. *Iewes in America, or, Probabilities That the Americans Are of That Race With the Removall of Some Contrary Reasonings, and Earnest Desires for Effectuall Endeavours to Make Them Christian*. London: T. Slater, 1900 [1650].

Toro, Alfonso de. *Los judíos en la Nueva España*. Mexico: Archivo General de la Nación, 1932. LCG

Torquemada, Juan de. *Monarquía Indiana de los veinte y un libros rituales y Monarquía indiana, con el origen y guerras de los indios occidentales, de sus poblazones, descubrimiento, conquista, conversión y otras cosas maravillosas de la mesma tierra*. Edited by Miguel León-Portilla, Estudio de Fuentes de Tradición Indígena. Mexico: Universidad Nacional Autónoma de México, Instituto de Investigaciones Históricas, 1975–1979.

Wolf, Lucien. *Jews in the Canary Islands: Being a Calendar of Jewish Cases Extracted from the Records of the Canariote Inquisition in the Collection of the Marquess of Bute*. Toronto: University of Toronto Press/Renaissance Society of America, 2001.

Secondary Sources

Academia das Ciências. *Dicionário da língua portuguesa contemporânea da Academia das Ciências de Lisboa, 2 2*. Lisboa: Verbo, 2001.

Alberro, Solange. *Inquisición y sociedad en México, 1571–1700*. México: Fondo de Cultura Económica, 1988.

Altman, Alexander. "Eternality of Punishment: A Theological Controversy within the Amsterdam Rabbinate in the Thirties of the Seventeenth Century." *Proceedings of the American Academy for Jewish Research* 40 (1973): 1–88.

Amelang, James S. *The Flight of Icarus: Artisan Autobiography in Early Modern Europe.* Stanford, CA: Stanford University Press, 1998.

———."The Reformed Spaniards: Tales of Conversion in 1620s London." Paper presented to the S.C. Davis Center, History Department, Princeton University, September 2013.

———. "Tracing Lives: The Spanish Inquisition and the Act of Autobiography." In *Controlling Time and Shaping the Self:Developments in Autobiographical Writing since the Sixteenth Century.* Edited by Arianne Baggerman, Rudolf Dekker, and Michael Mascuch. Leiden: Brill, 2011.

Arenal, Electa, Stacey Schlau, and Amanda Powell. *Untold Sisters: Hispanic Nuns in Their Own Works.* Albuquerque: University of New Mexico Press, 2010.

Baer, Yitzhak F. *A History of the Jews in Christian Spain.* Vol. 2. Philadelphia: Jewish Publication Society, 1992.

Beinart, Haim. *The Expulsion of the Jews from Spain.* Oxford: Littman Library of Jewish Civilization, 2002.

Berger, Shlomo. "Ashkenazim Read Sephardim in Seventeenth- and Eighteenth-Century Amsterdam." *Studia Rosenthaliana* 35, no. 2 (2001): 261.

Bernardini, Paolo, and Norman Fiering. *The Jews and the Expansion of Europe to the West, 1400–1800.* New York: Berghahn, 2000.

Bodian, Miriam. *Dying in the Law of Moses: Crypto-Jewish Martyrdom in the Iberian World.* Bloomington: Indiana University Press, 2007.

———. *Hebrews of the Portuguese Nation: Conversos and Community in Early Modern Amsterdam.* Bloomington: Indiana University Press, 1997.

Boer, Harm den. *La Literatura sefardí de Amsterdam.* Instituto Internacional de Estudios Sefardíes y Andalusíes, Universidad de Alcalá, Servicio de Publicaciones, 1995.

Caro Baroja, Julio. *Los judíos en la España moderna y contemporanea.* Vol. 1. Madrid: Istmo, 2000.

Castro, Américo. *La Realidad histórica de España.* Mexico: Porrua, 1971.

Certeau, Michel de. "Reading as Poaching." In *The Practice of Everyday Life*, translated by Steven I. Rendal. Berkeley: University of California Press, 1984.

Chajes, J. H. "Accounting for the Self: Preliminary Generic-Historical Reflections on Early Modern Jewish Ego Documents." *Jewish Quarterly Review* 95, no. 1 (2005): 1–15.

Cohen, G. D. "Esau as Symbol in Early Medieval Thought." In *Jewish Medieval and Renaissance Studies*, edited by Alexander Altmann. Cambridge, MA: Harvard University Press, 1967.

Cohen, Martin A. "Antonio Díaz de Cáceres: Marrano Adventurer in Colonial Mexico." *American Jewish Historical Quarterly* 60, no. 2 (1973): 169–84.

———. *The Martyr: Luis de Carvajal, a Secret Jew in Sixteenth-Century Mexico.* Albuquerque: University of New Mexico Press, 2001.

Colbert, Emily Sarah. *The Other Sephardic Diaspora: Feminine Representations of Sephardic Identity in the Early Modern Atlantic World.* PhD diss., University of California, Invine, 2012.

Costigan, Lúcia Helena. *Through Cracks in the Wall: Modern Inquisitions and New Christian Letrados in the Iberian Atlantic World.* Leiden: Brill, 2010.

Delany, Paul. *British Autobiography in the Seventeenth Century.* London: Routledge & K. Paul, 1969.

Domínguez Ortiz, Antonio. *Los Judeo-conversos en España y América.* Madrid: Istmo, 1971.

Elliott, J. H. *The Old World and the New, 1492–1650.* Cambridge: Cambridge University Press, 1970.

Friedman, Jerome. "Jewish Conversion, the Spanish Pure Blood Laws and Reformation: A Revisionist View of Racial and Religious Antisemitism." *Sixteenth Century Journal* 18, no. 1 (Spring 1987): 3–29.

Fuente del Pilar, José Javier. "Pedro Teixeira y su viaje por Mesopotamia." *Arbor* 180, nos. 711–12 (2005): 627–43.

García-Arenal, Mercedes, and Gerard Wiegers. *A Man of Three Worlds: Samuel Pallache, a Moroccan Jew in Catholic and Protestant Europe.* Baltimore: Johns Hopkins University Press, 2003.

Gerber, Jane S., and Miriam Bodian. *The Jews in the Caribbean.* Oxford: Littman Library of Jewish Civilization, 2014.

Gitlitz, David M. "Inquisition Confessions and Lazarillo de Tormes." *Hispanic Review* 68 (2000): 53–74.

———. *Secrecy and Deceit: The Religion of the Crypto-Jews.* Philadelphia: Jewish Publication Society, 1996.

Glaser, Lynn. *Indians or Jews? An Introduction to a Reprint of Manasseh Ben Israel's The Hope of Israel.* Gilroy, CA: R.V. Boswell, 1973.

González Echevarría, Roberto. "Humanismo, retórica y las crónicas de la conquista." In *Isla a su vuelo fugitiva: Ensayos críticos sobre literatura hispanoamericana.* Madrid: J. P. Turanzas, 1983.

———. "The Law of the Letter: Garcilaso's *Commentaries* and Origins of the Latin American Narrative." *Yale Journal of Criticism* 1 (Fall, 1987): 107–31.

———. *Myth and Archive: A Theory of Latin American Narrative.* Cambridge: Cambridge University Press, 1990.

Graff-Zivin, Erin. *Figurative Inquisitions: Conversion, Torture, and Truth in the Luso-Hispanic Atlantic.* Evanston, IL: Northwestern University Press, 2014.

Grafton, Anthony, April Shelford, and Nancy G. Siraisi. *New Worlds, Ancient Texts: The Power of Tradition and the Shock of Discovery.* Cambridge, MA: Belknap Press of Harvard University Press, 1992.

Graizbord, David. "Converso Children under the Inquisitorial Microscope in the Seventeenth Century: What May the Sources Tell Us about Their Lives?" In *Childhood in the Middle Ages and the Renaissance,* edited by Albrect Classen. Berlin, New York: Walter De Gruyter, 2005.

———. *Souls in Dispute: Converso Identities in Iberia and the Jewish Diaspora, 1580–1700.* Philadelphia: University of Pennsylvania Press, 2004.

Greenblatt, Stephen. *Marvelous Possessions: The Wonder of the New World.* Chicago: University of Chicago Press, 1991.

Gutwirth, Eliezer. "Towards Expulsion: 1391–1492." In *Spain and the Jews: The Sephardi Experience: 1492 and After,* edited by Elie Kedourie. London: Thames and Hudson, 1992.

Herculano, Alexandre. *History of the Origin and Establishment of the Inquisition in Portugal*. New York: AMS Press, 1968.

Herpoel, Sonja. *A la zaga de Santa Teresa: Autobiografías por mandato*. Amsterdam: Rodopi, 1999.

Huddleston, L. E. *The Origins of the American Indians: European Perspectives*. Austin: University of Texas Press, 1967.

Israel, Jonathan I. *Diasporas within a Diaspora: Jews, Crypto-Jews, and the World of Maritime Empires (1540–1740)*. Boston: Brill, 2002.

———. *European Jewry in the Age of Mercantilism, 1550–1750*. London: Littman Library of Jewish Civilization, 1998.

Jara, René, and Nicholas Spadaccini. "The Construction of a Colonial Imaginary: Columbus' Signature." In *Amerindian Images and the Legacy of Columbus*, Vol. 9, edited by René Jara and Nicholas Spadaccini. Minneapolis: University of Minnesota Press, 1992.

Kagan, Richard L. *Lucrecia's Dreams: Politics and Prophecy in Sixteenth-Century Spain*. Berkeley: University of California Press, 1990.

Kagan, Richard L., and Abigail Dyer. *Inquisitorial Inquiries: Brief Lives of Secret Jews and Other Heretics*. Baltimore: Johns Hopkins University Press, 2004.

Kagan, Richard L., and Philip D. Morgan. *Atlantic Diasporas: Jews, Conversos, and Crypto-Jews in the Age of Mercantilism, 1500–1800*. Baltimore: Johns Hopkins University Press, 2009.

Kamen, Henry. "The Mediterranean and the Expulsion of the Spanish Jews in 1492." *Past and Present* 119 (1988): 30–55.

Kaplan, Debra. "The Self in Social Context: Asher ha-Levi of Reichshofen's 'Sefer Zikhronot'." *Jewish Quarterly Review* 97, no. 2 (2007): 210–36.

Kaplan, Yosef. *An Alternative Path to Modernity: The Sephardi Diaspora in Western Europe*. Leiden: Brill, 2000.

———. "Amsterdam, the Forbidden Lands and the Dynamics of the Sephardi Diaspora." In *The Dutch Intersection the Jews and the Netherlands in Modern History*, edited by Yosef Kaplan. Leiden: Brill, 2008.

———. *From Christianity to Judaism: The Story of Isaac Orobio de Castro*. Oxford: Oxford University Press, 1989.

———. "Gente Política: The Portuguese Jews of Amsterdam vis-à-vis Dutch Society." In *Dutch Jews as Perceived by Themselves and by Others: Proceedings of the Eighth International Symposium on the History of the Jews in the Netherlands*, edited by Chaya Brasz and Yosef Kaplan. Leiden: Brill, 2001.

———. "The Travels of Portuguese Jews from Amsterdam to the 'Lands of Idolatry' (1644–1724)." In *Jews and Conversos: Studies in Society and the Inquisition: Proceedings of the Eighth World Congress of Jewish Studies held at the Hebrew University of Jerusalem, August 16–21, 1981*. Edited by Yosef Kaplan. Jerusalem: Magnes Press, 1985.

Kayserling, Mayer. "The Jews in Jamaica and Daniel Israel Lopez Laguna." *Jewish Quarterly Review* 12, no. 4 (July 1900): 708–17.

Kellenbenz, Hermann. *Sephardim an der unteren Elbe, ihre wirtschaftliche und politische Bedeutung vom Ende des 16. bis zum Beginn des 18. Jahrhunderts*. Wiesbaden: F. Steiner, 1958.

Leibman, Laura. "Poetics of the Apocalypse: Messianism in Early Jewish American Poetry." *Studies in American Jewish Literature* 33, no. 1 (2014): 35–62.

Lewin, Boleslao Gaspar de Alfar, Juan de León, and Francisco Botello. *Confidencias de dos criptojudíos en las cárceles del Santo Oficio, México, 1645–1646.* Buenos Aires: Talleres Gráficos Julio Kaufman, 1975.

Lieberman, Julia Rebollo. *Sephardi Family Life in the Early Modern Diaspora.* Waltham, MA: Brandeis University Press, 2011.

Liebman, Seymour B. *The Enlightened: The Writings of Luis de Carvajal, el Mozo.* Coral Gables, FL: University of Miami Press, 1967.

———. *The Jews in New Spain: Faith, Flame, and the Inquisition.* Coral Gables, FL: University of Miami Press, 1970.

Ludmer, Josefina. "Tricks of the Weak/Tretas del debil." In *Feminist Perspectives on Sor Juana Inés De La Cruz*, edited by Stephanie Merrim. Detroit, MI: Wayne State University Press, 1991.

Malkiel, Yakov. "Hispano-Arabic Marrano and Its Hispano-Latin Homophone." *Journal of the American Oriental Society* 68, no. 4 (1948): 175–84.

Martínez, María Elena. *Genealogical Fictions: Limpieza De Sangre, Religion, and Gender in Colonial Mexico.* Stanford, CA: Stanford University Press, 2008.

Martínez, María Elena, David Nirenberg, and Max-Sebastián Hering Torres. *Race and Blood in the Iberian World.* Berlin: Lit, 2012.

Melammed, Renée Levine. *Heretics or Daughters of Israel? The Crypto-Jewish Women of Castile.* New York: Oxford University Press, 1999.

Mintz-Manor, Limor. "Discourse on the New World in Early Modern Jewish Culture" (Hebrew). PhD diss., Hebrew University, 2011.

Molloy, Sylvia. *At Face Value: Autobiographical Writing in Spanish America.* Cambridge: Cambridge University Press, 1991.

Montezinos, Elizabeth Levi de. "The Narrative of Aharon Levi, alias Antonio de Montezinos." *American Sephardi* 7–8 (1975): 75.

Moriana, Antonio Gómez. "Autobiografía y discurso ritual: Problemática de la confesión autobiográfica destinada al tribunal inquisitorial." *Inprevue* 1 (1983): 107–27.

Mulsow, Martin, and Richard H. Popkin. *Secret Conversions to Judaism in Early Modern Europe.* Leiden: Brill, 2004.

Nalle, Sara Tilghman. *Mad for God: Bartolomé Sánchez, the Secret Messiah of Cardenete.* Charlottesville: University Press of Virginia, 2001.

Neher, André. *Jewish Thought and the Scientific Revolution of the Sixteenth Century: David Gans (1541–1613) and His Times.* Translated by David Maisel. Oxford: Littman Library/Oxford University Press, 1986.

Netanyahu, Benzion. "The Marranos according to the Hebrew Sources of the 15th and Early 16th Centuries." *Proceedings of the American Academy for Jewish Research* 31 (1963): 81–164.

Neubauer, A. "Where Are the Ten Tribes?" *Jewish Quarterly Review* 1 (1899): 14–19.

Nirenberg, David. "Mass Conversion and Genealogical Mentalities: Jews and Christians in Fifteenth-Century Spain." *Past and Present* 174 (2002): 3–41.

Parker, Geoffrey. *The Dutch Revolt.* Ithaca, NY: Cornell University Press, 1977.

Perelis, Ronnie. "Daniel Israel Lopez Laguna's *Espejo Fiel de Vidas* (London 1720) and the Ghost of Marrano Autobiography." In *The Jews in the Caribbean*, edited by

Jane S. Gerber and Miriam Bodian. Oxford: Littman Library of Jewish Civilization, 2014.

———. "Marrano Autobiography in Its Transatlantic Context: Exile, Exploration and Spiritual Discovery." PhD diss., New York University, 2006.

Popkin, Richard H. "The Rise and Fall of the Jewish Indian Theory." In *Menasseh Ben Israel and His World*, edited by Yosef Kaplan, Henry Méchoulan, and Richard Popkin. Leiden: Brill, 1989.

Popkin, Richard H., and Gordon M. Weiner. *Jewish Christians and Christian Jews: From the Renaissance to the Enlightenment.* Dordrecht: Kluwer Academic Publishers, 1994.

Proodian, Lucía García de. *Los Judios en America. Sus actividades en los Virreinatos de Nueva Castilla y Nueva Granada s. XVII., etc.* Madrid: Instituto Arias Montano, 1966.

Rico, Francisco. "Los orígenes de 'Fontefrida' y el primer romancero trovadoresco." In *Texto y contextos: Estudios sobre la poesía española del siglo XV.* Barcelona: Editorial Crítica, 1990. http://www.cervantesvirtual.com/obra/texto-y-contextos -estudios-sobre-la-poesia-espanola-del-siglo-xv--0/.

Ross, Kathleen. "Cuestiones de género en Infortunios de Alonso Ramírez." *Revista Iberoamericana* 62, nos. 172–73 (1995): 596.

Roth, Cecil. *A History of the Marranos.* Philadelphia: Jewish Publication Society of America, 1960.

Sá, Isabel dos Guimarães. "Up and Out: Children in Portugal and the Empire (1500–1800)." In *Raising an Empire: Children in Early Modern Iberia and Colonial Latin America*, edited by Ondina E. González and Bianca Premo. Albuquerque: University of New Mexico Press, 2007.

Salomon, H. P. "The 'DePinto' Manuscript: A 17th Century Marrano Family History." *Studia Rosenthaliana* 9 (1975): 1–62.

———. *Portrait of a New Christian: Fernâo Álvares Melo, 1569–1632.* Paris: Fundaçâo Calouste Gulbenkian, 1982.

Sánchez Rubio, Rocío, Isabel Testón Núñez, and Antonio Domínguez Ortiz, eds. *El hilo que une: las relaciones epistolares en el Viejo y en el Nuevo Mundo, siglos XVI–XVIII.* Cáceres: Universidad de Extremadura, 1999.

Saraiva, José António. *The Marrano Factory: The Portuguese Inquisition and Its New Christians, 1536–1765.* Edited by H. P. Salomon and I. S. D. Sassoon. Leiden: Brill, 2001.

Schmidt, Benjamin. "The Hope of The Netherlands: Menasseh Ben Israel and the Dutch Idea of America." In *The Jews and the Expansion of Europe to the West, 1450–1800*, edited by Paolo Bernardini and Norman Fiering. New York: Berghahn, 2000.

Scholberg, Kenneth R. "Teixeira, Pedro." In *Encyclopedia Judaica*, edited by Michael Berenbaum and Fred Skolnik. Detroit, MI: Macmillan Reference, 2007.

Scholem, Gershom, "Gilgul: The Transmigration of Souls." In *On the Mystical Shape of the Godhead: Basic Concepts in the Kabbalah*, translated by Joachim Neugroschel and edited by Jonathan Chipman. New York: Schocken, 1991.

Schorsch, Jonathan. "American Jewish Historians, Colonial Jews and Blacks, and the Limits of *Wissenschaft*: A Critical Review." *Jewish Social Studies* 6, no. 2 (2000): 102–32.

———."Mosseh Pereyra de Paiva: An Amsterdam Portuguese Jewish Merchant Abroad in the Seventeenth Century." In *The Dutch Intersection: The Jews and the Netherlands in Modern History*, edited by Yosef Kaplan. Leiden: Brill, 2007.

———. *Swimming the Christian Atlantic: Judeoconversos, Afroiberians and Amerindians in the Seventeenth Century*. Leiden: Brill, 2009.

Shell, Marc. *Children of the Earth: Literature, Politics, and Nationhood*. New York: Oxford University Press, 1993.

Shoham, Ephraim "'Vitam Finivit Infelicem': Madness Conversion and Adolescent Suicide among Jews in Late Twelfth Century England." In *"Slay Them Not": Jews in Medieval Christendom*, edited by Kristine T. Utterback and Merrall L. Price. Leiden: Brill, 2013.

Sicroff, Albert A. *Los estatutos de Limpieza de Sangre: controversias entre los siglos XV y XVII*. Madrid: Taurus, 1985.

Silverblatt, Irene. "New Christians and New World Fears in Seventeenth-Century Peru." *Comparative Studies in Society and History* 42, no. 3 (July 2000), 524–46.

Soyer, François. *The Persecution of the Jews and Muslims of Portugal: King Manuel I and the End of Religious Tolerance (1496–7)*. Leiden: Brill, 2007.

Stuczynski, Claude B. "Harmonizing Identities: The Problem of the Integration of the Portuguese Conversos in Early Modern Iberian Corporate Polities." *Jewish History* 25, no. 2 (2011): 229–57.

Studnicki-Gizbert, Daviken. "La Nación among the Nations." In *Atlantic Diasporas: Jews, Conversos, and Crypto-Jews in the Age of Mercantilism, 1500–1800*, edited by Richard L Kagan and Philip D. Morgan. Baltimore: Johns Hopkins University Press, 2009.

———. *A Nation upon the Ocean Sea: Portugal's Atlantic Diaspora and the Crisis of the Spanish Empire, 1492–1640*. Oxford: Oxford University Press, 2007.

Swetschinski, Daniel M. *Reluctant Cosmopolitans: The Portuguese Jews of Seventeenth-Century Amsterdam*. London: Littman Library of Jewish Civilization, 2000.

Temkin, Samuel. *Luis de Carvajal: The Origins of Nuevo Reino De León*. Santa Fe, NM: Sunstone Press, 2011.

Todorov, Tzvetan. *The Conquest of America: The Question of the Other*. Norman: University of Oklahoma Press, 1999.

Toro, Alfonso de. *La familia Carvajal: Estudio histórico sobre los judíos y la Inquisición de la Nueva España*. México: Patria, 1944.

Trivellato, Francesca. *The Familiarity of Strangers: The Sephardic Diaspora, Livorno, and Cross-Cultural Trade in the Early Modern Period*. New Haven, CT: Yale University Press, 2009

Yerushalmi, Yosef Hayim. *Assimilation and Racial Anti-Semitism: The Iberian and the German Models*. New York: Leo Baeck Institute, 1982.

———. *From Spanish Court to Italian Ghetto: Isaac Cardoso, A Study in Seventeenth-Century Marranism and Jewish Apologetics*. New York: Columbia University Press, 1971.

———. "Marranos Returning to Judaism in the 17th Century: Their Jewish Knowledge and Psychological Readiness." In *Proceedings of the Fifth World Congress of Jewish Studies, the Hebrew University*. Jerusalem: World Union of Jewish Studies, 1969.

Yuval, Israel Jacob. *Two Nations in Your Womb: Perceptions of Jews and Christians in Late Antiquity and the Middle Ages*. Translated by Barbara Harshav and Jonathan Chipman. Berkeley: University of California Press, 2006.

Zagorin, Perez. *Ways of Lying: Dissimulation, Persecution and Conformity in Early Modern Europe.* Cambridge, MA: Harvard University Press, 1990.

Zamora, Margarita. *Reading Columbus.* Berkeley: University of California Press, 1993.

Zemon Davis, Natalie. "Fame and Secrecy: Leon Modena's Life as an Early Modern Autobiography." In *The Autobiography of a Seventeenth-Century Venetian Rabbi: Leon Modena's Life of Judah*, edited by Marc. R. Cohen. Princeton, NJ: Princeton University Press, 1988.

Index

Abensur, Mosseh, 95, 153n77
Aboab de Fonseca, R. Isaac, 148n16
Acosta, José de, 104
Adler, Cyrus, 7
Adler, Elkan Nathan, 122
adolescents and conversion narratives, 84–85
Almeida, Jorge de: and arrests of Carvajal
family, 49, 58, 59; contact with family,
64; escape from Inquisitors, 58, 141n19,
143n39; financial assistance of, 57–58;
marriage of, 55–56; plan to marry two
sisters, 60, 142n31; relationship with
Carvajal family, 57–60
Amelang, James S., 129n18, 130n38, 131n44
American Indians: and appropriation
practices, 108; and brotherhood, 98, 108–10,
116, 120; and Christianity, 109; and European
colonialism, 115; identification of Montezinos
with, 107–9; and Jewish diaspora, 115; and
Menasseh's *Esperanza de Israel*, 98, 100–101,
116–120; and messianic speculation, 104–5;
Montezinos's relationship with, 75, 98, 116,
120; oppression and persecution of, 106–7,
108, 115; physical appearance of, 118–19; and
prison revelations of Montezinos, 107–10;
Reubenites's relationship with, 115, 116–120,
157n50; and Spaniards, 106–7, 115, 116;
speculation on origins of, 103–5; and
Thorowgood's *Iewes in America*, 99–100.
See also Francisco; Reubenites
American Jewish Historical Society, 7
Amsterdam: and acceptance of religious
community, 25–26; anxiety about "returned"
Jews in, 14; and Cardoso, 22, 75; and
collective amnesia of New Jews, 25;
ex-conversos/New Jews in, 22; literary
production in, 131n42; Sephardic community
in, 10, 22; and transition from Catholicism to
Judaism, 22, 131n40
Andrada, Leonor de: and Ana's throat disease,
66; on Luis as family's spiritual guide, 70;
Luis's book inspired by, 70, 145n69; Luis's
relationship with, 68, 70–71; marriage of, 52,
55, 56, 57, 58, 60; religious devotion of, 70;

trial testimony of, 68–70, 145n69; and uncle's
plans for nieces' marriages, 38; and *Vita*,
66, 70
Arbel, Mordechay, 7
archive (term), 10, 128n1
Archivo General de la Nación (AGN), 32, 33,
133n9
Arenal, Electa, 71
autobiographical texts and practices, 1;
Amelang on, 129n18; among Western
Sephardim, 22–25; audiences of, 103,
130n34; and confessional discourses, 13, 14,
15–20; dearth of, 7, 22–25, 132n48; details
included to bolster believability, 12–13,
26; eclectic narrative practices in, 29;
embeddedness in, 20–21, 73; family
dynamics illustrated in, 124; goals of, 103;
as "interested" texts, 21, 130n34, 155n21;
interrelatedness of genres in, 20; as mediated
practice, 17, 102–3; and self-expression, 16–17;
shared attributes of, 130n34; as source
materials, 121; third-person voice in, 14–15,
16, 27, 28, 33; written in safety of Jewish
communities, 8
autoría mediatizada (mediated authorship), 17

Bar Mitzva, 37, 135n22
Barrios, Miguel de, 25
believability in texts, 12–13
Biblioteca Española-Portugueza-Judaica
(Kayserling), 7
blood, bonds of: and apostasy, 84–85; and
betrayal, 59; and Cardoso, 74, 75, 78–80,
84–85, 93, 96; and Carvajal, 34
blood purity (*limpieza de sangre*): and
awareness of racial differences, 2; and
Cardoso, 79; and converso identity, 4, 125n5;
and heresy, 15; persecution associated with,
6; racial nature of, 79
Bodian, Miriam, 25, 34, 131n40, 132n47, 136n47,
147n2
Boer, Harm den, 131n42
Böhm, Gunther, 7
Brazil, 7

Inquisition, 9, 101; Jewish credentials of, 110–11, 113; journey with Francisco, 112–13, 114, 116; and Levi pseudonym, 9, 12, 13, 100; and Menasseh, 100–101; as messianist, 13; New-Christian status of, 102; oral testimony of, 102; origins of, 98, 100, 101; prison revelations of, 107–10, 112; publication of writings, 1; and purpose of text, 21, 128n9; and racial otherness, 74–75; religious orientation of, 100; self-fashioning of, 103; and veracity of narrative, 128n9. See also *Relación de Aharon Levi, alias Antonio de Montezinos*
Morales, Manuel, 40, 42–43, 48, 54

Nachbin, Jac, 133n9
Naphtalites, 117
A Nation upon the Open Seas (Studniki-Gizbert), 35
Naufragios (Cabeza de Vaca), 12–13
Netanyahu, Benzion, 127n11
New Christians. *See* conversos
New Jews: and blood purity (*limpieza de sangre*), 79; collective amnesia of, 25; educational literature for, 22; term, 128n8; transition from Catholicism to Judaism, 22, 131n40
Nirenberg, David, 148n14
Novitsky, Anita, 7
Nueva Granada (modern day Colombia), 9
Nuñez, Felipe, 63, 144n53
Nuñez de Carvajal, Francisca, 53–55; arrests and imprisonment of, 54, 61; biblicizing of, 54; and crypto-Jewish practices of family, 38, 40, 53–54, 67, 70; on Díaz de Cáceres, 61; and Isabel's testimony, 143n44, 143n48; and marriages of daughters, 58; penance assignment of, 67; religious devotion of, 54
Nuñez de Ribera, Guiomar, 36, 134n16, 143n44, 143n48
nuns' literature, 17, 19, 70–71, 103

Old Christians: and blood purity (*limpieza de sangre*), 79; conversos' transition into, 134n18; Inquisition's leniency with, 151n43; and marriages of Carvajal's sisters, 57; and social ostracism of New Christians, 5. *See also* Cardoso de Macedo, Manuel
Old Jews, 79
oral testimonies, 9, 16, 99, 102–3
oral tradition, 107

Orobio de Castro, Isaac, 79
ostracism of New Christians, 5

Parker, Geoffrey, 151n49
Pedro de Oroz, Fray, 23, 48–51, 54
Pelengrino/Peregrino, Abraham, 26, 95, 96. *See also* Cardoso de Macedo, Manuel
peregrino figure, 27–28
Peru, 7
picaresque narratives, 19, 20
Pinheiro, Rodrigues, 95
Pinto, Isaac, 25
Portrait of a New Christian (Salomon), 76
Prado, Juan del, 131n40
Protestantism, 75, 82–83, 131n44. *See also* Calvinism
Prudencio de Sandoval, Fray, 79

Race and Blood in the Iberian World (Martínez, ed.), 126n6
Ramírez, Alonso, 129n21
Reading Columbus (Zamora), 8
Rebecca (biblical), 78
Reformation, 25, 75
reincarnation, 148n14, 148n16
Relación de Aharon Levi, alias Antonio de Montezinos (Montezinos), 12–15, 99–102; audience of, 10, 13, 103; authorship of, 14, 102; and brotherhood, 105, 120; confessional mode employed by, 13, 14; details bolstering believability in, 12; eclectic narrative practices in, 29; on European colonialism, 115; goals/purpose of, 10, 128n9; as historical source, 121; hybridity in, 11; on Indian–Reubenite relationship, 115, 119–120, 157n50; and Israelite Indian theory, 103–5; and Jewish credentials of Montezinos, 110–11, 113; on journey with Francisco, 112–13, 114, 116; and Levi pseudonym, 9, 12, 13, 100; and Menasseh's *Esperanza de Israel*, 1, 9, 100–101, 102, 116–120; on message given to Montezinos, 113, 114, 116; and messianic speculation, 104–5; Montezinos's Judaism revealed to Francisco, 110–12, 156n38; on Montezinos's meeting of Reubenites, 100, 112–14; origins of, 99; on physical appearance of Reubenites, 118–19; and prison revelations of Montezinos, 107–10, 112; publication of oral account, 9, 99, 102; reporting function of, 12, 13, 103; and self-fashioning of Montezinos, 103;

RONNIE PERELIS is the Chief Rabbi Dr. Isaac Abraham and Jelena (Rachel) Alcalay Chair and Assistant Professor of Sephardic Studies at the Bernard Revel Graduate School of Jewish Studies of Yeshiva University.

www.ingramcontent.com/pod-product-compliance
Lightning Source LLC
Chambersburg PA
CBHW020811100426
42814CB00001B/25